Table of Contents

This book is dedicated to my wife, Dr. Sharon Wetherall, who led me to true happiness and continues to mend my wounds in every way imaginable.

Introduction

My life path took a major turn—to the right or to the left can be debated—in 1992, when a car accident resulted in the amputation of my left leg, five inches below the knee. I was twenty-five years old, fresh out of college, eagerly looking forward to what the future had in store. The future I had dreamt about didn't include a prosthetic leg.

Seven days after the crash—and five operations later—the doctors requested my signature to amputate. As I lay there in immense physical and emotional pain, I wasn't thinking about why this happened to me—I knew damn well why; I'd had a few beers at dinner and fallen asleep while driving home—I was thinking about what challenges would await me over the next fifty years living the life of Uniped.

I wholly expected to be far less active and, to some degree, less happy. Within the first few months, those perceptions had quickly shifted. I learned I could still strap on the skates and hack my way through a pick-up game of ice hockey. I could still bomb downhill on two skis. I could still slice a golf ball with the best of them. Those perceptions were smashed to pieces three years later when I ran the New York City Marathon and cried my eyes dry with sheer joy!

The finish line of that 26.2-mile run provided a solid platform constructed of a renewed self-confidence along with finely tuned muscles and cardiovascular fitness I hadn't known in years. I knew when I crossed that line in Central Park that I was meant for this: I was destined to be a disabled athlete. No joke.

I moved to Colorado a month later, in December 1995, to begin an earnest pursuit of the U.S. Disabled Ski Team, later renamed the U.S. *Adaptive* Ski Team. The goal was to be at the top of the hill at the

Paralympic Games in Nagano, Japan, three years later. As it was, that goal never materialized, without one ounce of regret, I might add. It just wasn't in the cards.

(The Paralympics, as some of you may already know, could be best described as the Olympics for the physically challenged, occurring at the same venues as the Olympics, held two weeks later. These Paralymics are actually the second largest attended and televised sporting event in the world, second only to their big brother. Unfortunately, this is not so in the United States. Write your congressperson.)

Without giving away the whole story, I shelved my ski-racing career and embraced the endurance sport of triathlon: swimming, cycling, and running. I also truly began to enjoy writing about my experiences on the road and on the course. These writings were mostly self-glorification crossed with self-degradation. These "race reports" traveled through cyberspace and landed in e-mail in-boxes across the country and around the globe. Many of my experiences resulted in pain, some of them in victory, most in some sort of comedy (primarily of the *Stooges* subgenre). The following pages reveal just what my life as an athlete has been like. All of which, I am proud to say, has been performance-enhancement-drug free.

Early in the race-report-via-e-mail days—sometime in 1997, I believe—I had no intention whatsoever of building any type of dedicated readership. They were sent out to keep family, friends, and sponsors abreast of my glories and failures—to let them know that my time away from a "job" was not spent in front of the tube. I wrote several, detailing my ups and downs as a ski racer. These were sent, forgotten about, and presumably lost forever.

In June 1998, I made my bike-racing debut at the national disabled cycling championships. A couple of weeks later, after my second bike race, I sent out an e-mail entitled "Bike Racing Can Be Dangerous." Then I forgot about it, never to be seen again. Therein, I entertained a budding e-mail list with the horrors of a particular criterium bike race in which I crashed … twice … going twenty-five miles per hour … wearing Lycra … in the first two laps … in the first mile. Think skin removal, blood, headache, etc.

A month later, in the midst of training for the Hawaiian Ironman, I sent the following e-mail.

Correction

September 1998

Bike racing is not dangerous. *I* am dangerous.

I picked up on this Saturday as I picked myself, my broken helmet, and my broken sunglasses off a downhill stretch of pavement early in the day's training ride. (The road's shoulder narrowed by about twelve inches without my noticing ...) I brushed myself off, examined the raw skin on my right hip and shoulder, and kept on riding. A few miles down the road, I stopped at the local convenience store to grab some Neosporine and Advil. Here, my body sat me down to have a few words. Moments later, I made it to the toilet and was on my knees. My body had become itchy all over, I was sweaty and cold, I couldn't feel my lips or my fingertips, and I had a god-awful taste in my mouth, one I'd never had before.

Body said, "You know something—I'm not one of those sponsored pieces of equipment you don't seem to have any respect for!"

"But ..."

"Shut up or I'll make you puke!" I almost did ...

(At this point, I'm on the concrete basement floor with a towel on my forehead.)

"From now on," Body said, "every time you abuse me, I'm gonna retaliate. How do you like the no-feeling-in-your-lips deal? Okay. I have your attention. I thought the loss-of-leg thing would have smartened you up a bit, but *nooooooo!* You gotta go and break me, skiing and jumping off bicycles at high speed. *Well, enough is enough!* Cut the crap or next time I'll make life a little more miserable. Good day!"

That being said, I started to feel a whole lot better (T plus 1.5 hours). To my good fortune, Susan Latshaw, a new friend and training partner, as well as 1997 Ironman Europe champion, was comforting me throughout the whole ordeal.

I got myself together, bid farewell to Susan, mounted the bike, and started my ride home, thinking the day's training was shot. However, with all the distractions in the form of traveling I've had during my Ironman training, I didn't want to lose any more quality riding time, so I turned up the road and put in another sixty miles, followed by a four-mile run.

I returned to the house and immediately jumped in the shower in an effort not only to freshen up but to clean the wounds. With the hot water stinging all over, Body had only one thing to say: *"Idiot!"*

Yes, as much as I wish it weren't true, I am far from graceful. However, I do like to dance—in an unstructured manner, of course. Over the years, I've fallen off ladders, hung precariously forty feet in the air from steel joists as an ironworker, been stitched up on many occasions, and have crashed more cars than most people own in a lifetime. Ten years after competing for the U.S. Disabled Ski Team, the former coach told me I remained the best crasher he'd ever seen. My bike handling skills were on par.

A week after the e-mail above, I sent another one.

News Flash

September 1998

This just in: Legendary bonehead cyclist Paul Martin is at it again. Just days after his notorious "body retaliates" crash, Martin eats it on his road bike for an unprecedented seventh time in a single season.

Our reporter on the scene, Heebee Bummin, has the report:

> It appears that Mr. Martin was the last in a line of three riders descending a hill on a sharp right-hand turn when they came upon a large dog and its owner walking up the inside lane of the blind corner. The first two riders, startled by the sheer mass of the large snarling animal, veered to safety, but Martin, his options lessened by the others, had no choice but to go down. And down he went on the shady gravel-strewn corner.
>
> The homeowner, whose driveway gravel was in the road and later embedded in Martin's hip, commented, "You know it's a bad crash when the guy's leg pops off!"
>
> We understand Martin holds no grudge since the homeowner did supply the necessary first-aid kit. Dr. Susan Latshaw, attending physician, lent these words: "There are two kinds of people in this world. Paul's the type that likes to dance with gravity." She made no reference to the second type.
>
> Paul's Body was unavailable for comment, apparently on a much-needed long weekend.
>
> As the group was preparing to finish the one-hundred-mile ride, Martin was overheard in a display of sick, masochistic humor: "Let's hit the road!"

Thank you, Heebee.

Martin was admitted to a local clinic for a tetanus shot and gravel removal. We are told the pea-size hole in his hip should close up in a few days.

In a related story, a recent poll suggests that America's fear of amputees is at an all-time high.

This report generated a frenzy of replies, with folks poking fun at my inability to keep the rubber side down, and many offering appreciation for a brief comedic respite in an otherwise uneventful day in front of the monitor. Some suggested I might try to do something with my writing, to try to get it published in some type of media. I considered their recommendations lightly.

My impending mission was solely athletic. I wanted to be branded an "Ironman." I was preparing to undertake the ultimate triathlon distance, with eyes on breaking the twelve-hour mark. I felt confident that this goal was within reach; perhaps I could even go a little faster. I have since witnessed this trait in nearly every Ironman rookie–big eyes and big goals rarely realized on race day. Part of the learning curve, I suppose.

At the time, I was also a newbie member of the U.S. Disabled Cycling Team, having enlisted with the team after winning both races at the national championships I mentioned earlier.

I approached those nationals with an unusual block of training: the Transcontinental Triathlon for Life—the Tri4Life. A male quadriplegic who rode a handcycle and a racing wheelchair, a deaf/blind woman on a tandem bike (with a sighted pilot), a man with full-blown AIDS and I swam, biked, and ran from Los Angeles to New York City to raise money and awareness for disabled youth. A rewarding experience, indeed.

The personal impetus for this undertaking was the fact that I didn't qualify for the trip to Nagano to ski with Team USA, and I had time and energy to burn, so I threw myself into training for a self-propelled cross-country adventure.

Those 3,100 miles in the saddle over a two-month span provided the legs needed to win both the time trial and road race—results far above my expectations. I had no idea that I could possibly be the best one-legged cyclist in America. I'm still wondering if there was a faster guy out there somewhere who didn't show up.

It just so happened that in September, a mere two months later, the disabled cycling world championships were held in Colorado Springs, down the highway a spell from my new home in Boulder. The U.S. team coach and the manager were both thrilled to have a strong new addition to the team. I still knew next to nothing about bike racing, nor was I all that excited about making the cut. My mind was already in Kona, on the Big Island of Hawaii, preparing for October's Ironman World Championships.

I let them know that I already had some major training plans ahead of me, which included lots of swimming and running, and that I couldn't commit to focused bike training. They understood, to some degree, and gave me some friendly ribbing for not being able to pick a sport.

After proudly accepting their invitation, on my terms, I stayed focused on triathlon training and approached the world championships—just three weeks prior to Ironman—as part of my training, my last big effort before I began my taper. (To "taper" refers to gradually decreased training, and hence more rest, before an endurance event.)

I took a bronze in the road race and a fourth in the time trial. Everyone was happy with that, although that fourth place took a few days for me to truly appreciate—I had naively expected to win.

A couple of weeks later, I boarded a plane headed to Kona for the toughest event of my life—the toughest athletic event, that is. I crossed the finish line of my first Ironman in eleven hours, fifty-five minutes, and thirty-seven seconds. Then I took off my leg, held it over my head, and declared quite proudly and loudly, "*I am Ironman!*" That race report is also among the missing.

That was quite a significant moment in my life. The change of course my life took afterward was a direct result of what I had just accomplished. You see, I had quit my well-paying job and budding career as a sales engineer to earn a spot on the U.S. Disabled Ski Team, and I was awarded that spot a few months earlier, shortly after the closing of the Nagano Games. Upon my return from Kona, I attended an on-snow training camp. (I had attended a two-week dryland camp with the team in July, which happened to be the weeks both preceding and following my weekend crash-filled criterium bike race described in the preceding pages. So, yes, the second week of training was a bit uncomfortable for me with two skinless hips, one skinless elbow, and an overall body ache.)

Immediately upon my introduction to the ski team's expectations and dynamics, I was let down by a lack of anticipated energy. I had just finished an Ironman; I was all about work ethic and athleticism. Triathlon provided something that was missing from the ski-racing scene. As I struggled with morale though my rookie season, my performances suffered. I injured my left hip in a downhill training crash, which drastically added to my poor form. To top it off, I had little respect for the head coach—and my feelings were reciprocated.

I quit the team before the season ended. I wanted to be a triathlete.

Furthermore, I couldn't wait to write a book. My first volume, my too-young-for-a-memoir memoir, was published under the title *One Man's Leg* in October 2002. And wouldn't you know it—this comes with an interesting little story.

In the winter of 1998 I was arrested for driving with a suspended license—suspended for a paid but past-due traffic ticket. As it turned out, driving in the state of Colorado with a suspended license is a mandatory five days in the county jail. After a year in the courts I was sentenced to do the time at the end of the ski season. The judge was respectful of my national team membership and allowed me time to compete.

With a shortened ski season by my own resolve, a burning desire to put my life on paper, and 120 hours looming ahead of me with not a whole lot to do, there was only one option. I called the jail superintendent three weeks prior to my scheduled arrival and asked to be put behind bars. I wanted to start writing.

In that book, beyond detailing childhood experiences and life with two feet, I wrote about the races in Colorado Springs and Kona, which I touched on above. I had sent out e-mails reliving these marvelous experiences when they occurred, but sadly, without intention ever to make further use of them, they are among those lost in cyberspace. Maybe the FBI …

With the incarceration behind me, I set out to continue my quest in triathlon. I also discovered that bike racing wasn't so bad. More directly, I realized that I possessed plenty of potential to compete as a member of the U.S. Paralympic Cycling Team headed to Sydney in 2000. With that as a motivator, I spent significant energy preparing for team qualification—more detailed than just winning a national championship. I raced primarily triathlon that season but hit a few bike races as well. Part of the latter process was attending the national championships in Arkansas. (I flew into Tulsa, Oklahoma—this stop in the Sooner State completed my "fifty states visited" quest—and drove from there to the race in Fort Smith, Arkansas.)

The team later traveled to France to compete in the European disabled cycling championships, open to the USA and a couple of other invitees. I'd been to Europe for the first time the previous winter, skiing for the national team. My second trip to Europe in one calendar year was detailed in the following e-mail.

Busy, Busy, Busy

August 1999

I was in Paris recently to witness Lance Armstrong and the U.S. Postal Service Professional Cycling Team win the Tour de France. From a tree branch high over the heads of hundreds of thousands of crazy cycling enthusiasts, I saw one of the most popular sporting events in the history of the world. Very cool.

However, I hadn't traveled all the way to France to witness a bike race. I was there to win one, or at least try to! It was the European disabled cycling championships in Blois, France.

I was fortunate to take third in the time trial—and not so fortunate to get dropped in the road race the day before. Chalk that one up to lack of experience. I didn't get up and go when I should have, and I missed the opportunity to hang with the lead pack. Half a dozen other riders and myself were "off the back" for the rest of the race.

Before jetting off to France, I jetted to Fort Smith, Arkansas, for the national disabled cycling champs. The road race result was nearly parallel to that of last year; I won due to a fellow competitor's mishap. Poor Gary—with thirteen miles left in the thirty-four-mile race, he crashed into another fallen rider. (He crashed just seconds away from the finish line last year, which secured my win.) As I did a year ago, I saw the opportunity and took off like a man possessed. I managed to hold the lead and eventually won the race by a couple of minutes.

The day before was the time trial in which Gary beat me by seventeen seconds. A couple of days later was the inaugural criterium race at nationals. I got third. I thought there was still a lap to go. Oops.

A week prior, I was home in Massachusetts, racing in the Fitchburg Longsgo Classic. This event, in its fortieth year on the Fourth of July weekend, was a four-day stage race (combined time of four days of racing determines the winner).

Fitchburg, Massachusetts, is crazy hilly, and I was dropped on the road race on the final day on the final climb. I was forced to miss the crit on the final day of racing to head to nationals in Arkansas, but after three days of racing, I was in ninety-fifth place out of 150 category 4 riders. Happy. (As I edit this piece nine years later, that result seems so poor. Oh, how our perspectives shift in time.)

And a week prior to these races, I competed in the Greater Hartford Triathlon. This race was two days after a fraternity brother's wedding, which was four days after my birthday, which was two days after another fraternity brother's wedding. I went into this race thinking it was a short sprint race (750m swim, 20k bike, 5k run) that I would be able to clamor through without much difficulty after the weeklong celebration. *Errrrnnnntt*, wrong. It was an Olympic distance race (1.5-kilometer swim, 40-kilometer bike, 10-kilometer run) with a difficult trail run that kicked my butt and had my guts wrenching. The challenging run put me on my face four times tripping over roots. It took me an hour and fifteen minutes to do that 10-kilometer run. I was bummin'.

And before that, I raced at the Bolder Boulder on Memorial Day. There were forty-three thousand people participating in this 10k classic. (Not all at the same time. Runners go off in waves of about five hundred.) I crossed the finish line inside the University of Colorado's Folsom Field in 43:29. Then I drank the free beer they gave me.

When I returned from France, I competed in the Boulder Peak Triathlon (1.5k swim, 42k bike, 10k run) on August 1 and had a decent day. Sparing some details, the valve on my run leg broke off before the race but unbeknownst to me until I started running; this causes the leg to lose proper suspension and get all sloppy. I was forced to MacGyver something to plug the hole. I yelled out for help from spectators: "Anyone got any chewing gum!? Chewing gum!? Anybody!?"

A man came running up next to me and offered a piece of Wrigley's Spearmint, fresh in the wrapper. I quickly chewed it into a gummy consistency and patched it up. That worked great for about a mile, until the growing bubble popped. The gum began to dry up and was soon not so gummy. I had to keep fixing it by folding and molding the pink material until I hit the finish line some forty-eight minutes later. Slow run. Big highlight, however: I beat triathlon legend Scott Tinley on the bike by two minutes, and a couple of the other pros by a minute or so! Again, very nice. I finished up in 2:28, five minutes faster than last year. Sixtieth of three hundred in my age group. Yeah, a big race.

Then, to wrap things up, I raced yesterday, August 8, in Brian Head, Utah, at Scott Tinley's High Altitude Triathlon. At the time it was the highest altitude triathlon in the United States: swim at 8,300 feet, mountain bike up to 11,000 feet and then down to 9,400 feet, and run a 9K bad-ass trail run. Tinley got back at me by finishing nearly an hour faster than I did and taking first overall. The highlight here: I finished third in my age group for my first event podium appearance! And at the toughest mile-for-mile race of my short career.

Today is Sunday, and I'm still in Utah, heading home in the morning. Say a prayer that my car with the burned-out headlight and a dead battery (I've been pop starting it for a couple of months now) gets me home by seven.

And to the rest of you—thanks for everything, as always.

My focus had returned to triathlon, a sport I was beginning to love—or become addicted to, I'm not really sure which. The time was approaching to take on the big fish once again. Back to Kona.

While I was happy with my performance on the Big Island the year before, an emptiness remained: *I can go faster.* I knew it. I eagerly looked forward to more self-induced pain. The inexperienced little voice in the back of my head last year told me that I might be able to complete the distance in less than eleven hours.

Now, a year later, I was no longer the rookie. And I wanted to go sub-eleven. I sent this note out before heading over.

Ironman, The Sequel

October 1999

The time has come to conquer once again the lava fields of the Big Island of Hawaii. I leave on October 15 to race at the 1999 Hawaiian Ironman World Championships (reminder: 2.4-mile swim, 112-mile bike, 26.2-mile run—in a row!).

There will be a race within a race this year—three BKs (below-knee amputees) looking to challenge each other as well as themselves. There's Dan Jensen, a Vietnam vet who raced there in '97 in twelve and a half hours; there's Joel Sampson, a twenty-seven-year old husband and father from Honolulu who's making his debut; and myself. Brian Leske, an AK (above-knee amp), is also racing, along with his able-bodied twin brother and their father. Clarinda Brueck, an arm amputee, will be racing for a third straight year.

Please follow along at www.ironmanlive.com the day of the race. The Web site will be updated every few minutes, or something like that. Enter a name and the site does the rest. I hop ... oops! Freudian slip ... I hope to break eleven hours this year. Last year I crossed in 11:55:37. I know I can shave a half hour off both the bike and run. Things will be going well if I can do the following:

swim in 1:10 plus a five-minute transition

bike in 5:25 plus a five-minute transition

run in 4:14:59

Wish me luck!

In September, I competed in Montreal at the ITU World Championships (Olympic distance: 1.5k swim, 40k bike, 10k run). Rivaldo Martins spanked me again. I recorded a personal best of 2:15 (my goal for the day), but the Brazilian crossed in 2:09. Sooner or later, I might learn how to swim. Or maybe I'll just have him taken out. I know people. People like Jack Barr, that ruthless SOB.

11

Six days later, I competed in the Colorado Relay, a 170-mile ten-person team run from Idaho Springs to Glenwood Springs, Colorado. I ran a 10k through Vail at 2:00 AM! Good fun. I still haven't heard how we did.

On October 3, I ran a 5k in Chicago on behalf of the Rehabilitation Institute of Chicago, who puts on the race. Each year, there is a 10k wheelchair race with prize money (five hundred dollars for first). The organizers are interested in starting an ambulatory challenged (stand-up gimp) division, so they flew me in, put me up, and fed me twin lobster tails in return for showing that it can be done. Maybe I'll win some money next year and won't need your money, Matt, Brent, Dr. Rob, Dr. H2Os, Dan, Pokey, Muddy, Dad … The list is endless.

I'm now in Southern California. I raced yesterday in Oceanside at the U.S. Triathlon Series National Championships. Biggest surf I've ever been in, but obviously, I managed not to drown. Rumor has it that the lifeguards had to pull fifty people out of the water. Furthermore, it was a hilly bike course and hotter than hell on the run.

Did well. First gimp.

Off to Santa Barbara later today to get some last-minute training in with all the fine folks from the Tri4Life—the cross-country swim, bike, run team that I've been a part of the last couple of years.

After Ironman, I hope to be strong enough to race (walk or crawl may be more appropriate) in the Xterra World Championships on Maui on October 31. This is referred to as the infamous "Double." I'm looking for the feather in the cap.

I hope all is well with all of you. As always, thanks for being there.

He knows not his own strength that hath not met adversity.
—Ben Jonson

A week later, with the race in the record books (my journal), I sent the following to the followers.

Finis!

November 1999

Ironman was good to me once again.

The sub-eleven hour thing didn't happen despite having shaved "SUB 11" onto the back of my head several days before the race. The comments came frequently, typically from behind, and they were always appreciated: "That's awesome!" "Good luck!" "Who's Sue 11?" "What does Sub U mean?"

The good part is that my splits were close to my predictions. I came out of the water in 1:09:09, transitioned to the bike in three minutes (so far ahead of schedule), biked a 5:46:46 with another three-minute transition to the run (now fifteen minutes behind schedule, with just under four hours left to run to break eleven hours), then ran a 4:20:22 marathon. I crossed the finish line at 11:22:49. That's the bad part, which really isn't so bad.

You may recall from last year's report that when I crossed the finish line, I raised the prosthetic leg overhead in victory and exclaimed, "I ... am ... Ironman!" Well, I did it again. I guess that's gonna be my thing.

Dan and Joel, the other BKs in the race, finished in 12:22 and 12:32, respectively. Good job, gentlemen. Brian Leske, the only above-knee amputee (AK) to ever run the marathon here on a prosthesis, crossed in about 16:45. Just under the seventeen-hour deadline. His good leg went bad on the bike, which made for a stressful marathon, as you can imagine. Kudos to you, Brian. Clarinda finished just ahead of Brian, I believe.

I then headed to Maui for the Xterra World Championships. The year's off-road triathlon series (1.5k swim, 30k bike, 11k run) wrapped up at and around a resort in Wailea. We swam 750 meters, got out of the water, and hopped 75 meters to swim it all over again, then biked a gnarly mountain bike ride with a ton of vertical and hairy descents over loose lava rocks that, had you gone down, would cause bloodshed. (Brent Ruemaker of B&L Bikes in Kona was kind enough to lend me his full-suspension bike, which made all the difference on the downhills as I passed dozens of hardtail riders over the lava rocks.) The bike section was followed by a challenging run that took us over trails, under low-hanging tree branches, over lower-hanging tree branches, and through soft beach sand, which I walked through. I was tired.

I completed the race in 4:12:04 and became the first challenged athlete to conquer The Double. For this, the race directors gave me a sweet pair of Spinergy SPOX cross-country mountain bike wheels! Thank you very much.

Check out the January broadcast on ESPN. I interviewed with them prior to the event, and they followed me around with a camera on race day—I'm hoping to make the final cut.

Sunday I participated (as opposed to "raced") for the fourth consecutive year in the San Diego Triathlon Challenge in La Jolla. Our team, Two Gimps and a Freak, consisted of Joel Sampson swimming, myself on the bike, and duathlon (run, bike, run) legend Kenny Souza on the run. I was so spent from the previous weekends and the interim celebrating that what should have taken 2:45 on the bike took me 4:30. I guess napping along the course in fluffy grass and soothing sunshine is no way to set course records. When I came into transition, Kenny had already left on the run.

After the race, the not-so-surprisingly unexpected occurred. The Honda's timing belt snapped and caused irreparable damage to the engine. The junkyard is installing a used engine tomorrow, and I should be back on the road to Boulder by Friday morning. You know, always an adventure. And thanks to Billy Garcia for buying those new Spinergy wheels from me. Now I only have to come up with another couple of hundred bucks to get my car back!

Until next season ...

The preceding wrapped up 1999's passages. The winter was spent training—mostly on the bike. You can ride in Boulder in the winter despite what you might think. It can get quite cold, but my water bottles only froze twice. Layers, it's all about layers. I was looking forward to a good showing at the Paralympic trials in May, doing whatever it would take to get there, feeling quite confident that I would earn a spot on the Sydney squad the following October.

Training went well. I'd spent three days at the Olympic Training Center in Colorado Springs with other Paralympic hopefuls. We were tested and poked and prodded, and the technicians came back with their numbers: body fat of 8.6 percent; weight at 156 pounds (without the leg); VO2Max of 66.5 (whatever that means); and a resting heart rate of forty-two beats per second (that's good). All enzymes, proteins, cholesterol, etc. in perfect balance. Doc said, "Stick with whatever diet you're on." (Eggs and ice cream!)

Up to this point, I had yet to ride a track bike, and in Sydney there would be more medals up for grabs on the velodrome than on the road. The coaches and I agreed that my country and I would be best served if I'd dedicate some time riding a bike with no brakes and a fixed gear in counterclockwise circles on a forty-degree banked oval.

In April, I attended a one-man accelerated debut track camp that took place on an old cement velodrome in Houston and the near-new wooden one in Frisco, Texas, just outside of Dallas. At this track, in a mere three weeks, Paralympic track trials would take place, and those who qualified here would automatically be eligible for the Sydney road races as well. Road trials were in June so knocking out the qualifier now would relieve a little stress for the next couple of months.

Suddenly, it was time to put the pedals to the metal and see if those frozen bike rides were going to pay off. You must be so excited! Let's see what happens …

Flu-Ridden Track Debut

May 2000

Another slightly less-than-ideal chain of events. The month of April began with a six-day bout with the flu, or something similar. Of course, I didn't actually go to the doctor to find out. My good friend Michele mixed up a bunch of nasty liquefied herb things to get me back on track, quite literally.

As my illness began to fade, I flew to Dallas to learn the skills of the sport with cycling coach Ryan Crissey. He offered scant sympathy, and on day one, I was riding those laps to the left. The next day I entered a local Category 5 (entry-level) race. Track racing, I soon learned, is high heart rate, high power stuff. Minutes into it, I thought I might puke or pass out, as I still had plenty of bug left in me. With the Paralympic trials just a couple of weeks away, I felt I had no choice but to ride. In the four days spent in Dallas/Houston, I learned what I had to do to prepare for the April 25 four-kilometer time trial that could make or break my Sydney track racing hopes.

On April 23, I returned to Dallas to put four solid months of training to the test. I had logged about thirty-two hundred miles on the bike and sixty hours in the gym since December 1, with November completely off after Ironman/Xterra. With a number of student presentations throughout the New Year, my finances were indeed more stable than they had been in the recent past; nevertheless, I had yet to purchase a track bike. Therefore, I was forced to beg for a rental bike at the track (these bikes are only allowed for training and not racing, so I had to act desperate—I was desperate, so I guess I wasn't acting). Rental bikes come with your basic spoked wheels, which are immensely slower in time trialing than pricey aerodynamic carbon disc or three-, four-, or five-spoke wheels, so I had to borrow a pair. I was able to hook up with a fifteen-hundred-dollar set from a friend in Boulder who, expectedly, told me "not to fuck 'em up."

We gimps were lucky to have complimentary flights to the trials from Disabled Sports/USA's sponsor, United Airlines. Well, the baggage handlers are not quite as respectful as the brass; when I arrived in Dallas, the wheels, in a made-for-rough-handling travel case, were completely crushed, along with the container. Pretty sure that the jet itself actually rode over them. They would replace them ... so they said.

So there I was, without the necessary equipment and a certain amount of concern regarding my buddy's impending disappointment, about to enter an important five-minute-plus bike race. Previous life experience had trained me to regard these situations as ultimately beneficial, and I knew that something good would result.

A representative from Shimano (a bike accessory manufacturer providing neutral support at the race) was gracious enough to let me use a fast rear disc wheel and a prototype six-spoke front wheel—these wheels were potentially even faster than the ones I had borrowed. The next day, at the track, my shorts and wallet mysteriously disappeared from my bag of stuff—a bit of a drag. I wasn't overly concerned. I have learned that such an occurrence, in and of itself, cannot create stress unless you let it. Two days later, after the big race, on a wet morning at the track, I found them both in a pile of random soaked clothing on the other side of the infield (my fault somehow, I'm sure).

To qualify for Sydney, a rider needed to come within 15 percent of the world record (WR) time of his/her disability classification in one of three events *and* be a top fifteen overall contender. Twenty riders from six different classes were chasing these slots.

I'm ecstatic to say that my 4k ride placed me fourth overall and earned me a trip to Sydney in October!

Finally. Six years and four sports later, I'm a Paralympian-in-waiting. I'm happy.

🚲   🚲   🚲

Tragicomedy was once again the feature; the crushed wheel situation brought in $5,200 from United! I replaced my buddy's equipment, bought myself a set of wheels, and had enough money left for a couple of months worth of bills and rent. The trials were behind me. All I had to do was focus on fitness and experience on the bike. So that's what I did.

More of the Same

July 2000

June 24

So there I was, racing in the Colorado State Road Race Championships, at mile 10 of a forty-eight-mile race, when my own teammate tried to throw an elbow at a passing competitor. The elbow missed its mark and the elbow thrower's front wheel did not miss the other guy's rear wheel, which sent my teammate crashing to the ground. Since I was being a smart and savvy racer, a mere six inches off his rear wheel, I went down too, taking out a mailbox in the process. I suffered a little elbow damage, the leg popped off, and the chain was a tangled mess. It took about four minutes to get myself back together. (All the while feeling little to no sympathy for my teammate, who lay there in pain, with a mild concussion and dislocated right thumb—a quick glance made that obvious, as it pointed nearly ninety degrees to the right!) I rode the remaining thirty-eight miles solo for the most part, picking off about thirty racers in the process, finishing in the middle somewhere.

July 1

So there I was, descending Mount Wachusett in Central Massachusetts, down a steep and bumpy road, when a shadow-cloaked pothole buckled my gimpy side and sent me crashing to the ground. The derailleur hanger bent a little, but luckily my steel Schwinn Peloton was easily rebendable. This was *after* the day's race was over! It was the third stage of the four-day Fitchburg Longsjo Classic, where we finished the road race with a charge to the highest point in Central Massachusetts. There were 150 category 4 riders (Cat 4s) in the race, and I finished fortieth overall. Had I not been late for the opening day's time trial by forty seconds (I have an uncanny ability to lose track of time), I would have been around thirtieth. As Led Zeppelin's Robert Plant might say ... *N-n-n-n-nobody's fault but mine.*

July 9

So there I was, fresh out of the saddle and turning on the sprint for the finish line of the Attleboro (Massachusetts) Criterium, when a competitor "hooked" me (illegally cut my line of travel, clipping my front wheel with his rear) and sent me crashing to the ground. The scabs from last weekend's crash on my right forearm and hip were mercilessly ripped from my already tender skin, and blood proceeded to leave my body at a rather rapid rate. No major physical or psychological damage—the only race that matters is not until October, in the fine city of Sydney, Australia. Every race until then is an opportunity to sharpen my never-been-sharp-to-begin-with skills. I was actually in a position to take at least a top five finish, if not a possible win. Safe to say, I was having the smartest race of my infantile career before …

For those of you still reading, this is the part where I back up chronologically and detail some crashless races. I know, these just don't provide those same exciting, vicarious sensations. Forgive me.

May 5–7

Tour of the Gila (pronounced *hee*-la), Gila National Forest, southwest New Mexico. For the Cat 4s, it was a three-day stage race (road race, crit, road race) with a total of seven thousand feet of vertical climbing, or something like that. My rear tire went flat at mile 1, day one, at the base of hill one. I spent the next two and a half hours at 90 to 95 percent effort, continually thinking that at any moment I would catch back onto the pack. (I can be so wrong at times.) Again, I picked off about thirty riders and finished twenty-ninth of sixty-something.

In the next day's crit, I finished thirteenth. I was about ten meters from my first prime (pronounced *preem*: a premium lap that offers some sort of material reward to the first across the start/finish line) when the eventual winner came around and got me by a wheel.

On the final day, another not-so-good climber and I put three minutes on the field to start the climb of the Gila Monster, the category 2 climb that concluded the race. (A category 2 climb is *really hard*; a category 1 climb is the toughest and is *really, really hard*). Fifteen of the little guys—the better climbers—caught us before the summit, but my sixteenth place finish couldn't have tasted sweeter. I finished the stage race nineteenth overall.

May 21

A couple of weeks later, I traveled to Bellingham, Washington, to compete in the Ski to Sea race on Memorial Day weekend. This eight-member relay race consists of, in this order, downhill skiing (which is really a hike up a black diamond run with ski boots on and skis in hand, and then a ski down a "cat track" to complete the section); cross-country skiing; an eight-mile, eight percent grade downhill run; a thirty-six-mile road ride (that's me); an eighteen-mile two-person canoe; mountain bike of some distance; followed by a two-mile sea kayak finish.

Team USAble has assembled fully disabled teams over the last twenty years. This year they asked if I would bike for the team to try to break the top ten for the first time. Their best finish to date is fifteenth ... of 250 teams! (I assembled a fully disabled team that same year, 1997, and we came in 101st.) This year, there were 400 teams, and we came in 39th. We were 25th going into the kayak section. Proud to say I set a new course record for gimps and got one hundred dollars! I even tried to buy the beer that night but the boys wouldn't let me. (That was the second time I'd ever won money racing in anything. The first time was two weeks earlier in a track race in Colorado Springs. I won twenty dollars that night.)

May 28

A week later, in Seattle, Washington, I biked for a triathlon relay team and had the fastest bike split of all 145 two-legged freak competitors. It was an Aussie-style race where competitors swam 0.5 mile, biked 7.5 miles, then ran 2.5 miles—then did it all over again.

July 10

I raced in Central Park just a couple of weeks ago ... at six o'clock in the morning. Halfway through the thirty-mile five-lap race I was doing okay, until a mechanical problem on the bike sidelined me. Thrilled to be getting all these little annoyances out of the way now.

July 13

I raced a triathlon last Wednesday night in Connecticut—the 14th Annual Pat Griskus Memorial Sprint Triathlon. Pat was the first amputee to complete the Hawaiian Ironman and the first to run the Boston Marathon. In 1987, he was killed on a training ride in Kona, just days before his third Ironman. There had never been an amputee competing in his memorial race, but this year there were two: Ray Viscome—another below-knee amp and bronze medalist last year at the world championships in Montreal—and myself. I raced the 0.5-mile swim, 10.5-mile bike, and 3.1-mile run in 1:13:39. At 1:19, Ray was not far behind. He beat me on the swim and run, but the hours I've logged on my bike this year were tough for him to match. He's one of those amputees with a day job.

Off to Seattle again this weekend for a ride/run race. Then to the national road championships/Paralympic road qualifiers in Indiana at the end of the month. Wish me luck.

And pray I don't write so much next time.

🚲   🚲   🚲

I gotta believe I'd written up some sort of e-mail on the happenings at the road qualifiers, but I didn't seem to have one saved anywhere. In short, since I was already on the track team, all I needed to do was be sure to finish in the top three to ensure I'd compete in all events in Sydney. That I did, scoring a bronze medal in the effort.

After nationals, I didn't do any more racing; the quality time preparing for Sydney was spent at the Olympic Training Center in Colorado Springs. In the short time afforded me—two years—I learned what I could about bike racing. It was time to represent the USA in AUS.

En route to Sydney, the entire U.S. team made a stop in San Francisco for team processing. We received our uniforms, opening and closing ceremony parade wear, and general swag. (Swag is free stuff that comes with a race, typically a T-shirt, a water bottle, an energy bar, etc., which comes in, yes, a swag bag.) This process took several hours, after which we boarded another plane to head to Australia. We spent a week or so acclimating: resting our minds and bodies after the thirty-plus hours of traveling and swagging.

Most members of the cycling team skipped the opening ceremonies since we had a race the morning of the opening day of competitions. Cycling is all about the legs, and so we were mandated to sit and watch the festivities that took place inside Sydney Olympic Stadium on closed-circuit television.

The morning's event was the kilo, which I wrote about from the Surf Shack, the athlete computer lounge.

Fourth Fastest Kilo

October 2000

Today I raced the kilo. I'm the fourth fastest kilo racer in the world. That's nothing to sneeze at. A medal would have been sweet, but seeing how this was my second kilo, and those who beat me have ten to twenty races each under their belts, it gives me a little comfort. I'm telling *myself* this to feel better.

Sunday's 4k pursuit is a bit more my style. While it's still anaerobic, at least it's longer and, well, maybe that's good for me … The top dogs in the kilo will probably be the same who qualify for Monday's pursuit finals—the top four. I sure hope to be one of them. Remember: vibes. Now I gotta go check out some racing.

🚲 🚲 🚲

I raced the pursuit qualifiers two days later and ended up in sixth, out of the finals. I probably sent out a report on that, but if so, it's lost. Sixth is nothing to write home about anyway.

The following day was the road race. Of the small number of road races I've been in, I've tended to overthink them on the days leading up, then, when the chips fall, I find myself spacing out and miss the break. I expected to do well nonetheless. I was physically and mentally strong—a state of being that the competition always fears.

The race turned out to be quite remarkable. The following e-mail is but a brief glimpse of the day's exciting struggles. I detailed the experience in *One Man's Leg*, with the account recalled from both my memory and my journal.

That's All Folks!

October 2000

Hey, sports fans!

I'm hanging out in the IBM Surf Shack in Olympic Village, recovering from a post-final race and twelve-hour beverage/dance fest. You get the picture.

With five hundred meters left in yesterday's hard-fought road race, which had my heart rate pegged on several occasions, I was sitting pretty in third in the lead-out to the finish line, with plenty of juice to bust out a medal-chasing sprint to the line, which was to begin in about two seconds. I was tight against the right-side temporary steel fencing, out of the left-side wind.

Aussie Dan Polson had half a bike length on the world's best apparatus-wearing cyclist, Czech Republican Jiri Jezek, who had half a bike length on me. With the eyes on the prize, Dan made a quick jump right (oh, how I wish he would have gone left) to throw wind into the face of this chaser, which forced Jiri into me, and me into the fence. As my knuckles rattled the barriers and my momentum carried me farther into them, it looked like I was going down. In a move to regain my balance, I threw the bike sharply to the right, intensifying the knuckle rattle, and managed to stay up. Unfortunately, in the process, my prosthesis unclipped, and in the miraculously quick two seconds it took me to click it back in, those precious three or four pedal strokes lost me four spots, and I crossed the line behind six other riders.

I was *so* bummed ... for about thirty seconds. Then I congratulated myself for riding one hell of a great race!

🚲　　🚲　　🚲

Upon returning stateside, I had less than a month to whip myself back into running shape. This time it was a race for actual money—like three-months-of-rent-money money! The race was the inaugural Silver Strand Half Marathon in Coronado, California, just outside of San Diego. This event has a five-thousand-dollar purse, something unheard of in our sport. Lord knew I was broke, and as a competitive prosthesis-wearing distance runner, I wasn't about to miss it.

Silver Strand

November 2000

My back hurts …

The Silver Strand Half Marathon is one of the fastest halves in the country. I can say this because I just posted a 1:31:50 there yesterday and won my division. Credit for this relatively fast-ass time goes to the course, the new killer run leg I've recently been fit with, and a healthy set of lungs from all that cycling I've been up to lately.

A dose of credit also goes to fifteen-year-old Andrew Lester, who went out like a rocket. He forced me to run just under seven-minute miles for the first seven miles before he realized he was going a bit too hard and buckled. Not knowing his strength, I had to hold close to his pace to keep him in sight. A pace about thirty seconds faster than I'd expected. My previous personal record (PR) was 1:42, and that was three years ago, when I focused on the run. Ah, the new leg's a beauty.

This race also happens to be the first national championships for leg amputees for the half-marathon distance. The medals eluded me in Sydney, so a nice little championship title at home feels good.

Next Stop ... Malaysia

January 2001

The best gift I received over the holiday season was an invitation to Ironman Malaysia ... *all expenses paid!* The race is January 28, and while I'm nowhere near ready to go the distance, a chance like this one doesn't come around every day. This will put a slight damper on my off-season strength program, but I gotta do what I gotta do.

Coach Kathy put me on a three-week crash Ironman program to get me as ready as possible. I've been running since November, so I'm not totally screwed. I can, however, guarantee that the ride and the marathon are going to hurt! I leave for Malaysia somewhere between the twentieth and the twenty-third (minor miscommunication), returning on the thirty-first. You can expect competition details in your mailbox soon thereafter. So while you're sleeping—resting before your big Super Bowl party—I might be puking somewhere on the other side of the world.

A big thank you to all of you who have helped me be the one who was fortunate to be invited. The support you give allows the work to be done and the racing to be fast enough for the race organizers to take notice.

Hope your holidays were full of friends, family, and lots of love. Happy New Year to all of you.

Thirty-eight hours after pulling out of the driveway, I reached the hotel in Langakawi, Malaysia—a touristy place just off the northwest corner of the country, less than ten miles south of Thailand. I don't typically sleep well on a plane, which makes transcontinental traveling even tougher than it needs to be.

I arrived at the newly built and aesthetically impressive Kuala Lumpur Airport twenty-four hours into the trip, at 2:00 AM. My layover there before boarding the one-hour flight to Langkawi was another eight hours, with pretty much nothing to do and nowhere to get comfortable. More reading of whatever book I was reading. Then, at, like, 5:30, a sketchy guy sporting a blazer and bloodshot eyes came sleazing up to me, asking where I'm from.

"U.S.," I answered politely. "You?"

"Pakistan. What brings you here?"

"I'm here to compete in a triathlon on Sunday. You?"

"Just came back from Thailand. I come to fuck the young girls. Twelve-, fourteen- year-olds."

What the … ? Holy crap … You fucking scumbag! I was thinking. "Excuse me," I said, making my way to another corner somewhere, wondering why it is that such people exist (though I'm not completely naive to the reason), hoping he finds himself scratching later on.

Fortunately, nothing else nearly as disturbing happened while I was in town. (The night after the race, in Kuala Lumpur, I understood exactly why countless beautiful Asian women were hanging out with fat old white men at the bars.)

The week in town was relaxing. The locals were hospitable beyond expectation. The sun was hot. The air was humid. The food sucked. But what an amazing experience the race turned out to be: hot, tiring, miserable, humbling.

I Love This Sport

February 2001

What can I say? I love triathlon. The overwhelming joy I experienced, once again, when I crossed the finish line of Ironman Malaysia on January 28, had me in tears. To push yourself physically, which requires, de facto, mental fortitude, is perhaps the most spiritually satisfying endeavor I can imagine. It leaves you feeling in control of your surroundings ... and your life.

The day's nemesis was the heat. The humidity passed 90 percent, while the temperature exceeded 105. This made for an extremely difficult race. Lothar Leder, the first man to break the eight-hour mark at an Iron-distance race, told me that this was the most difficult race he'd ever done, finishing second in eight hours, forty-seven minutes.

My race started on a high note: one hour, four minutes in the 2.4-mile swim. That bettered my previous best time by more than five minutes. I think I'm finally starting to dial in the technique. I got back in the pool in December after nearly a year off, go figure. The big swim scare of the week was the jellyfish. Four competitors got stung early in their race, including a guy a few feet from me, before the flare gun got things under way. Of the 290 starters, I came out of the water in seventy-seventh place. Woo- hoo! A 2:30 transition and I was off, hopefully, to crack five hours on the bike.

This would require riding the 112 miles at an average speed of just over 22 miles per hour. Well, that didn't even come close to happening. I was on pace for the first thirty miles, and then the hilly section and heat humbled me. The bike section was a two-lapper. By the close of the first lap, I averaged 20.7 miles per hour and resigned to clocking whatever the day would give me. After all, I was on the three-week Ironman training program. I couldn't expect the world.

Near the end of that first lap, my aero-bar elbow pad came loose, and I had to stop there, at what is also the finish area and main stage for spectators, in search of a bike repair. No luck, no tools. I rode on, having noticed several auto repair shops along the course. I was concerned that perhaps the race marshals would not allow me to stop in for an Allen wrench. (Outside assistance is not allowed in triathlon.) But this was a safety issue; had that piece come off while in the aero position, I certainly could have eaten the pavement. (All too familiar to me.) A motorcycle-riding marshal finally came by me, and I requested to seek help. He kindly allowed it—I'm not sure if he was supposed to, but he did. I soon found a shop and got back to business in just a couple of minutes. The rest this provided was kinda nice. Then the damn thing got loose again near the end of the ride and snapped right off at mile 102!

Riding the last ten miles with one arm pad wasn't so bad. I got off the baking bike in 5:38, breaking my PR by eight minutes, averaging 19.7 miles per hour, and posting the forty-fourth fastest bike split of the day.

A sweet 1:41 transition and I began the run feeling relatively fresh, considering the circumstances. This feeling lasted approximately one mile. The heat buried me—along with 290 other sickos. I walked quite a bit early in the run; the heat and the 4 percent grade from miles 2–5 had many of us doing the walk-a-little, run-a-little thing.

Before reaching the 6.55-mile turnaround in the run, I found some energy, and my pace held steady. The run was also a two-lapper. The mostly downhill return to the finish area wasn't much faster than the way up. Total round trip: two hours, twenty-five minutes.

I did my best to impress the crowd as I ran steadily into the finish area. Whit Raymond, the race announcer, pumped up the crowd when I came through, so I kept it up until I was out of sight two hundred meters later ...

Then I walked ... a lot.

Walk-a-lot, run-a-little, walk-a-lot, run-a-little.

I nearly shut down at mile 14—I had a heavy head and heavier legs. This was gonna take a whole lot longer than I had hoped. It looked like I would be walking the majority of the final 12-plus miles. I kept thinking repeatedly, *Overheated and undertrained. Overheated and undertrained.* I know, not the best mental imaging, but gimme a break.

Ever so thankfully, the heat backed off with the added tree shade around the corner, an occasional cloud cover, and a settling afternoon sun. Ninety degrees seemed like cool conditions. By mile 15, going back up that hill, the legs came back with a third or fourth wind.

Along the course, I found respite in my now-ritualistic pouring-of-the-ice-water-all-over-Stumpie. Gawd, that felt so good. Must've done it a half dozen times. More running, less walking. By the time I reached the turnaround at mile 20, I felt strong. Much credit goes to my kick-ass run leg: it's comprised of a Flex-Foot C-Sprint pylon, ALPS South EasySleeve suspension sleeve, and comfortable socket and liner by TEC Interface—love that thing.

Miles 20–25 were the fastest of the day, something like nine-minute miles. The original finishing goal was an aggressive ten hours, thirty minutes. That changed to eleven hours when I got off bike at a total time of 6:45. That changed to simply finishing the damn thing at mile 14 of the run. At the final turnaround, feeling good, the new goal was for this not to be my slowest race ever, to be faster than the 11:55:37 I posted at my first Ironman in '98. By mile 25, the goal was to break twelve hours.

The final mile was so hard. I pushed and focused and pushed and focused until about a quarter mile out. Then I sat down, took the leg off, and thought about how long I could sit there and still break twelve. I got back out there, ran for maybe five hundred feet, and then sat down again, doing the fuzzy math to see how long I could sit. The finish line stretch, twenty meters from where I sat, was eighty to ninety meters, and I wanted to run in strong, to look like I had it all together. I got up and ran. I ran strong into the finish line chute. I could hear Whit on the PA from seventy meters out. "Here comes Paul Martin! Let's hear it!"

The crowd of a few hundred locals and family and friends cheered and cheered some more. My eyes began to water.

I crossed in eleven hours and fifty-eight minutes—half crying, half smiling. Sixty-sixth overall finisher, and my first daytime finish. Good thing we started in near darkness. (You might be wondering if I "won." I was the only one-legger out there, so there wasn't any winning going on, but I did finish eighth of forty-two starters in my age group, 30-34).

Then the Ironman finish line bit that appears to be becoming routine: when I crossed the line, I took off my leg, raised it overhead and exclaimed, "I've said it before, and I'll say it again: *I ... am ... Ironman!*" The crowd, as it has in the past, went nuts! And I started crying, for, like, ten minutes. I immediately sat with the CEO of the race organization for a TV interview and managed to answer the questions while continuing with the half-smiling, half-crying emotions.

Q) "How do you feel?"

A) "That was so hard. That was so unbelievably hard ... I love this sport."

Thanks for the vibes. I know many of you were out there with me. I sincerely hope that every one of you, by whatever means necessary—be it giving birth or climbing Mount Everest—can experience the feelings I did last Sunday.

I was so glad to get that race over with, and I pretty much committed to never doing another Ironman without proper training! But there I was, suddenly and unexpectedly whipped into shape, so I opted to ride the fitness wave awhile. I kicked it back into gear after a couple two three weeks off (that's French Canadian talk) and started training for a marathon. The race known as The Race. The Boston Marathon.

In the meantime, as I'd been doing a fair amount of lately between races, I spoke to kids of all ages around the state and a few around the country, spreading the message of *this* Ability.

Boston Marathon

April 2001

Here's the lowdown.

Good news: smashed my marathon PR.

Bad news: didn't come anywhere close to the WR.

Conditions leading up to the gun were less than stellar but not so poor that I can excuse my performance because of them.

I had run in the pouring rain in LA a few days earlier and caught a nice little cold that stuck with me up to race day (I know, supposedly you can't actually catch a cold from bad weather, but experience tells us there's some correlation). But even that was not much more than a psychological glitch. The next day I spoke at a school in Southern California, last Tuesday, a week ago today. I had gotten up at 5:00 AM that day and driven two hours north from Santa Barbara to Santa Maria. (Got a speeding ticket from CHiPs on the way.) Did two talks at the school and got back to LAX for a 4:00 PM flight back to Denver. Got home, repacked for the next morning's trip to Boston, and was in bed by 11:30. Then up at 4:30 AM and on the road to DIA at 5:30 in a wicked snowstorm. DIA was shut down, so I visited a friend in Denver for a couple of hours, and the TV told us that United Airlines canceled all flights before 6:00 PM. I spent a couple hours back in Boulder and got back to DIA at 3:00 PM, hoping to get on a flight ASAP. (I had a speaking gig the next morning in Fall River, Massachusetts—adjacent Rhode Island—at 8:00 AM and another in Norwell, just south of Boston, at 12:30. These two talks paid more money than I earned in all of October through December of last year! I *had* to be there.)

So I got on a flight from Denver to *San Francisco* at 8:00 PM to catch the red-eye to Beantown at 10:15 PM, scheduled to arrive at 6:45 AM—cuttin' it a bit close. The plane out of San Fran had some mechanical problems, and we ended up on another plane at another gate, leaving at 11:30. Got to Boston at 7:45 AM and finally made it to my first talk almost two hours late, doing two twenty-minute talks instead of three forty-minute talks ... and still got *paaaaiiiiid!* Made it to Norwell a little late and did one talk instead of two, and this time I received half the original fee, which left me little room to complain.

I finally made it to Mom's couch at 8:00 PM that night.

On Saturday morning, I did a little three-mile run with the folks from Brooks, my shoe and apparel sponsor, near Boston. My stump was bothering me a little on that run but I thought nothing of it and headed to the race expo at Boston's World Trade Center for an hour at the Brooks booth, signing autographs on these cool little photo cards they had made up for me. (This shouldn't impress you very much—in an hour, I signed, like, ten of them.)

Now, I've run about five hundred miles since Sydney on my Flex-Foot C-Sprint running pylon, and about a thousand miles in the socket, but for some unknown reason, my leg was *killing* me on Saturday night. Some sort of pinched nerve thing on the posterior medial aspect (inside-back side) of Stumpie. I've had some discomfort in that area before, but nothing I couldn't handle. All of sudden, I couldn't walk more than twenty feet. Not cool.

The next day—the day before the marathon—Stumpie was feeling a little better, and I broke out Uncle Eddie's Dremel bit to grind away some of the socket wall of my running leg to give Stumpie a little more room. That night Aunt Rachael performed Reiki (holistic energy healing, pronounced RAKE-ee) on Stumpie and the rest of me, and Monday morning it felt *wicked fuckin' pissa*—that's Boston talk for "good."

Marathon weather conditions were nearly perfect, fifty-fiveish at the start, with blue skies. Got a little chillier with a headwind near the finish, but nothing crazy. With the massive crowds in the first couple of miles, I started out just slightly ahead of pace. The communal excitement crept in, and I ended up ahead of schedule at mile 5 and still a bit too fast at mile 10. Five miles later, I was right on, and by the time I got to Heartbreak Hill at mile 20, I was a couple of minutes behind a world-record pace.

The hill was a grind, but the way down the steep hill that followed was tenfold worse. I'd already begun to waver, and I felt a side stitch coming on as I crested the hill. The downhill pounding sent my guts into an uproar. By mile 21, with hopes of a world record (3:18) all but gone, the pain in my side had me standing still, leaning against a tree, trying hard just to breathe. I held up for a minute or so and then tried simply to trot along, but every foot strike had me cursing the pain. I went through this uncomfortable scenario for the next two and a half miles, which took about forty minutes. Between miles 23 and 24, the pain had subsided and I could breathe, for the most part, but my legs were already fried.

I ran an 8:30 to 9:00-minute-per-mile pace for the rest of the race and crossed in 3:38:07. I ended up first among the gimps—I'm pretty sure; I couldn't seem to get an answer—and about 5,200th among the 15,500 starters. Within the hour, I called my dad, a few of my longtime buddies from Gardner, and my buddy Puck and his friends, including his wife, Erica, who also ran, and they all just happened to be at the same bar! A couple twenty-two-ounce Sammy's later, and I was very, very happy to have just run the Boston Marathon.

I came to one conclusion at the top of Heartbreak: If I intended to be the fastest gimp marathoner the world has ever known, I gotta put in more miles. I gotta figure out how to run more without beating up Stumpie, or I gotta run through pain a little more than I have been. A little more focus. A little more motivation.

And finally, congrats to Amy, Jack, Ivan, and a couple of other one-leggers for a great job yesterday. Way to go!

Thanks, as always, for what all of you do for me. It doesn't go unnoticed.

The best part of journaling, and this might be painfully obvious, is picking up that bound version of your past and reliving it. That's what happened just now, in real time, on March 29, 2005, 4:53 PM Mountain Standard Time. I just reread the Boston e-mail that I had sent over cyberspace four years ago. I had forgotten about the whole episode, this not-so-out-of-the-ordinary minor calamity my life turns into every now and then. (There's more to come, I'm sure of it.) In reliving the experience, I am reminded of how much fun this trip has been.

With the last couple of e-mails, you might have noticed the expansion in length and detail. I'm not sure how or why the phenomenon came about when it did, but I was really beginning to enjoy writing.

I got a little crazy with this next installment. Hope you like it.

Germany and Then Some

July 2001

I spent the better part of last week in Germany. To do an Ironman. Went well.

I thought it might. I'd spent six consecutive weekends riding long miles. Mostly by myself. Thinking about who knows what. I'd run on Sundays for, like, three hours.

I'd been feeling good ever since I'd run Boston. Back in April. I raced in California on May 5. A crunchy race called Wildflower. Naked girls. I didn't see them. I'm told they were there. I came in eleventh of 251 in the 30-34s. Almost shit myself when I saw the results. Almost shit myself in Germany too. Read on. I raced in Memphis in May at a race called, for some reason, Memphis in May. That's in Tennessee. Near Alabama. South of Kentucky. Didn't come in eleventh. Came in twenty-third, out of 109. Had my second fastest race ever. In my life. And yours too, for that matter (2:17:??).

So I felt good at the onset of Sunday's Ironman Europe. In Roth, Germany. North of Austria. I did my homework. I ate lots of ice cream in June. I finished in 10:41:43. Forty-one minutes faster than I'd ever gone before. Happiness. Joy.

Satisfied. Yes. But I still didn't win my division. Rivaldo Martins crossed the line, breaking his previous world record of 10:22, with a time of 10:10:05. He's Brazilian. He's probably not even human. Totally freakin' incredible. Congratulations, Rivaldo. Again. I've raced him three times. Each time it's a new personal record for me. But honestly, I'd much rather beat him.

Everything worked on Sunday. Had a good swim. Didn't swallow anything funny. It was raining. Got out of the water in one hour, four minutes. Rode kinda fast: five hours, twenty-four minutes. And, of course, ran like a steed—that part took four hours and six minutes.

There's this half-mile hill on the bike course. Called Solerer Berg. With twenty thousand people on it. Un. Believable. Shoulda seen it. Riding into a funnel of people is cool. Loud people. Naked girls. Not on the course this time. I was just thinking about them.

First lap of two on the bike: I closed the eleven-minute gap Rivaldo put on me in the water to nine minutes. I felt as if I'd already won. The second lap of the bike got a little windy. Believe it or not, winds at 130 miles per hour. Don't believe it. More like 20 to 30 miles per hour. In the face. Took the average speed down from 22.3 miles per hour to 21.0. That sucked.

I completed the first lap in two hours, thirty-two minutes. The second in two hours, fifty-two minutes. I was then twenty-two minutes behind the one disguised as human. "I can cover that." I actually said that to Martin Goetz. Martin was my host, my taxi driver, my chef, my maid ... By mile 10 of the marathon, Rivaldo was up by twenty-four minutes. That sucked. By mile 20, twenty-seven minutes. I had clearly lost the race. Was not going to win. That wasn't a big deal. I was so pumped. I was flying. (Speaking of flying, I flew first class to Paris. That did not suck.) I had actually trained hard. I'd better have. It's not like I have a job.

The training appeared to be helpful. I was on a 3:50 marathon pace at the halfway point of the run. At mile 20, a 4:00 pace. It was right about then that my legs decided not to go so fast. The last 10k took over an hour. Other than right at the end there—at the end of 2.4 miles of swimming, 112 miles of biking, and 26.2 miles of running—I felt great. No major pain. Other than an unhappy lower back fighting that bastardly wind on the bike. Well, that and the cramps I had in my intestinal track. At about the same time my back hurt.

The Goetzes, my host family—possibly the greatest family in the history of mankind, next to mine, of course—fed me too damn much. Well, maybe I just ate too damn much. I don't know. Anyway, when you eat too much, there's too much in you. See where I'm going with this? There I was at, like, mile 85, fighting the winds, having to poop like you would not believe. I pulled over to the best spot I could find.

Talking to self: *There's an old cart path. A big bush. Excellent.* I dropped the bike. Hobbled over there. It was a pricker bush ... With no options, I did my thing. I smiled. I laughed. With shorts tucked around ankles, with athletes zipping by, I duck walked around in a little circle, looking for anything without spikes for the cleanup. I had my hand, clutching a few green leafy things, up my butt. I looked up into the eyes of a female racer passing by. I felt silly. I then hopped on the Schwinn and cranked my dirty little ass up as fast as I could go. Passed her as if all was normal. Nothing going on here. Without looking over. Hoping never to see her again.

On the run course—the entire run course—people were yelling "Soooo-pah." Means "super" in English. I was still seeing naked girls.

The race wrapped up with a strong finish. Into the finish area. Shaped like a horseshoe. Big grandstands. People cheering. I crossed the line. Held leg overhead and proclaimed loudly, with German hair ball–clearing accent, *"Ich ... bin ... Ironman!"* You translate.

The 10:41:43 finish put me 631st of 2,700 overall—193rd of 600 in the 30-40s. Happiness. Joy.

Peak Experience: Myself and five other gimps were on the stage for awards the next morning. Thousands of people gave us a five-minute standing ovation. Smiles. More smiles. Rivaldo was standing to my right. He was faster than I am. *I must keep competing. How can I do anything else?*

Thanks, you guys and you girls. Special ones to Bill Beiswenger and Bill Teague from Abilities Unlimited—prosthetic shop in Colorado Springs—for the moola. And to Mike Godfredson at Road Runner Sports/Athletes Helping Athletes for the rest of the moola.

The moola came less than three weeks before the race.

But as I've come to learn, no need to panic. I had no flight before Mr Godfredson stepped up and, with two weeks to go, no place to stay in mid-Bavaria. A friend of a friend found a friend to provide housing—the fabulous Goetz family. Got a cheap ticket online and flew to Paris. Took trains from there to Germany. Train tix provided by my roommates Tracy and Lisa, who work for RailEurope here in Boulder. Kudos to John at RE for making that happen.

Put your head where you want the rest of you to be. It *will* follow.

Off to Edmonton in six days for Triathlon World Championships. No. I don't have a flight or a place to stay ...

Two thousand and one was my busiest year to date. Lots of traveling and lots of races. And lots of trying times of the adventurous sort.

No Rest for the Stoopid

August 2001

Some of you might have read the big ol' e-mail about Ironman Europe. It gets worse.

Exactly thirteen days after that Ironman in Germany, I raced the Olympic distance world championships in Edmonton, Alberta, 1,200 miles north of Boulder. I got there via *my* car. To know the typical Paul car, in this case, a fifteen-year-old Toyota Camry, is to know that arrival at the planned destination is far from guaranteed.

I made the trip in three somewhat enjoyable days.

I camped each night along the way, cooking dinner over open flames. I really do love that scene. Gotta learn to play guitar.

Things got sketchy right from the start. Apparently, I needed a new thermostat. The car was overheating and the immediate no-cost temporary solution was to *blast* the heater to cool the engine as I drove seventy miles per hour in the ninety-five-degree Wyoming sun. Nothing like a good sweat to make one feel fresh.

Upon my successful arrival at Edmonton, I drove the bike into the hotel garage overhang! You should have heard the expletives ... should have seen the witnesses. Funny from a distance, I'm sure. Turned out all was good with the bike; only the bike rack was in pieces. Breakaway racks: genius.

I won the race—my division anyway—in 2:23. I beat all but one of the wingers; those are the one-arm/no-arm dudes. That's always the race within the race, trying to edge as many of the "faster" gimps as possible. I sprinted another winger down at the finish line. He was waving; I was running. One-arm Willie Stewart was, as he often is, first to the line. He's fast. And his wife, Lindsay, is extremely cool.

The eight-foot brass version Wayne Gretzky posed with me for a photo right outside the rink where he made himself famous. Seems he's not well liked by all those Edmontonians, something to do with being a defective. Then I made my way home via Jasper National Park, where humongous elk with humongous antlers live. One of those big bastards crossed the road three feet in front of my car. I got a photo. If this here scanner worked or if I knew how to use it, I'd attach it, but it doesn't/I don't ... so I won't.

I stayed at a hostel that rainy night and drove toward Calgary the next day via Lake Louise. While there, it only seemed fitting to rent a canoe and tool around the lake with a friend who hitched a ride with me from the hostel. All of sudden, out of nowhere comes a crazy friggin' hailstorm. It was phenomenal. And very cold.

We brought in the canoe, grabbed some lunch, and then headed off to Yellowstone and Old Faithful.

A great trip.

A week later, back in Colorado, I raced Xterra Keystone—an off-road triathlon. The one-thousand-meter swim was at nine thousand feet; my lungs were useless. The eighteen-mile ride had two parts: (1) straight up to eleven thousand feet, and (2) straight down. (I hadn't mountain biked in a year and a half; I sold my mountain bike for rent last winter—damn!) The rear tire flatted on the straight down part. I didn't have a pump, which sucked. (That's where the stoopid part comes in.) A fellow competitor and friend rode by and helped me break the rules by lending me his pump. I only lost about ten minutes.

The 10k run was rooty and rocky and hot and miserable and endless. All those adjectives were borne directly from the "I'm tired" factor. I had to walk some of that tricky terrain stuff. I finished up in 3:17 and then lay down in the grass, legs convulsing.

I rested a week and a half at home before heading out to San Diego for the International Challenge, a track-and-field event for the disabled. I hadn't raced at a track event since '97, and for this reason alone, I was excited. I ran the fifteen hundred meter on Thursday in 5:10. Not too bad. On Friday, I ran the five thousand meter in 18:49. Not too bad. I broke the official national record by nearly a minute (I would imagine there's gotta be at least a couple of faster unofficials out there. I mean really, at least one.) And guess what! I won $150!

Saturday I raced the Muddy Buddy, a 10k two-person mountain bike/run event at Camp Pendelton. I had no intention of doing that when I headed to Southern California, but since discovering that Brooks, my shoe and apparel sponsor, was sponsoring the event, and since the beneficiary of the series is the Challenged Athletes Foundation, it was clearly the thing to do. The race was *so* much fun. Crawling-on-our-bellies-through-eight-inches-of-mud type fun! Then I met a girl in the outdoor community shower. She hasn't returned my calls.

My muddy buddy and I won our division, an able-bodied division, and a cool frog trophy.

That night I flew home to Boulder, got to bed at 12:30AM, got up Sunday at 5:15 AM, and raced a PR at the Boulder Peak Triathlon at 7:56 AM, a just-ever-so-slightly-longer-than-Olympic-distance race. I didn't quite meet my goal, however. I was hoping for a 2:25 and finished in 2:25:02.

So that's what I've been up to. How 'bout you? Let me know. I would love to hear. Vanity only gets you so far.

Being single and unemployed certainly has its advantages. At the top of the list comes freedom. Freedom to go anywhere and do anything. Anything that doesn't cost much money, anyway. I was having such a rewarding year racing all over the world, posting fast times in the process. The year wasn't nearly over yet, and I still had plenty of steam, enough to jump on a plane headed for Hawaii for a double dose of suffering.

The Double

October 2001

I just got back from Kona. I spent nearly three weeks there, with the unique pleasure of completing both the Hawaiian Ironman and Xterra world championships. Let's be brief, shall we?

I arrived there nine days early and slept on a friend's futon. I didn't do much last-minute training—a couple of little swims, little bikes, little runs.

On October 6 around 6:55 AM, I was in the water for the 7:00 AM start of the 2001 Ironman Triathlon World Championships. On cue, the goggles fogged as soon as I stuck my size seven head in the water. Then I swam as fast as I could, stopping a couple of times to defog myself. I reached the 1.2-mile turnaround in twenty-nine minutes, fifty-nine seconds and returned to the pier, a matching 1.2 miles later, in forty-one minutes—must've been a current ... The 1:11 swim was a tad disappointing. Rivaldo, my nemesis, swam it in fifty-five minutes. Then, as I began my hop up the swim exit ramp, I fell flat on my face and said the F-word at high volume. Sixteen minutes down from the get-go.

Then I rode as fast as I could, which wasn't terribly fast. It's been said in the past, and will undoubtedly be said again, but the winds out on the Queen K were the worst *ever!* By mile 38, my back was killin' me, and I suddenly felt overly undertrained. I got off the bike and lay on the road's shoulder for thirty seconds to relieve my aching lumbar number four. First time I've ever done that. I must say, it did wonders, and I felt so much better when I got back on it. "It" being the new Griffen Vulcan boron carbide super high-tech, recently top-secret declassified material rocket ship bike. I'd have been bumming more if I weren't on that thing.

As I approached the turnaround in Hawi, I saw The Nemesis leaving it. I made note of where I'd seen him, and I also took note of my watch. I was then able to ascertain his eighteen-minute lead when I later passed that point. Since we were battling side winds and headwinds all the way to Hawi, the tailwind-aided return would be well received. But alas, that never came—the entire fifty-plus-mile return was somehow nothing but side winds and headwinds! Not good, not welcomed. I had to get off the bike again for a thirty-second R & R at mile 90. The hoped-for bike split was 5:30. The actual bike split was 6:06. Knockered and sore, but still ready to run, I took a leak, and in four minutes, six seconds, I began whittling away at the next task.

I was now down by thirty minutes to the Brazilian. (I found out after the race that he was a pro triathlete when he lost his leg. My ego was *thrilled* to hear this.) By mile 4, I had whittled his lead down to twenty-four minutes. By mile 11, it was twenty minutes. Then some random guy on a bike coming the other way said, "The other guy's only got three minutes on you!" At the next aid station, a volunteer volunteered, "At least you're running through here; the other guy was walkin' ..."

The I BEAT RIVALDO e-mail was being written.

I kept running hard—around nine-minute miles, as hard as I could—and looking up the road to find his crumpling ass ...

But nada.

At mile 16, someone told me I was ten to fifteen minutes down.

"Crap!"

Near the final turnaround at the Energy Lab (an actual scientific facility specializing in the study of renewable energy), I saw Studly running strong with a fourteen-minute lead.

I kept pushing. I *really* wanted to beat him. I kept pushing the pace. But he kept pushing too. He *knew* that I wanted it. He finished in 11:09. About that time, I was at mile 24. But I didn't know that. I had no choice but to keep hittin' it, hoping that he'd buckle.

When I got to mile 26ish, I saw a happy Joel and Diane (more about her later), who informed me that I was down twenty minutes. No matter. I was smiling and damn happy to have just about finished my fifth Ironman. I made the bend onto Ali'i Drive and saw the people. The smiling, happy, cheering people. I almost shed a tear, but not quite.

I slowed the pace and took it all in. I high-fived a few, then let one guy pass me to be sure the stage was all mine (yes, preparing to showboat). One step across the line, a look to the left. "You know who I am? ... You wanna know who I am? ... (with leg overhead) ... I ... am ... *Ironman!*" The crowd roared, as did I. Joel and Diane and my handler, Sandy, were all right there with hugs and hollers.

It's amazing how the feeling comes back repeatedly. That "just finished Ironman" feeling. No other experience has matched it.

I finished in 11:31:33. My finish was nine minutes slower than in '99, but I moved up from 841st to the 613th finisher of fifteen-hundred-plus starters, a testament to the tough conditions that you don't like when you're out there, but which make the finish taste that much sweeter.

Okay, that part's done. Not really all that brief, and we're not quite done yet …

Before Xterra, eight days later, I earned my scuba certification in Kona. This is needed for Expedition BVI, a four-day adventure race I'll be part of in the British Virgin Islands in December, which, of course, you'll have the opportunity to read about in a couple of months, if interested.

Xterra wasn't as fun as I'd hoped it would be. Problems included the following:

Malfunction of the walking leg suspension mechanism the morning of the race, literally causing me to walk out of my leg a few times, accompanied by a hopping save.

Bike leg suspension mechanism broke in the first crash of many on the day, resulting in immensely frustrating problems that I'd rather not revisit.

Bike leg pedal cleat broke in a hike-a-bike across the lava, causing me to ride without being clipped in, which caused me to crash at a high speed onto sharp, unforgiving chunks of lava, resulting in removal of skin, lost blood and overall discomfort.

Lying there on the side of the course, I briefly felt thankful that I was in enough pain to quit the race. A race marshal was at the bottom of this particularly nasty descent for the sole purpose of taking care of competitors who would inevitably "eat it" there. He rushed up the hill, prepared to administer the necessary first aid. He asked a few questions and determined that I was nothing more than banged up. He grabbed my bike while I hobbled down the hill. My race was over so he called, at my request, for a ride to the bottom. Then I walked up the hill, looking for my Rudy Project eyewear. That took a while, and by the time I found them, the truck was there with my bike in the back. I looked at the fellow competitor, who had also quit the race, due to a ripped-open shin, and said with an air of stubbornness, "Fuck!"

Then I looked at the driver and told him to give me my bike back. I fixed the handlebars and the twisted cables, and fifteen minutes after my back, entire left arm, and left hip began to bleed, I hopped back on and descended somewhat cautiously—I had learned moments ago that not being attached to the pedals is a bad thing.

On the run, I hyperextended my left knee (prosthetic side) over and over and over due to the crazy trail terrain—the run leg is designed for flat surfaces. Mental note made over ... and over ... and over: get a trail running leg.

Then the toe edge of the sole on the bottom of my prosthetic somehow peeled half off, and I was digging up dirt and rocks and tripping and swearing and completely miserable. I got to aid station that had, yes, duct tape. Thank God!

I finished the race and have yet to DNF (did not finish) a triathlon—and I'm in no hurry to do so. (Thanks to the powers that be for giving me the wherewithal.)

With all this behind me, I headed home via LA and San Diego, where I spoke at a couple of schools, earning a few dollars to pay back all the people I've bummed money from in the past several months to keep doing what I do. Thanks to George, Mary, Paul, Jim, Ron, and especially Jon, whom I've owed money to since the birth of the Internet, and to Matt, whom I've owed money to since computers came onto the scene.

While in LA, I visited my prosthetic sponsor, Össur/Flex-Foot. We spent time discussing modifications for a mountain bike foot and a trail runner. I would like my next Xterra to be F-word free!

Soon before heading off to Hawaii, I received another one of those all-expenses-paid-to-an-exciting-destination race invitations. This time for an adventure race: new territory. I had been thinking about tackling one someday, so when the invite arrived, I was all over it.

Adventures in Humility

December 2001

I spent last week in the British Virgin Islands. Relaxing? Hardly. I took part in Expedition BVI, a four-day adventure race in the Caribbean islands just east of Puerto Rico.

The Challenged Athletes Foundation was granted two four-person team entries, worth a total of nine thousand dollars, in exchange for providing a challenged athlete for each team. Supposedly, we became the first disabled individuals to take part in a major expedition race. I was the gimpy part of Team DuPont/CAF and One-Arm Willie Stewart competed with three able-bodied athletes on Team Metabolife/CAF.

I interviewed with the media on several occasions, stating that I had ambitions for a top-ten finish among the twenty-four teams who made the trip. And I meant it. I had strong intent to show the two-legged freaks a thing or two about endurance. My teammates were all experienced adventurers, which provided me with even more confidence. By noontime of the first day of competition, I was eating my words.

The race began on Tuesday, December 11 at 8:05 AM, on the north side of the island of Tortolla. By 8:06 AM, I had already flipped my kayak on the beach. It was a tandem kayak; I took the front seat and Marshall Ulrich took the back. I got in first, and one little bump from Marsh put my ass in the sand. Teammates Lisa Jhung and Greg Thomas—our team's head navigator—were well on their way before Marsh and I began to paddle. We were on our way to our team yacht—yes, yacht—where we were to tie up the kayaks and swim to the beach to checkpoint I (CPI).

We coasteered the next leg to CP2. (Coasteering consists of making one's way along the coastline via trekking across beaches, climbing along large and small rocks, and wading and swimming through the water. Try to picture any conceivable

Paul Martin

type of ocean/land interface, and we had to make our way across it.) The deadline to CP2 to continue with the entire race was 12 PM. We got there at 12:25 ... The possibility of not completing the entire course never crossed my mind. Humility lesson number one.

This event brought a new format to adventure racing. Throughout the race, teams were ranked in one of three classes: Competition, Expedition, and Adventure, with the number of checkpoints required to stay ranked within that class declining respectively. The course designers wasted no time in weeding out the weaker teams; ours being one of five teams assigned to the Adventure class at CP2. From there, we skipped CP3 and kayaked directly to CP4, where we began a trek to CP6, the rappelling section of the race. Getting to CP6 was no easy task. We began the trek at around 2:00 PM and didn't get to the rappel until 9:00 PM.

The fastest way to CP6 was to swim/coasteer. Choosing the fastest way is a critical aspect of adventure racing—you're not told which route to take; you're just given a map and checkpoint coordinates, and it's up to you to get there, within the rules. Mistakenly, we chose to bushwhack through thick and prickly underbrush instead of taking the water route.

In and of itself, this was a new experience for me. We entered the brush when the road ran out, adjacent to an old house being rebuilt. We asked a local for some trail advice. His incredulous reply: "No one's been in there in twenty-five years. Nothin' but goats go in there now." He peered inquisitively at us, not sure what to make of these fools in matching outfits. "You need a machete to get through that."

I soon became a machete-less bushwhacker. For hours, we pushed through heavy growth comprised of a few friendly flora and several unfriendly cacti. Thank God for the thorn resistant pants and jerseys Marshall had scored for us. One of the top teams passed us in the section, and that team's lone female, Karen Lundgren, was sporting a pair of shorts. At the end of the day, I can honestly say that I've never seen *half* that many scratches on anyone's legs in my entire life. She didn't complain for a second, and the smile never left her face.

The sun had set by the time we got near the rappel site. We had covered 90 percent of the distance of that particular leg in a few hours. The next 10 percent took a couple more. We got lost a bit trying to reach our destination at the tip of the island; the rappel site was only reachable by one gnarly path down a steep face of loose growth and looser rocks. The waterproof headlamp I'd brought along wasn't so waterproof, and it wasn't working when I needed it to. The descent to the water along that steep face without a headlamp and a gimpy leg provided the greatest fear I've experienced in quite some time. I expected to push myself physically on this trip, but I really didn't expect to be frightened at any point. Once again, humbled.

We made it to the bottom, to the rocks by the water, only to have to scale a seventy-foot steeper-than-we-just-came-down trail to the rappel site. We dropped from that point into the ocean and soon began a swim back to where we'd dropped off the kayaks. It was now past 10:00 PM, the stars were out, the sea was calm, and I was floating on my back, looking up at the sky (we wore PFDs—personal floatation devices—for most of the race), and the next thing I knew, I was speaking aloud to the universe, expressing my gratitude for putting me there.

Marshall was fifty meters in front of me, and Lisa and Greg were fifty meters behind. I took in the wonder of the situation at hand and thanked my Maker for putting me there, for giving me the gumption to get off the couch and try my hand at adventure racing. For my prostheses and my teammates who were willing to take the risk of competing with me. It was cool. Soon we were climbing along big ol' rocks in the black of night.

We made it back to the kayaks at 1:00 AM, but we still had a long trek and coasteer to CP 7 before our day could end. The top teams had made it there and back by 10:30 and were now sleeping in their yachts just off the beach—and they had made it to all the CPs. Clearly, I was not the badass rookie adventure racer I thought I would be. The ego sat back and said little. To CP7 and back would be, at minimum, five to six hours round-trip. The boats would be departing at 8:00 AM. This didn't leave up a lot of time for error. We ate and drank, and we were making our way by 1:30. By 4:30, we were still an hour from CP7. We decided it would best to bite the bullet. We weren't going to get there and back in time, and that meant we were going to miss a CP. Missing a CP means dropping out of the official ranks. It means you lose. Marshall had never missed a CP. He'd never been unranked. Marshall holds the record for the Badwater Quad, a 136-mile race from Death Valley to the top of Mt Whitney—done four times back-to-back. That's right, a five-hundred-and-forty-four-mile race on foot. Marshall had all his toenails surgically removed to prevent problems on the run. Marshall Ulrich doesn't miss checkpoints. We all swallowed the same pill.

While we were no longer officially ranked, we were allowed to continue—just for the fun of it!

At 7:00 AM, we were back at the yacht and preparing to set sail at 8:00; day two would begin with a regatta. Greg was the only one to forego any sleep to help the skipper prepare to sail. Lisa, Marsh, and I got a little shut-eye before the boat began rocking back and forth and up and down. At 8:30, I was on deck, having a lot more fun than Lisa, whose entire stomach contents now lay at the bottom of a small trash can. It turns out that four of the teams dropped out of the official ranks that morning due to seasickness. Lisa toughed it out. After an hour of misery, a few minutes on land brought her back to normal. We began what was to be by far the most miserable experience I've voluntarily put myself through in a long, long time: a twelve-mile sea kayak into the wind.

The problem: back pain. Lots of it. A sea kayak provides little to no back support. This isn't a big problem for most people, and for those who do find it an issue, they install a lumbar support apparatus. Most likely, these people actually spend time in a sea kayak and discover the need—they are people who actually prepare themselves. My first inclination was to blame the misery on the compression fracture of a lumbar vertebra back in '88. In reality, I slept in the lack-of-training bed that I had made.

Sitting hunched like that for four hours while rotating and grinding away at the water and wind nearly had me in tears. Marshall, steadfast and sturdy in the rear seat, refused to entertain the thought of pulling over to shore to let me lie down. I wasn't the least bit happy about that, but I didn't want to sound like any more of a wuss than I was feeling like at the time, so we continued to plug to the next checkpoint. When we finally got there, I rolled out of the boat and lay there wriggling for a few minutes, ecstatic to be on land, having sworn an hour or two ago that I would never volunteer to paddle ever again. I think I actually cried. *Wuss.*

The kayaks weighed about ninety pounds apiece with our gear, and we had to portage (carry) them a couple of hundred meters to the bike transition, which required a 5:00 PM checkout time. We got there at 4:59:30. Too late, too bad. No bike ride for us. The weather was nasty, it was getting dark, and the course had been modified anyway, to less than twenty miles. We didn't miss much of the race, but the fact that we were missing checkpoints was painful to accept. I'd thought we'd be kickin' ass, and here we were, getting our asses kicked. A lot of that was my fault. Greg and Lisa had reached the shore about a half hour before Marshall and me. Had I been able to do my share of paddling (I sat up front writhing in pain, not contributing much to our forward progress for the majority of that section), we probably would have been pedaling, something my ego greatly looked forward to.

After the bike, teams were to get back in the kayak and paddle something like eight miles to another island. The thought terrified me. *How in the hell will I be able to hack it?* Such anxiety was foreign to me—but I was *frightened*. Then the race organizers opted not to send out any teams due to the bad weather: winds, high seas, and rain. Many of the faster teams had already set out and nearly completed the crossing. Some had already made it there and were safe and dry on their yachts that awaited them at Norman Island. After much deliberation on the administrators' part, the lagging teams were told to spend the night, that we'd pursue the island at first light. Fortunately, this latest CP was back at the hotel, and we were able to get a good meal and a good night's sleep before resuming at 5:00 AM.

Awoken by an unwelcome alarm, we prepared to get back in the boat and were soon informed that the start would be delayed until they could locate a missing team. A team of rookies from New York City took off for Norman Island the previous night just before it was called off, and they had yet to reach their destination. All were concerned. Apparently, they went off course a bit and ended up spending the night on Saint John, an island several miles out of the way. Around 7:30 AM, a helicopter saw them paddling toward Norman Island, and the rest of us were given the go to start making our way. While waiting for word to send off, I had rigged up a lumbar support pad out of rope and my foam seat cushion. Lumbar number four loved me for it.

While we made our way toward the island, the athletes who'd made it there the night before were treated to another regatta start, and we met them at their boating finish. Once on land, we swam to a nearby cave along the coast, where we had to swim in to find a posted code word for that CP. In the process, I lost my small bag of mandatory personal gear, which also held forty dollars and my credit card. I was so pissed at myself for losing it; if we were still ranked, that would have disqualified our team. *Schmuck.* Another team ended up finding it floating in the cave, and I received it at the finish line. It was my only credit card with any remaining credit left on it ... (Why was I carrying it? Buying food or supplies along the way is legal, and preparation is clearly necessary.)

Soon we were back in the kayaks for the trip to the scuba section. We reached it at 4:00 PM, only to learn that it closed at 4:00 due to the strong current that was causing poor visibility underwater and taking teams way off course. It was raining again, and the staff opted to load all the kayaks onto the huge media boat and bring those of us trailing far behind the leaders to the next CP. When I'd headed out to the scuba course, I'd left my trekking leg on shore, fully expecting to return for it. Only two members of each team were allowed to scuba, with the other two remaining on shore. When Lisa and I got to the scuba boat, they sent us directly to the media boat. The administrators directed those athletes left on shore to grab all their team's gear and meet the others on the boat. They radioed over to the shore to have my teammates grab my leg. In doing so, they left my interface liner on the rocks, without which I'm SOL. The boat was a clusterfuck of athletes and media and staff, and the word never got to shore to have the last team grab my liner. Fortunately, I was prepared for such a scenario. I'd given Greg a package of prosthetic spare parts for him to haul for me, including a liner, socks, and suspension sleeves. (It behooved our team to have the others carry my stuff and lessen the burden on Stumpie, bettering our chances for a strong finish, which had already reached farcical proportions.).

The next CP was phenomenal. Again, two teammates were designated—in this case, Marshall and myself—to climb and crawl along a rope-guided course though *huge* round boulders, like fifty feet high, perfectly smooth and round. *So cool.* It was like being shrunk down to ant size and walking through a pile of pebbles. This required a lot of crawling, which totally trashed my suspension sleeve. Again, the spare parts came in handy.

Back in the kayaks for a night paddle into a strong headwind. Nearly four hours of paddling got us to just outside the next CP, when it was decided, mistakenly, that we went a bit too far. We backtracked to the previous bay, a few hundred meters around the corner. As we entered the bay, a shallow reef challenged our passage, and the darkness added to the experience. Greg and Lisa were nearly toppled by a wave along the reef, but they made it through. Marsh and I then attempted to cross, but a wave came and tossed the inexperienced rookie onto the reef, leaving Marsh in the boat, shaking his head. I was okay with getting painfully dumped onto my back on a coral reef, but not okay with losing my new fresh-out-of-the-box Petzl waterproof headlamp I'd picked up back at the hotel the night before. I started cussin' like a peg-leg pirate and didn't let up for quite some time. When we finally made it to shore one hundred meters later, we discovered that the original point we were headed to was the right one. Then the lost Petzl really set me off, and I started spewing loud, lewd words all over again. A couple of minutes later, I laughed at myself and took it in stride.

It turns out we were beached on the beach of an exclusive private resort. We were warned in the rulebook not to trespass there, lest we wish to be arrested and fined. The staff didn't seem to mind, but they were perplexed as to what the hell we were doing paddling in pitch blackness in the rain. "Aren't you tired?" the late night front desk woman asked. "Yes," we answered. Then we paddled back through the channel and made our way to the proper CP.

There, we were fed well by a friend of Marshall's—a local woman and former adventure race team crewperson who had been out there all day, feeding hot soup, drinks, and cookies to the athletes. It was now about midnight, and our race was in such a shambles that we took up an offer from Bob, another local, to drive us to the next checkpoint, where we could grab a ferryboat to the evening's final CP—the Bitter End Yacht Club on an exclusive island. The last boat left at 1:00 AM, and we got there at 1:15. We opted to catch a few ZZZs and catch the next ferry out at 6:00 AM. My three teammates had no problem falling asleep with their compact emergency space blankets (the aluminum foil–looking things), but mine had floated away in that cave. I found a bundle of newspapers and stuffed both my shirt and pants with them. I was happy and toasty. The weather continued to be sketchy, so we opted to stay under cover. Under cover came with a slight sacrifice: we had to sleep on a slab of concrete. I got in two hours at best.

The next morning's 8:00 AM start marked the last day of competition. It began with a swim/coasteer section before a welcomed trekking leg that took us to the top of Virgin Gorda, then up an observation tower with a spectacular 360-degree view of islands and ocean. From there, we descended back to where we'd left the kayaks the night before. We headed back out to sea around noon and, fittingly, took a wrong course to our last CP, probably an hour or so out of the way. It was a three-mile paddle to the finish line from there. Thankfully, this final kayak section had a strong tailwind, something teams were deprived of for nearly the entire race. Being in the front of the boat, I was the one to hold up the small triangular handheld sail brought with us for such occasions. Holding it up was indeed a strain on the biceps and forearms, but it was a hell of a lot faster than paddling.

The finish line showed up around 4:30 that afternoon. People cheered. We felt good, glad to be done. I can't speak for my teammates, but I suspect they share a similar sentiment: we're a competitive sort and somewhat ashamed for just getting our asses handed to us. Finishing was nice, but we weren't exactly ecstatic about it. I looked for a little fun and humor in the situation; I'm sure I offended a few people, while making a few laugh and leaving a few wondering if I had actually said what I said when popping the cork: "Feet are for pussies!"

🚲   🚲   🚲

That was good stuff. Good stuff that keeps you motivated to get better. When you get out there and come up short, you usually want retribution. Retaliation. Redemption. For the next several months, I was certain adventure racing was in my future.

In the meantime, hockey was back in my life, and I loved it. I still don't feel that I'm very good, but playing with the other guys and gals from around the United States last year left me hungry to get better at that too.

The immediate focus of the team's mission was to become a Paralympic sport. We needed other countries to put together teams, and we needed the leaders at the International Paralympic Committee (IPC) to know that amputees skate at a competitive level. To this end, we played an exhibition against the Canadians during the Salt Lake City Paralympics.

And, of course, I was still a passionate triathlete. Since the invitation was there to head to Hawaii for an Olympic distance race, and since I couldn't think of a reason not to go, I went.

Ice and Lava

April 2002

Aloha,

Just did my first triathlon of the year and was once again reminded during the baking-hot 10k run that one should train for such endeavors …

The 5th Annual Lavaman Triathlon is an Olympic distance race located at the scenic Waikoloa Resort on the Big Island of Hawaii. I decided on this one for several reasons:

Obvious.

I had a free place to crash with Joel and Gina Sampson in Honolulu for as long as I liked. Joel's another one-legged Ironman guy. Their daughter, Lauren, is four (she told me she loves me, so I have that going), and their son, Carter, is sixteen months (he loves me too; he just doesn't know how to say it).

I actually made money on the trip speaking at a school in Honolulu and by getting some green from my sponsors for being one of the highlighted athletes on the Outdoor Life Network's (OLN, currently known as Versus) coverage of the race on April 24. (If you happen to catch the show and think I look fat and sunburned, it's because I'm fat and sunburned.)

There was also some golf to be played. Joel and I were a team in a Challenged Athletes Foundation fund-raising round of *speed* golf. That's right, speed counts here. Golfing against the clock, the lowest combined minutes and strokes wins. We shot a 116 in an hour flat for a score of 176. The team thing works like this: one guy plays the hole and the other drives the cart; the cart driver grabs the ball out of the hole as soon as the putter sinks it and takes off for the tee. Tons of fun! Highly recommended for you A types.

The final motivation for this much-earlier-in-the-year-than-I've-ever-raced before event was to kick myself in the ass to get training.

You see, last year was a little out of the comfort zone for me, and I got a bit burned-out—three Ironman races (the first of which was in January), a marathon, a slew of Olympic distance events, and in December a debut at expedition-length adventure racing—that was cool. By calendar year's end, I just wanted to play hockey. So that's what I did for the majority of January, February, and March.

I was getting ready, as were the rest of my U.S. Amputee Hockey teammates, for a Paralympic exhibition game against the Canadians in Salt Lake City on March 16.

We lost 8–0.

But I believe we accomplished our mission: we showed the International Paralympic Committee that gimps can play stand-up hockey, and because of this one game, we just might be a medal sport in the 2006 Paralympic Games in Torino, Italy. (As of the 2010 Games, this milestone has yet to be met.)

This winter has also brought me to quite a few middle schools and high schools, where students and faculty pretend to enjoy listening to me talk about myself. The questions remain the same, for the most part:

Q) If you could, would you want your leg back?

A) No, losing the leg gave me so much, but I'd like to have the leg *and* the learning that losing it provided, but that's just not possible.

Q) Can you jump?

A) Not very high. I'm white.

I received a stack of letters a few days after a sixth-grade presentation. One young man posed a difficult question: What do you do all day? I laughed—but not as hard as my housemates did when I relayed the story.

Next mission will most likely be St. Anthony's Triathlon (Olympic distance) in St. Pete, Florida. Pops lives near there, and the race is April 28, his birthday. Seems like the thing to do. Then it's Memphis in May Triathlon (Olympic) on May 19. Then Buffalo Springs Lake Triathlon (half Ironman) in Lubbock, Texas, in late June. These races are all preparation for Ironman USA in Lake Placid, New York on July 28. Would love to see some of you New Englanders there.

One last thing: the book. It's called *One Man's Leg*. It comes out in the fall. Before coming to Hawaii, I spent nine days in the Northeast, speaking at schools, visiting friends and their new babies, and doing a photo shoot for the book's cover. GreyCore Press will publish this memoir, covering everything from misspent teenage years and time spent in a foster home, to life as an ironworker, to college, to the corporate world, to amputation, to athletics, to God. All this with a little sex, drugs, and rock 'n' roll mixed in for a spicy meal. I'll certainly keep you posted on the date it hits the shelves.

In the meantime, take care of yourselves. No one else wants to.

Must Continue

May 2002

It's been an Olympic distance spring season. I did that Lavaman race in Hawaii on April 7, which I wrote about not too long ago. Three weeks later, as I said I would, I traveled to St. Petersburg, Florida, to cover the distance on April 28 at St. Anthony's Triathlon. The impetus for said competition was my locally habitating father's coincidental birthday. Unfortunately, he opted for a trip to Holland, so I had his house and wheels to myself. (If you know anything about my vehicular history, you'll be surprised to hear that the truck went unharmed over four days of use—the scratch, Dad later admitted, was already there.)

The race in St. Pete went well for the most part. Slow swim: twenty-eight minutes. The PC (physically challenged) athletes again started the day in the first wave, and I was out in front by myself, going a bit off course. I biked a 1:06 despite the back pain—a reasonable split. Then I ran a forty-five-minute 10k—satisfactory. Total time: two hours, twenty-five minutes. Three minutes slower than I covered it in '99. At the awards presentation a few hours later, a physically challenged competitor, George Smith, competing with both legs, nearly completely paralyzed below the knee, told me that he'd taken up triathlon after meeting me a few years ago—that I was the reason he was there. Wow!

"Me? You race because of *me*?" Yep, on the right track …

The following weekend, I was in Manhattan at the Book Expo of America (BEA), promoting *One Man's Leg*. Al Gore was signing his book downstairs at the Jacob Javitz Center. I was upstairs signing mine. The publisher and I went through the fifty advance review giveaways (galleys) in forty-five minutes. People lined up to have me sign my book for them. (Two people constitute a line, you know.)

A couple of weeks later, I rode the sixteen-kilometer Cherry Creek Time Trial in Denver in an attempt to qualify for the U. S. all-expenses-paid team and a trip to the disabled world championships held this August in the Bavarian region of Germany. The qualification standard was a 38.8-kilometer-hour effort of no less than sixteen kilometers.

I met the challenge at a tad under forty-one kilometers per hour, and at this point, I'm an unofficial member of the A Team—me and Mr. T. (The U.S. team is currently in the opening days of a two and a half week training camp that started yesterday in Colorado Springs, at the Olympic Training Center. I'm committed to a few speaking gigs this week, so I'll get there on Friday.)

Last weekend, I raced at the Memphis in May Triathlon and posted an unofficial fastest Olympic distance race of my tri career: 2:13:20—twenty-fifth of 165 in the 30-34s. The swim was a wetsuit-assisted personal best (23:08). I might have broken twenty-three minutes if it weren't for the massive volume of urine I jettisoned in the first 150 meters. You see, this race is unique in that it's a time trial start: athletes line up and get in the water in five-second intervals; I couldn't much relieve myself in line. Once in the water, a wetsuit makes it tough to loosen up so I did sort of a right-hand stroke/left-hand piss/stroke/piss/stroke/piss thing 'til all was gone, perhaps losing up to nine seconds. I know, too much information, but isn't such info the reason why you take the time to read these e-mails in the first place?

I biked a back-painful 1:02. (In the next few weeks, I'll be getting a new Griffen bike and a new bike fit. Sure hope that helps.) The course was a mile and a half short, hence an unofficial PR, due to a last-minute course change. (A change mandated by the U.S. Army: the course has traditionally gone through their local base, but since 9/11, no civilians are allowed.) Then I ran a 43:18. That last part made me happy. What made me even happier were the words of a 230-plus-pound relay team runner:

"Can I say something to you?" he asked. For a moment, I thought I was in some sort of "stay away from my girlfriend" trouble.

"Sure," I responded with concern.

"I've never run six miles in my life. I was suffering at mile four, wondering if I could finish, then I saw you hauling ass, and I *knew* I could. Mind if I get a photo with you?"

Again … Wow!

Thankfully, the occasions are seldom these days that I second-guess my occupation. George Smith and the big guy (in conjunction with *the* Big Guy) reminded me that my job is the proper one. Thank you, gentlemen.

Next tri is Buffalo Springs Lake Triathlon in Lubbock, Texas, on June 30. Notable: I turn thirty-five on June 21, so into the 35-39 age group I go. That has its pros and cons. Speaking of cons, I haven't been arrested in a while. That's a good thing. I hope you can say the same.

Ironman USA, Lake Placid

July 2002

I do not claim to be the most organized person around, as evidenced by my lack of detailed preparation the morning of the race. I remembered my ankle chip (a race timing device) just as we pulled out of the condo parking lot at 5:45 AM; I stood in the mandatory stand-here-for-longer-than-you-thought-you-would-have-to Porta-Potty line for fifteen minutes, emerging from the stinkhole just minutes before the nearly half day of self-induced punishment was to begin. I got to the start line realizing that I had no swim cap … and had yet to get body marked, i.e., to have a race volunteer write my race number on both my legs and arms in permanent black magic marker that I consistently forget to scrub off and so must endure the never-ending "what's the number on your arm for?" question from those not in-the-know. The full hour I gave myself to prepare at the race site—to deal with the aforementioned, to set up my leg at the water's edge, to direct my father on how to assist me through transitions (to make sure my prostheses were where they needed to be when I needed them to be there), bullshitting with everyone I hadn't seen since whenever—just wasn't enough.

I jumped in the water, after scrambling for a cap and a magic marker, at approximately 6:59 AM for the 7:00 cannon blast and swam over to a good starting position: the right side of the start line, several rows of swimmers back, away from the major congestion but tight enough to require several minutes of deliberate elbowing to establish my piece of liquid real estate. I think I might be getting more comfortable with this aspect of triathlon since I earnestly enjoyed the physical aggression required to hold my own.

The swim course was a two-lapper in Mirror Lake. The first took me thirty minutes and some number of seconds. Between laps, the athletes hop out (I was probably the only one literally hopping) and cross a twenty-meter strip of land before beginning the next lap. That next one took me just under thirty-four minutes, and according to my watch, I was at the water's edge in 1:04:02. Solid.

I immediately popped into my run leg, preparing for the four-hundred-meter haul to the first transition, but was forced to pop it off again just as quickly since I'd forgotten to take what's left of my left leg out of my wetsuit before donning the prosthesis. I then hurried over to the volunteers, who directed me to sit so they could peel the suit off my right leg with one quick yank. Fittingly, these volunteers are referred to as "peelers."

Six minutes after exiting the water, I was on my Griffen Classic road bike, with Profile AeroStryke clip-ons, of course. (I chose the road bike over the Vulcan rocket ship triathlon bike for the sake of the hills. In hindsight, I think either choice would have had equal merits.)

The bike course was also a two-lapper, the first of which took me 2:35. Just as I completed that first lap, at the top of the little hill adjacent the "1980 Rink" (site of the infamous defeat of the notorious Russians in the semifinals by the hands of the kids on Team USA en route to defeat the Finns and secure an Olympic gold medal), my family—Mom, Dad, sisters, nieces, aunt—cheered for me. Way cool.

Considering the hills, I was having a great ride. Of the eighteen hundred athletes, I was four hundred and something out of the water and, like, 150th to complete the fist lap of the bike. I might have gone out just a little too hard, as I ended up somewhere around 190th at the second transition (152nd fastest bike split overall). I probably lost ten to twenty spots sitting on the side of the road at mile 105, serving a three-minute spanking for my first-ever-in-fifty-triathlons drafting penalty, which, as I'm sure you've already assumed, wasn't my fault.

It went down like this: I was going uphill at twelve miles per hour, a bike length and a half behind another rider, looking down, looking for some steam. "Seven nineteen!" I heard the marshal bark from the backseat of the motorcycle over my left shoulder. While I felt his call was questionable, I didn't complain for a second—after more than five hours on a bike seat, I welcomed a three-minute break with open legs. (Did I just say that?) Jinxed myself is what really happened. At mile 30, I witnessed quite a few riders drafting—you almost can't help it when hundreds of athletes emerge out of the pond at about the same time—and told myself I'd probably never get a drafting call since I'm so damn anal about it. *D'oh!*

Positive note: The hilly ride, which allowed me to get out of the saddle often, along with the newly adopted raised stem and resultant lesser strain on my lower back, albeit a less aerodynamic position, made for a nearly pain-free back. This was huge. All five of my previous Ironman rides had been compromised by back pain misery.

Funny note: It had rained hard on several stretches of the second lap. This provided opportunity to take a leak while descending a hill, while the riders around me were none the wiser, as the product was discreetly washed away. It's the simple things, really.

When I got off the bike, Dad was there with the bike leg and some words of praise. Two and a half minutes later, I headed out for a 26.2-mile run. Right out of transition, the athletes were reminded of the value of the undertaking: thousands of spectators cheering for you, wishing you a successful race, while each of us inspires each of them in some unique way. I love that shit.

I felt good straight out of the gate and managed an 8:30 pace for the first few miles. (The course, another two-lapper, primarily descends to a turnaround at mile 5.5ish.) By mile 9, I was averaging nine-minute miles, working a sub-four-hour run, looking like I might break eleven hours. Then, a couple of climbs later, I was at the halfway point in 2:05, pulling over to kiss my mother. By mile 15, I was bumming out and kicking twelve-minute miles, walking all the aid stations, taking in calories, wondering if I wanted to do this again on October 19 on the Big Island of Hawaii.

Dozens of spectators reflected the respect I offered the Empire State: "We love New York too!" (I had sewn "I♥NY" across my blue-suited butt. A photo of the graffitied blue moon made the paper the next day.) All due respect to the Red Sox, of course. I do hate the Yankees.

The remaining miles remained steady, and the feet kept moving. I even managed to pick it up on occasion. The last trek through town with the cheering crowds instilled the same feelings of appreciation and accomplishment they always do. By mile 25, the can't-friggin'-wait-to-be-done mind-set began to fade, the pain subsided, and I felt like an Ironman finisher. The final two hundred meters around half of the Olympic speed skating oval were fabulous. The stands erupted as I came into view (gimps get such a full-blown ovation from the gallery!)

I crossed the finish line after a 4:35 marathon (second slowest ever) with an overall time of 11:25:38. Still not too shabby. I was the 313th finisher, 52nd of 323 in my new age group: 35-39. Happy. Gimpy. Sore. I removed the leg and raised it to the crowd, and breaking the traditional "*I ... am ... Ironman!*" proclamation, I let them all know this: "*I love New York!*" That seemed to go over well.

All said and done, a good race. Glad to have undertaken the undertaking. Ready to head back to Kona. Not so secretly gloating over the fact that my condo-mates from the Boulder Triathlon Club—Cathy, Scott, and Larry—all finished behind me!

Thanks for taking the time to read this. Now go do something productive ...

2002 Disabled Cycling World Championships

August 2002

There were four races to try to win over there, two on the velodrome and two on the road. I expected exactly zero medals. *That's no way to go into a World Championship!* you say. I understand your disappointment. Sorry about that, but I had just finished an Ironman eight days prior. I was tired. I went there to help my buddy Ron Williams win the road race. That was about it.

So why had I tackled an Ironman just days before the gathering of the world's best one-leggers on bikes? 'Cause I love triathlon, and this race was the one Ironman that my mother, who'd yet to see me race triathlon, could get to, that's why.

Team USA gathered at Dulles Airport in Washington, D.C., on July 31. From there, we all headed to Munich Airport and were then bussed to Altenstadt, a two-hour ride. We spent the first few days acclimating and feeling out both the track and the road courses for the time trial and road race.

On day one of the races, I lined up on the indoor velodrome without nerves, without expectations, without concern of how fast I could ride one thousand meters. I thought I might ride a 1:17 or so. I'd ridden a 1:14:88 at the 2000 Sydney Paralympics after much preparation and focus. I'd just completed a diametrically opposite race in Lake Placid. My training was all diesel, no nitro. One thousand meters and 1:14:13 later, I was sitting in first place. *Where the heck did that come from?* I asked myself. Coaches and teammates alike seemed to do the same, shaking their heads with those little smiles of surprise.

But there were a bunch of strong riders still to come. I kept my enthusiasm in check. The next guy, the German, was slower, as expected. The Spanish guy, the new guy who was a junior national rider when he lost his left foot to a guardrail in a freak bike accident a couple of years ago, was slower. The French guy was slower. My fellow American and one of my favorite people, Ron Williams, was up, and I figured he'd bump me; he's been training his butt off for these races. He was half a second slower. Three riders left, three medals available. The Czech rider, number one ranked Jiri Jezek, was faster, half a second faster. Then another French guy was ... *slower!*

I'm on the podium! I'm on the friggin' podium!

Then the other American, Dory Selinger, the kilo world record holder, posted a 1:12:68, and my bronze medal was complete. *Bejesus! Who woulda thought?*

Ron finished fourth.

The next day was the qualifier for the four-kilometer pursuit. Two riders on the track at once, on opposite sides of the straightaways, "pursuing" each other. Of the seventeen athletes competing, eight would make it to the semifinals the next day. I lined up against a Swiss dude, passed him with eight laps left of twenty and rode a personal best 5:10, half a second faster than I'd ridden in Sydney. *Why? How? I'm confused. I didn't really even train for this.*

The following day in the semifinals, I lined up against the new Spanish guy, Roberto. Coach Craig Griffin told me to go hard, put a little scare into him, and hope he spent a bit more energy than he expected to, so that the next day's final would be that much tougher for him, so that Dory had a better chance of getting the win. In his qualifier, he'd ridden six seconds faster than I had, and he was therefore clearly favored to win. By this time, I was feeling almost confident, not ruling out an upset. I went out hard, a little too hard, and led the race for fifteen laps, putting a scare into Roberto, as I rode a 5:00 pace. Then I faded ... hard. He increased his lead on each lap and beat me by four seconds, posting a 5:02 to my new PR of 5:06. Sans disappointment, however—I was thrilled I had just pulled that one off. *Woo-hoo!*

The next day, Roberto beat Dory in the finals, by 0.2 seconds.

So then I had three days to rest before Saturday's time trial on the road. I was feeling much more confident than expected, getting ready for what I would have thought—before that kilo ride—to be my strongest event. Still not expecting much, I didn't get too amped up during warm-up; I wasn't too nervous before I rolled up onto the starting ramp. I looked at Jiri, our assistant coach, and said, "I love racing."

He smiled. "Of course you do," he replied with a Polish accent.

With my Sidi shoes clipped into my Look pedals, I looked up and did what I usually do before any sizable race: I asked for my best race and said a couple of words to my grandfather and my childhood best friend, Rob Maillet, both up there and looking after me. Then I pedaled my ass off for twenty-three kilometers.

Early in the ride, like three hundred meters into it, there was a tight left-hand turn that I took a bit too aggressively. I wasn't gonna make it without either hitting the brakes or bunny hopping the curb onto the sidewalk. I opted for the latter, hopped onto the curb, got a charge out of the cheers from the crowd, and felt this might be a good ride. I had a team car behind with a coach, a mechanic and wheels in case of a flat. The mechanic later told me that he wondered why I went out so hard (twenty-six miles per hour), harder than he thought I could handle, concerned that I might blow up.

In this time trial, riders left the ramp every minute sharp, and just seven kilometers into the ride, I caught my "minute man." That's a good thing. He was a Frenchie. Then I reached the base of the one sizable climb on the out-and-back course that led to the turnaround. I kept the cadence high for a climb, in the high nineties (cadence is bike talk for pedal rpm). Most of the ride I was in the mid to high one hundreds, sorta Lance-like—I actually thought about him as I kept the aggressive rhythm. I saw the gap to my two-minute man closing as I climbed the hill. (I also picked off a guy from India, my six-minute man, at the base of the hill. This guy was great. He came to Germany without a bike, without a coach, and without any friends. Just wanted to represent his country in sport. He came in dead last in every event, and like so many athletes I've encountered in recent years, the smile never left his face.)

Just before cresting the hill and reaching the turnaround, I saw Rivaldo Martins descending it. Some of you might recognize the name; he's the guy that spanks me in triathlon. He looked strong. I barreled down the descent on the Griffen Vulcan boron carbide rocket ship, my Rudy Project glasses fogged and full of sweat, blazing at forty-four miles per hour. Then I picked off my three-minute man, then my two-minute man, then my four-minute man, then my five-minute man. *Damn! This is looking like one hell of ride!*

The last little hill to the finish line consumed everything I had, emptying the tank. I crossed in 32:38, and it took another thirty seconds to get the strained grimace off my face. I was making my way back to the Team USA corner when Coach Griffen said, "I think you might have won."

"*Might* have won? I'll be back." I had no desire to sit there stirring, waiting on official results. I knew I'd ridden hard. I figured I'd probably reach the podium. There were a few strong riders to go. I needed to get out of there. I jumped on my road bike and tooled around the quaint little residential neighborhood for a good ten minutes. I didn't get too excited, no sense in setting myself up for disappointment. I saw Coach Jiri looking quite anxious.

"There you are," he said. "Where's Sarah? You need to go with Sarah to doping control."

"Did I win?"

"Of course you did."

"*Niiiiiice!*"

I'd just beaten every prosthesis-wearing rider the world could muster up. Every rider in the *world*! I'd just beaten 'em all. It was an amazing feeling. There was deep competition among the guys in my class, the LC2s. It was anybody's race. I was only five seconds ahead of Roberto from Spain, who finished second, and eighteen seconds ahead of Jiri Jezek, who took third.

I saw Ron moments after hearing the good news. He gave me a respectful smile, a thumbs-up and a "Nice work." Ron's my biggest competition, and he's been touted as The Man, by myself and many others. Ron finished fourth, again, twenty-eight seconds behind me.

I went off to doping control, filled out some paperwork, and peed in the cup on command. Wolfgang, a one-armer from Austria who'd just won his division (and the only amputee to beat me—arm, leg, or other), was sitting there waiting to have to go. Three hours later he peed in his cup.

Then the rains came and the flooding of Eastern Europe began. The award ceremonies were moved to the next day.

The next day was the road race. The flooding of Eastern Europe was *well* under way. The LC2 race began at 11:30 AM. At the gun, Rivaldo took off, and Dory chased him, along with Morten Jahr, an eighteen-year-old from Norway, my two-minute man.

The rains returned from a short break, and we raced the entire 66k in soaking wetness. Classic stuff. My job remained unchanged: help Ron win. He's a much more effective road racer and tactician. He had the world's fastest BK to work for him (vanity? where?). He was feeling comfortable.

Dory and the other two were thirty meters ahead as I led the chase group up the one significant little hill that led to the finish line—the first of twelve laps. The crowd cheered as we passed the banner. On that first hill, we'd already dropped seven of the twenty riders. On the second lap, Dory buckled. He no go long. A couple others also fell off pace, and there were ten of us. By the fourth lap, there were seven of us: Ron, Jiri, Morten, Roberto, Patrice and Sebastien from France, and me. I looked at Ron. "That was only four laps? Damn ..." He shook his head with a smirk, and we both knew this was gonna be a rough one. I kept the pace high and attacked a couple of times, causing others to chase and allowing Ron to sit in, conserving energy for the sprint. That was the whole plan.

With seven laps to go, as we negotiated a left turn on a wet corner, I sat right behind Roberto as we all leaned into it ... just before he dropped like a rock. He slid toward the right side of the street we were taking the left onto. I had no choice but to go straight at the sidewalk and do another bunny hop right through a little corner store parking lot, banging a hard left, yelling at the pedestrian walking down the sidewalk in the midst of my line as I headed back onto the road.

Ron was leading, with Morten right behind him and Jiri taking chase. I chased back, and Patrice was on my wheel. Sebastien didn't go down but did get caught up; he had to stop while we pedaled away.

Ron and I were wired to Coach Griffin's radio, and he gave us orders and other info. He told us that the Spaniard and the French guy were dropped, so I picked up the pace to make sure they stayed dropped.

With four laps to go, moments after leading an attack up the hill, I fell off the back as the others rounded the corner toward the finish area—I was running out of juice. The pace was high going up that last hill, and my weight was playing a factor; I had ten to twenty pounds on all those guys. They had just dropped me on the climb. For the next two laps, I chased the pack and kept a steady gap of thirty to fifty meters without blowing myself up as I tried to get back on. The finish line crowd threw me support on each pass.

With two laps to go, I began to close the gap as the foursome eased on the hill. Shortly after starting the eleventh lap, I snuck up to Patrice, who was fourth in the file, and sat in, making absolutely as little noise as possible, then cracked past them with most of what I had left—the shock factor can sometimes be quite helpful. They thought I was toast until I made them chase for a quarter mile, while Ron sat in. We rolled up the hill together; once again, they rode away, and I chased. The crowd at the banner cheered as the bell lap rang, and the pack was moving ... and I was *still* chasing. (The crowd had no idea that I had caught them on each lap, attacked them, and been dropped again.)

This time I didn't catch them until just a few hundred meters from the hill. Jiri later told me that he told the peloton, "Paul is gone." That was about three seconds before I caught them, three seconds before I gave it all I had and launched a vicious attack. That put a huge panic into the group, and they all hammered. All but Ron; he sat in. They caught me while I climbed the hill. And the moment they caught me, my system shut down. They were flying, I was flat and had just finished doing my job.

"*Win this fucking race, Ron!*" I yelled. That was all I had left.

I soft-pedaled up the hill, looking over my shoulder on occasion to make sure the others were not sneaking up behind me. I listened intently as Griffin coached

Ron over the radio. "Put it in the big ring ... wind it up ... They've got the wind ... *Go! Go! Go!*"

Ron went at one hundred meters out, but that was a microsecond after Jiri and Morten went. Then Morten dropped. Ron caught Jiri's wheel. They went hard. Ron won a silver medal at the world championships.

Nice work, Ron.

Later that day, they held the award ceremonies for the previous day's time trial. On my left stood Roberto, former heir to the Spanish cycling throne. On my right was Jiri, number one ranked rider in the world. They played "The Star-Spangled Banner." At "home of the brave," the tears began to flow.

🚲   🚲   🚲

Quite the busy summer doing what I love to do, and the race season wasn't quite over yet. After returning from Europe, I jetted out to Honolulu to participate in a fund-raiser for the Challenged Athlete Foundation.

The event, Ironman Revisited, was a newbie on the calendar and conceived to both honor the original Hawaiian Ironman and to give triathletes a chance to retrace the course the original fifteen competitors followed back in 1978. (Quick bit of history: Navy Captain John Collins, his wife Judy, and a couple of their buddies were enjoying a few beers and arguing over what was tougher, the Waikiki Roughwater Swim, the Around-Oahu Bike Race, or the Honolulu Marathon. With no clear winner, they decided to stage all three events consecutively and a few months later the "Ironman" was born. Three years later, the race moved to Kona.)

I rode the bike portion of the Revisited event as a relay team member with two other challenged athletes. Then I returned a couple of months later for another solo Ironman in Kona.

IM, TV, and XT

November 2002

Been travelin' some more. This time to Kona ... then to LA ... then to Maui ... then back to Boulder. Got home this afternoon, Wednesday, and tomorrow morning around 6:00 AM, I'll be driving to San Diego for the annual pilgrimage to the San Diego Triathlon Challenge.

Here's what's been going on.

The Hawaiian Ironman

Ironman was a couple of Saturdays ago, October 19. Happy to say that it went well overall. Actually, of my four starts over there, it was my worst finish among the rank-and-file athletes, finishing 907th in 11:48:10. But of those starts, it was the one in which I had to work the hardest to finish first among the one-leggers. My training wasn't so hot leading up to the event, with both Stumpie and back issues, not to mention a distinct lack of motivation to put in the miles.

One man in particular made this race a special one. He brought an effort out of me I had yet to experience. Toshio Futuhara (or Furuhata, I forget), a forty-year-old below-knee amp from Japan, who qualified for the world championships in Kona as an *able-bodied* athlete, coming in third in his age group at Ironman Japan, finishing in just over ten and a half hours. Mofo ran a 3:35 off the bike! Mofo has a personal best open marathon time of 2:55! Yeah ... that's what I said. Some of you may have read what I'd written about Jim MacLaren, that he holds the unofficial marathon world record with a time of 3:18. Well, clearly, I was wrong. Seems Toshio's the fastest marathoning peg-legger to date. Then again, who knows, maybe there's another out there somewhere.

So, I figured on crossing the finish line on Ali'i Drive sometime after this guy, my original game plan changing slightly after learning more about him. I was going to take it easy on the bike (I've been riding strong lately so wasn't too worried about those 112 miles of the race) to save a little something for the run, but I ended up pushing hard to establish a solid lead for the marathon in order to minimize the damage by the Gifted One.

In the eight weeks leading up to the race, I managed only 109 miles on the run. Folliculitis (infected hair follicles), atypical blistering behind my knee, and this crazy-weird bulbous lump of junk proximal to the trim line of my socket made for painful runs, which took away from the desire to go through the motions. Point being that I figured on a less-than-stellar foot race and knew I would need to save something for those miles after the bike. Well, the winds were calm this year, which played nicely into shooting for a personal best on the bike, and I ended up with a record time out there in the lava fields, getting off the machine in five hours, thirty-four minutes.

My swim was a personal worst at any Ironman: a 1:14 to Toshio's 1:12. It rained hard the morning of the race, and there were some big ol' swells out there. Swim times were slow in general. My problem was the low back. I have some sort of muscle/tendon problem, where one of those major muscles that are so critical to the freestyle swim stroke attaches near my lower spine. It's something that doesn't bother me on the bike or run, only in the water. And since I'm not the biggest fan of swim training to begin with, time spent going back and forth staring at a black line was significantly compromised.

I'd gotten off the bike not knowing how far I was ahead of Toshio (I later learned it was forty-five minutes). The first turnaround was at mile 5, and on the way back, I kept an eye open for him, figuring he'd be whittling away at my lead and I'd be able to gauge at what point he'd run me down. I saw him at around mile 7, so I had about a four-mile lead, i.e., the forty-five minutes had already dropped to something like thirty to thirty-five minutes.

I was plugging away at ten-minute miles, about what I thought I might be able to handle for twenty-plus miles, slower than I'd ever started a marathon in the past. I kept this pace—probably slowing to 10:30s—right up until mile 18, at the final turnaround in the Energy Lab. At this point, I was still a bit surprised that Toshio had yet to pass me; three or four minutes later, I saw him coming the other way, which meant my lead was less than a mile. My spirits took a hit; the legs suddenly felt heavy, and the uphill climb out of the Lab was at snail's pace. At the aid station just past mile 20, I looked back to see what was taking the imminent passer-to-be so damn long. I was stuck between wanting him to pass me, to get this anxiety and punishment over with since I was sure to start walking some once I fell into second place, and hoping he'd buckle or something … and I might actually win.

There he was, one to two hundred meters behind me, looking as if he had plenty of steam left. *Just a matter of time,* I thought to myself.

A mile later ... nothin'. *Keep running; keep the legs moving. Can't give up until he catches you. He just may have buckled. Probably just slowing a bit, but he just may have buckled.* I looked back a couple of times, but I couldn't see him. It was getting dark, and I was getting a bit delirious, so maybe I just wasn't seeing him ... or maybe he'd already passed me. I couldn't be sure. So I had to keep running. By mile 24, I was so friggin' shot that I stopped looking anywhere but forward, didn't acknowledge any of the well-wishing athletes passing me or the smattering of fans alongside the Queen Kaahumanu Highway. Eyes wide open, staring forward in a daze, running a ten- to eleven-minute pace.

At mile 25, he still hadn't passed me. It was getting very dark, and I looked back as I made the right-hand turn at the top of Palani Hill. I didn't see him, wasn't convinced that I'd held him off just yet. From the top of Palani, it's pretty much all downhill to the finish line. The road is fairly steep, and I let the legs go, doing my best to stay focused, not looking at the cheering fans. Not smiling, not waving, not nothin'. I just kept the legs moving, hoping not to trip and fall. With a half mile to go, I saw a man in a wheelchair from the corner of my eye. It was Australia's John MacLean, the first man to complete this race in a wheelchair within the official cutoff times, this year's inductee to the Ironman Hall of Fame. "Go, Paulie!" I heard him yell. No smile, no wave, no nothin'. *Keep the legs moving. Do not fall!.*

Then the top of Hualalai. Just before making this right-hand turn down the little hill to Ali'i Drive, I stopped to look back on the well-lit street, and I didn't see Toshio. I turned and began running down the hill, and in the midst of accepting the feeling of victory, with the crowd cheering louder and louder, I cracked a smile. Then I held back the downward-turned lip emotions and sucked up the wonder of Ali'i Drive.

As hard as that was, deeper than I've ever dug before to win a race, I thought about how fortunate I am to have what I have, and I just about committed to doing this again, not exactly sure when, but, man, did I ever relish in the magnificence of that finish line chute. The only way to get it back is to do it all over again ...

In the end, I'd crossed the finish line some thirty minutes ahead of Toshio, who had some sort of stump or prosthesis problems that caused him to slow down considerably just after I saw him last.

The Best Damn Sports Show Period

My publisher, Joan Schweighardt, is also my de facto PR person, and she'd set me up with a speaking gig in LA, an avenue to help promote the book. It was a pro bono talk for Safe Harbor, an organization that promotes non-drug alternatives for mental health rehabilitation—healthy diet, exercise, etc. A couple of weeks after booking this, Fox Sports Net's *The Best Damn Sports Show Period* returned Joan's call and wanted me on the show. We picked October 23 since I'd already be in LA. And just to make the trip a bit more efficient, I set up a book signing at Cal State Dominguez Hills.

The show was a cool new experience. Big celebrities. Couple of funny guys. Just before going on the set, I bumped into John Sally (one of the hosts, former LA Laker) and the first thing he did was pull up my shirt and grab my belly to see how lean I was. *Interesting.* Then he shook my hand, introduced himself, and immediately said, "I bet chicks love to lick your stump!" Yep, that's what he said. Then, without hesitation, he went into a story about Verne Troyer ("Mini Me") and himself at the Playboy Mansion, and how all the girls—how can I say this without being too vulgar?—were doing nasty things to the short one, while he couldn't get no satisfaction. *Bizarre.*

Then I went on the set.

I sat between John Kruk and Tom Arnold. I was sporting my "Got stump?" T-shirt, which brought out a couple of comments. They asked me the typical questions, and when the opportunity arose, I ripped on Tom for being a non-athlete, and we all laughed. Fun stuff. Live studio audience too. Cool. Then I left. No good "beers with the boys" stories here.

In theme with the odd celebrity insider story, at the Safe Harbor talk the next night, I was rapping with one of the psychiatrists, who, without hesitation, asked me if I "get a lot of action on the road," in those very words. *Hmmm.* Then he goes on to tell me how in his early med days he was intern in the ER, and he and the others, to keep on their toes for thirty-six hours on/twelve off, would do lots of coke to stay up and hard liquor to get some sleep. *Hmmm.* Disturbing? A little. After the Mini Me story, I just had to laugh.

Xterra

From LA, I flew straight to Maui for a third crack at breaking four hours at the Xterra World Championships. Four hours not only for the sake of four hours, but also to beat my good friend and fellow BK Joel Sampson's record time of 4:01 he'd posted two years ago. This year I had a new mountain bike leg and had made a modification to the run leg (a heel), feeling confident with the goal. Last year I had a nasty crash on the bike, which added twenty-plus minutes to my ride and resulted in a 4:25 finish. This year's crash wasn't so bad.

The day started with two laps of a 750-meter swim. Water was calm. The day was beautiful. The stretch to the first buoy was mayhem, with too many flailing arms and legs in too little water, but fortunately, no black eyes or kicks to the midsection. I think they made the beach run between laps a little longer than it was in years past. That seventy-five-meter hop in soft beach sand left me legless. Toward the end of the long hop, I nearly broke and took a knee, but I managed to stick it out. When I hit the water, I simply fell into it, struggling to move the arms in some type of swimming motion. By that first buoy, I'd found the rhythm again. I hopped out, put the bike leg on, went to and through transition, and mounted the bike in a total of twenty-eight minutes. Decent but nothing to write home about—sorry for the contradiction, Mom.

The crash went down like this: I'm letting it go down the first real descent of the 30k course, and I'm on the left side of a steep and wretched cart path. Up ahead on the right is some goober looking well below the comfort level while attempting to negotiate the lava rocks. (We're riding on chunks of lava ranging in size from dust to grapefruits.) I'm coming up on him, and it's clear that his inability to hold a straight line might very well send him into my lane. I bark out the necessary "On your left! On your left!" and just as I'm about to pass, just a few feet behind him, going nearly twice his speed, he loses control and pulls ninety degrees to his left, directly into my line. My brakes did little, and post-T-bone impact with his front fork, I sailed through the air, unleashing expletives, and landed smack-dab on the top of my noggin.

The Giro helmet did exactly what it was designed to do, receiving a couple of telltale dents in the process, and the bell ringing lasted only a couple of seconds. Well aware of the athletes bombing down the hill behind me, I reached out and grabbed my leg, which was hanging on completely backward by a hair (perhaps literally) and pulled it out of the others' way. I then took a moment to survey the damage ... There was none, except for some skin missing from my back, near the right scapula. I made a quick mental note of the sore neck I would be experiencing in the morning, put the leg back on, yelled at the guy again, who was now beyond earshot, stood up, yanked my bike out of the bushes, hopped on, and pedaled.

Other than the flat tire with a mile to go, which I rode in without fixing, this was the day's only real problem. The truthful reasoning behind not bothering to fix the flat was that it was a rental bike from B&L Bike—not my rim, not my worry. I know, disrespectful, but I was in a hurry.

I got off the bike in 2:18 and took off running on the wiry trail of logs, beaches, pavement, grapefruits, small cliffs, grass and bushes, etc. This type of terrain is not my forte, and I ended up walking the more technical sections, happy to say that I didn't trip even once. The 11k run took a whopping 1:06, and I didn't know 'til I got to the finish line that the goal was reached, crossing in 3:58 and change. (I didn't know because I wasn't wearing a watch. I didn't wear one in Kona either, and I'm not so sure I'll ever wear one to race again. Not knowing how badly you're doing removes a tremendous amount of anxiety.) I crossed the line, and the first guy I saw was Joel. He was happy for me. He's a good guy. He was hoping I'd come in a few minutes later, but happy for me nonetheless. Did I mention he's the new manager at B&L Bikes? Did I mention that it was kinda fun to bash his rim then break his record? *Ha-ha!*

A productive and enjoyable couple of weeks. To top it off, at the airport in Maui, I grabbed a seat waiting for my flight, and the guy next to me was reading *One Man's Leg.*

As always, thanks for taking the time to read this. And as always, I hope all's well with you and yours, and that good things are happening.

With *One Man's Leg* on the shelves a couple of months now, I was spending a good amount of time traveling around to various markets peddling the volume, getting on the set of a good number of morning local news programs, and doing readings at various bookstores, mostly Barnes & Noble. Some I'd driven to and some required a flight. The best part of these trips is that I found a way to turn them into revenue: each TV broadcast was a chance to flaunt my prosthetic hardware on the airwaves, which led to nice media incentive payments from Össur, my prosthetic sponsor.

Tales from the Road

February 2003

I pulled into Boulder last night after a ten-hour drive from Cedar City, Utah. Very happy to say I made it through both states without a single traffic ticket. My travels over the last couple of months have provided several moving violations and generally entertaining stories.

Let's look at a few just for fun:

In February, I drove to Texas to sell some books, to meet some kids at Dallas Shriners Hospital for Children, snagged a scalped ticket to a Stars/Kings game (that's National Hockey League play), and reunited with two high school friends, one I hadn't seen since graduation day, May 1985. Relatively non-notable trip until I received the ninety-five-dollar speeding ticket doing eighty in a seventy on the flatness of the Texas plains. Fittingly, I got myself on TV in San Antonio, Austin, and Dallas, which earned me a few media dollars from Össur/Flex-Foot and PowerBar to pay for said ticket.

Two days later, I flew to Boston for a U.S. Amputee Hockey Team training camp. I received some ink in the *Boston Globe*, did a local TV gig, got more rent money. Then I headed off to New Jersey and New York and sold some books, met kids with disabilities in Manhattan, and got some airtime on CNN New Jersey.

On the way out of the Big Apple, I incapacitated my rental car. Arguably, not my fault … I had another book signing in Upstate New York with scant time to spare; I was on the phone with Avis in a matter of seconds. The boys in blue showed up and I told them that I'd be back in ten minutes—that I had to go pick up my new car. They looked at me as if I had two legs. In just shy of nine minutes, I was back with my new car, before the tow truck had dragged away the severely dented one. The cop ridin' shotgun looked at me and said—in a classic New York accent—"You gotta get me a car sometime!" Needless to say, I impressed them as well as myself, signed a book for them, to "NY's finest," and as they pulled away moments later, they yelled, "Good luck, Paul!" I was on the road upstate and got there just a few minutes late.

Sometimes I wonder …

Why I was following that guy speeding on Route 2 in Massachusetts, resulting in, you guessed it, a speeding ticket, penalizing me two hundred dollars.

Then back home for a couple of weeks, where I spoke to five hundred students at the University of Colorado before heading to D.C. for a wedding. We'll leave that one alone.

Two days later, I was driving to LA via Las Vegas with my housemate Ethan, who was on spring break—he's back in school ten years after graduating from CU. The cheap room we scored off the strip eased the pain of losing my allotted fifty bucks on blackjack. I won a little back on craps—kept hitting the hard eights—and then I stuck a lone dollar bill into the nickel slots and pulled three sevens—a red one, a white one, and a blue one. With that, I was thinking gas money, and I put all those nickels in the plastic cup for big winners and headed to the cash woman. All seemed just grand until my leg fell off and the nickels went way far up before being dispersed about the carpet! One little bonus we one-leggers have is the oh-so-comical view of others' faces in such a circumstance. Ethan's stomach had now all but fallen out, the concierge went from wide-eyed to smiling wide, and in the end, we retrieved every nickel. Good. Clean. Fun.

I dropped off Ethan in Pasadena, and then I began my three-week book tour. The Barnes & Noble in Alisa Viejo was one such stop. I stayed with Jen Eibert—a certified prosthetist, Flex-Foot product specialist, and a jolly good friend who lived a matter of feet from the bookstore. I pulled into her garage completely oblivious (again) to the bike strapped to my roof. Upon registering the first nanosecond of *crunch!* I slammed the brakes while simultaneously jumping out to view the damage. As I learned the last time I did this less than two years ago, if you're going slow enough and hit the brakes soon enough, the rack will break … not the bike. Thank Goodness. Griffen spent the rest of the trip inside the Pathfinder.

Sometimes I wonder …

A week later, I was riding the Griffen—the Vulcan boron carbide rocket ship, I might remind you—on San Pablo Dam Road in the Oakland Hills, in the aero position. (Aero position on the bike means having your hands outstretched in front of you, holding onto your aero-bars while your elbows rest on pads mounted just above the handlebar stem. This makes you more aerodynamic and thereby more efficient and faster on the bike.) I was riding and smiling three and a half hours into a four and a half hour solo ride through personally uncharted territories when a car buzzed me at forty miles per hour and clipped my handlebar!

Oh my God! Does he crash? Is he maimed? Drain bamage perhaps?

Nope. The breakaway mirror on the sedan folded in; the driver probably never knew he/she just hit me and kept on driving. Most notable here is that my heart rate never jumped; the bike didn't even bobble or swerve, never mind nearly crash. Then I thought, *Wasn't that supposed to scare me? Why am I so comfortable with near-death experiences? Does having previous experience with near death lessen the discomfort?* Probably.

Between the Texas and Boston trips, I wasn't so lucky on the bike: There I was, last in a line of four riders and in the aero position, opening up a PowerBar, intensely focused on doing so, going relatively slow, when I clipped the wheel in front of me, going down hard on the left side on freshly chip-sealed pavement. In order of relative damage: hip, elbow, shoulder. What do I, the master of "step in shit, smell like roses," get out of this? Three nights of solid right-side sleeping practice, that's what.

The three weeks in California provided some fantastic bike rides, runs on the oceanfront, swims in the magnificence of the outdoor pool, a presentation at an East LA Catholic church, thirteen beds (couches, floors) in twenty nights, and 216 books personally sold. All in all, a good trip. Then I drove home.

No tickets, no accidents. I pulled in for gas at one of those gas stations on Interstate 70 in Utah, which approximately five hundred people visit each and every hour. To be smart, I brought my life, i.e., my planner—the one that happens to have nearly a grand in cash and checks inside—to deter those crooks who hang out at places like that. All was good, I brought it in, I brought it out, I put the gas nozzle back in the rack and drove away … with my planner on the spare tire on the back of the truck! (Embarrassingly, I did the same thing—the roof version—six years earlier, with seven hundred dollars. In some circles, this is known as "déjà stupid.")

Unfortunately for me, I realized this an hour later, just as I got through a five-mile stretch of five-mile-per-hour traffic due to an accident. I pulled over and searched the car, like five times. Then I called 411 from the cell phone and got the gas station's number ... They had nothin' for me. Then I considered my options: go back and look for it (fat chance) or drive away and hope someone finds it. Someone honest. Someone who will find my business card inside and call my cell phone. Fat chance. In considering the turn back, I thought about the rubberneck traffic jam on the other side of the highway. *Aaarrgghhhhh!*

Not one to get *toooo* permanently upset about this type of stuff (the biggest headache was that the cash was going to repay the loan from George, who was going to pay his taxes. *I let him down ... I'm such a loser ...*), I resigned to the loss, punched myself in the head (I most certainly did), and chose the turnaround option ... just in case.

I headed back, and just as soon as I hit the traffic—again—the phone rang. It was George. Not indebted-to-George, but George who also gets gas at the I-70 station in Bailey, Utah ... Found it! Has it! Woo-hoo! He found the card, he had a cell phone, and with it he called mine (notable: not everyone had a cell phone in 2002). George was headed in the other direction, pulled over to a rest area, and waited there for me for forty-five minutes. George the angel and his wife, Pam. Both angels. The book I signed over to them said exactly that.

Sometimes I wonder ...

I don't, however, wonder as much as I used to. Letters I get from people I meet and those in the audience when I lecture remind me that as chuckleheaded as I might be, I'm doing something right.

I have not lost any limbs, yet I do live with a neurological disease called neurofibromatosis. It is a disease that affects one in every thousand people. One of the disease's side effects is that I have birthmarks all over my body. And I have a tumor behind my eye, but it just sits there and does nothing (except make my life hard once a year when I have to get an MRI; yes, I can still see out of that eye). Over the years, I have come to grips with my disease, yet by reading your book, I saw a whole new light. It was almost like you proved to me that people with disabilities can do anything. I have always been told I could do anything even though I had a disability but never believed it, until I read your book and saw that you did it.

—Amanda Biddle, a young woman who wrote to me via my Web site

What greater way is there to achieve self-realization than to be a 'One-Man Enterprise'?
—Maggie Liptak, University of Colorado Business Student

You have made the entire semester in this class worth it.
—Breanne Kotz, University of Colorado Business Student

Helsinki to Alcatraz

April 2003

Last we talked, I'd just gotten back from an April trip selling books in California. Later that month, I headed to Finland to play hockey in the inaugural Amputee Ice Hockey World Championships. It was a four-game tourney against the Canadians, Finns, and Russians. We, Team USA, played great in a couple of the games, not so good in another, and lost to the Canadians in the finals in our best performance to date, 4–2. I scored a goal in three of the four games, including the second goal in the final game. That felt good. Anyone who knows my hockey talent knows it's not in scoring goals. It's having a motor that takes me long into the third period, gives me an edge on the backcheck, and helps me cause havoc on the forecheck throughout the game. In doing the latter, a couple of goals went in. Good stuff.

I departed Helsinki on May 5, traveling solo and not with the team travel deal because I had scored some flyer miles from an old high school buddy. (Elementary school, really. Mo Cormier. He was chubby way back when. Now he races twenty-four-hour mountain bike relays. Kudos, Mo!) I didn't actually leave for several hours after I got to the airport; missed my flight—there's a shocker. They told me right off the bat that I'd have to catch the same flight the next day, that they weren't able to change the routing since this was Finnair, and I was flying with American Airlines flyer miles. So I said, "Shit!" Then they told me to hang out a couple of hours to wait for American Airlines in America to open since they were the only ones able to reschedule frequent flyer flights ... I don't know. Then they got me on a flight to New York via London. Then the flight was canceled, and they told me the next London flight would get me in quick enough to still catch the flight to New York. Then they said, "Oh, since we goofed, we have the authority to send you nonstop to New York in a couple of hours."

79

Sweet. Then I found out it was the flight with the rest of the team. Sweet! On that flight, I played some cribbage with Scotty. Read a book. Couldn't sleep. Then our goalie, Mike Ginal, told me that the barley or the hops or something in beer has some sort of stimulant effect the next day. *Hmmm* ...

Upon arriving in New York, I rented a car and drove to Boston to hang out with the family. Then I hit Queens, New York, again a few days later to speak at Public School 207, a middle school. They had a band and a chorus singing songs as my opening act. A fifth grader played the drums and remained at his kit while I spoke. Upon telling my first joke, he quickly responded with a *ba-dum-tishhhh*. Funny stuff.

Then I spent three weeks in Boulder getting ready for my first triathlon of the year: Escape from Alcatraz. That's right. We had to swim from The Rock.

But first I headed to Philly/D.C. to sell some more books. I had nine book signings in nine days—exclusively at Barnes & Noble. Sold 123 books. At one of the signings, three out of four people (not on average, but four people who happened to walk in within a matter of minutes) said they'd seen me on TV. Often when I meet someone who has seen an endurance sport athlete on TV, they think they saw me. And I'm sure every other one-legger in the media experiences something similar.

While in Annapolis, I swam in an outdoor pool with my friend Katie Jereza. She was getting ready to swim the frigid 4.4-mile Chesapeake Bay swim with our mutual friend M.C. Brennan the same day I was to race Alcatraz. So we both took advantage of the opportunity to toughen ourselves a bit by training in a freezing-ass-cold outdoor pool. We swam an hour. Then I sat in front of her fireplace, drinking hot chocolate and shaking, chattering, shivering for a half hour. Preparation is key. On race day, the fifty-seven-degree water of the San Francisco Bay felt like a bath.

While in D.C., I received a forty-five-minute tour of the Pentagon with my cousin Richard Robichaud, a twenty-year Air Force veteran and chief sergeant at the time. We checked out Rumsfeld's and Powell's offices—well, the doors to their offices. Rummy came out and asked me what I thought of the Iraq war.

That didn't actually happen. What really happened was that Powell had this booger hanging from one of his medals, and I asked him if that was some sort of Green Beret thing.

No, that didn't actually happen either.

But seriously, the Pentagon tour was indeed an honorable experience. The headquarters of our national defense is quite a sight.

From there, I headed to downtown D.C. to meet with some of the staff at Leading Authorities—one of the nation's leading speakers bureaus. It was one of the biggest meetings of my financial career. (They talked of selling my presentations at five thousand dollars a pop.) I was late for the meeting—another shocker. I spent half an hour with them, and they said, "You're in," in so many words. That was cool with me. Doesn't mean a whole lot until they get me some gigs.

A couple of days later, on Thursday, I headed back to Boulder. On Saturday morning, I went to a wedding: my friends Aaron Clark and Lindsay Huck. Beautiful 10:00 AM wedding. Really, congrats to you both. I'm glad I had a chance to swing it. (I have a *whole year* to get a present, so sit tight.) After an hour at the reception, I busted out to DIA for a 2:30 flight to Oakland—had to be at the Marina Green in San Francisco by 6:00 PM for an interview. I was fortunate to be one of three athletes getting some airtime on the October 5 CBS broadcast of the Escape. They told me last year's broadcast was the highest-rated triathlon ever outside of the Olympics. I said, "Better than Ironman?" They said, "Better than Ironman."

So I got to the airport at 4:00 PM PST, but my bike didn't make it. I said "Shit!" They said it'd be in at 7:30. "Do you want us to deliver it?"

"Nope, I'll be back."

I got my rental car and made it to the marina at 5:45 for the interview. One of the questions asked whom I look up to in the sport. I mentioned Jim MacLaren, the below-knee amputee turned quadriplegic turned PhD. I said, "He wasn't the first amputee to race Ironman, but he raced hard on."

I said "hard on" in a CBS interview.

When I got back to the airport at 8:30, the baggage guy was kind enough to meet me at the curb with my bike; he had given me his number ahead of time. I pulled over, went around to put the bike in the backseat, and found the passenger side rear door locked. I went back around and hit the unlock button and shut the door and went back to the other side, and the side door was still locked, so I went back to the driver's side and the door was locked ... and the keys were in the ignition ... car running! I'm such a jackass!

I said, "No sweat!" to a cop who was laughing at me. Enterprise was about one hundred feet from me. (I was so lucky.) So I went over past the National people. They were open; they were happy. Budget. Same. Open. People were working. They were happy. I got to Enterprise. They were closed. I said, "Shit!" yet a third time.

So I called 1800 Rent-a-Car and got Enterprise roadside assistance on the line, and they told me they'd have a guy over to unlock the car within forty-five minutes.

It was now 9:00. I had to get up at 4:30 AM, and I hadn't assembled my bike yet or gotten to my friend's place in Berkeley, where I was staying. I took advantage of the time to build my bike on the curb at passenger pick-up. I'm in the way of, like, everybody. *Don't bother me. I've got things to do.*

One woman did come over to say hello. Her name was Tamara. She'd just started triathlon recently, and she said, "Are you the guy I've read about in triathlon magazines?"

"Maybe," I said.

"Can I have your autograph?" she said, and she handed me her new triathlon-training book, written by some triathlon trainer, and a pen. I told her I'd sign my own book for her, but it was locked in the car.

Dumb ass.

So the next day I was there at 5:30 AM, and I was all ready and all was good; I was on a boat headed to Alcatraz and I was wearing a wetsuit. I jumped in expecting freezing coldness, but, like I said, it wasn't that bad at all. Really. That fifty-seven degrees wasn't the least bit uncomfortable, an extremely pleasant surprise, thanks to that outdoor pool in D.C. What did suck was the choppiness of the water. But I expected that.

The swim section ends about a half mile "downstream" of Alcatraz. Typically, there's a nasty current going out to sea, and if one heads directly toward the beach exit, one will end up *waaaaay* past the intended target. So the best approach is to swim nearly ninety degrees across the current, which will take you most of the way across the bay. As you approach the other side, the current lessens, and you end up swimming mostly with the current, at a slight angle, to the beach exit.

The swim took me just shy of forty-five minutes. Upon reaching the beach, sitting in my previously arranged leg-donning chair, I grimaced through an all-too-familiar calf cramp as I removed my wetsuit. While running to the bike (this race is a little different than most in that you must run a half mile to the bike transition), I noticed that I couldn't really see out of my left eye. For some reason, it was burning from the swim.

The switch into the bike prosthetic went quickly, and I was on the eighteen-mile hilly bike course in no time. That ate up fifty-five minutes. Of the 1,223 finishers, I was eighty-fourth overall on the bike. Happy. Unlike Lance, for me it's all about the bike. Eye was still burning.

The eight-mile run was tough. As happens more often than not when I get off the bike, I had bad gut cramps early in the run. (They were also with me for most of the bike, which rarely happens.) I opted to stop at a public restroom at mile 1 to see if I might be able to exorcise some demons. Not much happened in there. Then came some difficult terrain for a mile or so. I was having leg problems too, and I had to reboot every ten minutes or so—mostly due to pain problems.

At the highest altitude point on the course, the road turned to steep pavement, and about that time, my gut problems subsided and I was able to turn it on some. Now, I can't run downhill slowly even if I want to. It's a carbon foot thing. So I was running fast and passing a bunch of competitors while the camera motorcycle followed me down the hill. If you see this on CBS, don't be fooled; this footage is not indicative of my run. Keep this between us. The rest of the country and all those sponsors don't need to know.

While running I tried closing my right eye—the good one—to see if I could even see out of the left one. It was as if I had glaucoma: all foggy. Like looking through wax paper. Really thin wax paper. Kept running.

Then down to the beach for the two-hundred-foot section of soft sand. That sucked. Then onto hard pack at water's edge to the turnaround and back from whence we came, toward the Sand Ladder—a notorious section of steep steps made up of logs and sand. Thankfully, with a wooden rope "rail" along the edge to help you along. That was hard too.

Then back over the difficult trail terrain and onto the last 1.5 miles of flatness. Feeling good at that point, I ran down several competitors, who then passed me back when I had to stop to reboot, and then I passed them back again ... and then there was the finish line.

Three hours and two minutes. Pretty good. I was 78th of 229 in the 35-39s—325th overall.

Believe it or not, I do like racing. It feels good ... when you're done.

Hey, thanks for taking the time to read this. I appreciate it. If any of you are in Alpharetta, Georgia, on June 22 for Dannon Duathlon National Championships, maybe I'll see ya there.

🚲　　🚲　　🚲

Outside of racing and training and skating and traveling to promote the book, I didn't have much more of a life. For the most part, that was fine with me.

Eight Races in Eight Weeks

August 2003

I'll start with yesterday's Boulder Peak Triathlon—an Olympic distance race with an extra 2k on the bike. It's great to do a race right in your own backyard: sleep in your own bed, eat your own breakfast (as opposed to eating someone else's breakfast?), and spank one of your housemates who drove you to the race. (It's too bad, really, for Randy's a nice guy.) Another housemate, and fixer of my bikes, Ivy Koger, spanked us both.

This was my fourth go at this particular race, and as with the previous three, I beat my prior time—not training much is working out well this year. The swim was okay, the bike was solid, and the run was great, relatively speaking: forty-four minutes. I finished in 2:23:42 and truly couldn't have gone any faster. It's called "leaving it all out there."

On a side note, thanks to all of you who kicked in for the multiple sclerosis fund-raising aspect of this race. My goal of five hundred dollars was smashed, and we gave the good people at MS over eighteen hundred dollars! You guys rock!

The race also has free beer. Then we had a little party back at the house.

And now for one of my all-time favorite stories: I'm driving down Moorehead Street here in Boulder, notorious for speeding tickets—got one there a couple years ago on my way to register for the race. I'm cognizant of such, and I'm looking around for the bad/good guys and at my speedometer and in my rearview mirror, and sure enough, there they are, right behind me. I monitor the speed, think about my car registration and insurance for a moment, acknowledge that I'm all paid up, think about what they're gonna pull me over for—they *always* pull me over. (A conservative estimate on lifetime pullovers: seventy—no joke.) I get to the end of the street and no lights, no sirens … phew. A couple of turns later and … *What the hell? They're still behind me.* Then, like the geyser in Yellowstone, colorful lights flash behind me. (The reference to the geyser was "reliable" not "colorful.")

I didn't use my blinker to make that right at the end of Moorehead. The right I took from the special lane with a semi-curved median on the left-hand side that, in my humble opinion, signifies the fact you're about to turn right. It's truly the only option. I guess I must've been so concerned about what they could possibly get me for that I missed the basics.

So the officer headed back to the cruiser to ascertain my legal status in the community, while his partner stuck her elbow in my passenger door and said, "Cool leg." I said, "Not as cool as my other legs, but thanks." We went through some idle chitchat, and she said, "Sounds like you made the most of it." I said, "Even wrote a book about exactly that."

The other officer returned from the car, said that I'm a good person, and didn't give me a ticket. The officer chatting it up with me asked if she could buy a book and if I'd personalize it to her, make it out to "A-I-M-E-E." I said, "Sure. Nothing like getting pulled over and turning a profit!" Then they wished me luck in my race. That's the story. Hope you liked it as much as I did.

Things didn't go quite so well for me the weekend before at the PanAm Disabled Cycling Championships in Brooklyn/Bronx. I didn't take this race too seriously; there were little to no consequences in this race other than finishing and ensuring our team certain Paralympic points for Athens next year. I actually flew in the night before from Seattle, where I was doing a couple of book signings in addition to some TV in Portland.

The road race was Friday, August 1. It was a 49k race—nine laps of a 6.5k course. I attacked near the end of the first lap, without being all that warmed up, then pulled out to let someone else take the lead for a spell. A Canadian winger obliged, and moments later, as we were approaching the base of the only real hill on the course, and he had about half a bike on me on my left, we came upon a right-hand turn that went off the course, which, for God knew what reason, he thought he had to take. In heading that direction, he forced me onto that road. The other options were to crash into him, crash into the sign that reads GO STRAIGHT, or crash into the curb and bushes. He managed to correct his bearing at the last moment, as I did a not-as-quick-as-I-should-have 360 on that off chute. Then I had to chase them up the hill.

Well, I had just finished an attack, which I probably shouldn't have since I wasn't sufficiently warmed up yet, and then I had to chase a peloton up a hill. That didn't work so well, and I spent three or four laps way above threshold ... and I blew up. Never caught 'em. Spent the next six laps riding easy for the sake of the finishing points. And to save myself for the time trial the next day in the Bronx.

That sucked too. Got beat by a few people who've never beat me before. 'Nuff said.

Just after the weekend of racing, I flew back to the Left Coast for more book signings and some more TV. I know, seems like a silly itinerary. Short story is I was supposed to do the AmeriCana Relay on August 1 and 2 (a 212-mile, twelve-person run relay from Nelson, British Columbia, to Spokane, Washington), but six of my teammates dropped out a couple of weeks before the race, which gave me an opportunity to race with the U.S. Elite Team obligation in New York City. I was originally exempted since I'd already committed to the relay team and had lots of press and signings planned around it.

So I flew to San Francisco and drove down to Santa Cruz for a signing at an independent bookstore called the Book Café in Capitola. Sold some books, had a good crowd, met a recent amputee named Britta, who seemed happy to hear my story, and just might have scored a speaking gig at a local high school. The next day I ran on the beach before I rode my bike along the Pacific Coast Highway into some cool country twenty-five miles north of Santa Cruz. I made my way up to Oakland that night for a signing at Barnes & Noble—three people showed up ... sold three books. By the numbers, my worst signing to date; by the experience, no worse than any other. I got to sit and rap with cool people, and I truly enjoyed myself.

I stayed with my friend in Berkeley and got up early for an interview with the morning news in downtown San Fran. KRON, Channel 4. Good questions, but the photo they put on the screen of an amputee cyclist wasn't me. Oh well, who knew? So I was free until 7:00 PM that night: had a speaking gig at Stanford University for a summer internship program called University of Dreams. The students are all business and finance majors interning at corporations in the city, and they bring in non-money people to show them a little something outside of capitalism. Go figure, I'm a "non-money" guy.

In the meantime, I cruised up into Marin County, just the other side of the Golden Gate Bridge. I got keen on walking along a beach for a spell and pulled up to Muir Beach. I had sandals in hand, walking along the edge of the water, cool brine splashing on my feet (foot), sun shining on me, feeling very pleasant. Then I walked through some rock croppings and found myself at none other than a nude beach. *Hmmm.* Then I find myself prolonging my gaze … at two old men.

With ego restored after some self-questioning, I got in the car and drove the switchback-y drive up to Mt. Tam (short for something that I don't know) and hiked the final quarter mile up to the coolest view of a city I've ever seen: low clouds rolling onto the tiny peninsula that houses the city of San Francisco. Highly recommended. Much more than naked old men.

The Stanford engagement went well. This was a gratis gig; at this event, if you do well the first year, they invite you back with pay the next year. They invited me back for next year. The big boss guy even gave five hundred dollars to the multiple sclerosis fund-raiser I mentioned earlier in this e-mail; the money was supposed to go to REI for some camp gear the interns had damaged. He said REI would just have to suck it up. Thanks, Eric. Then I sold the poor-little-not-getting-paid-all-summer-interns a bunch of books.

At the start of this whole Left-Right-Left Coast trip, I had a little mishap. Yep. I was at the Denver airport just in time to get my luggage checked in. At first, they wouldn't take it. Said fifty minutes before the flight wasn't enough. After some pleading and a call to the higher-ups, she took my bags and bike, and as she passed the first bag onto the belt, she said, "Oops, forgot to tag that one. That's what happens when you rush." I gave a little smile and held back all the fun words. Then I headed toward the gate, but not before feeding my face. Shoulda got it to go. Got to the gate eight minutes before scheduled departure time, and they'd already given away my seat. Missed the flight, along with a book signing in Eugene that night. *Stupid.*

So I'm killing time before my next flight in two and a half hours, and in the midst of making phone calls, I discover that my credit card is not in my wallet. The credit card I rent cars with, i.e., the one with enough "space" on it. Yeah, left it at home somehow. So I have no choice but to head back to Boulder, get the card, and drive back to the airport, catching the final flight of the day at 8:15 PM. But the aforementioned tagless bag didn't make it, as suspected, and I didn't get it until the following night. I got to my buddy's place at 11:00 PM and was up at 7:00 AM for a Portland TV thing—in my stinky clothes.

The show was *AM Northwest*. In the greenroom, I meet Tanya Brown, Nicole Simpson Brown's sister. She was there promoting her father's book on domestic violence. (He's eighty; he can't hang.) Just got a letter in the mail from her today. She said she got a bunch of her family members to buy the book. Cool.

Moving along, I raced the 5430 Triathlon—a half Ironman—on July 20 here in Boulder. Good swim, good bike, tough run. Very hot and sorta difficult terrain on back roads and, at times, gnarly washboard-surfaced dirt roads. My 2:11 half marathon was much slower than I'd hoped for, and I once again failed to accomplish the sub-five-hour half Ironman distance. I did, however, finish fifth of thirty-three in my age group—fortunately for me, everyone was bummin' on the run—my best percentile finish at this distance. I think.

Right around this time, I finally got around to reading a stack of letters from fourth graders—not even kids I'd spoken to. Their teacher found my Web site somehow and asked if his students could send me letters. I absolutely love getting letters from kids, so I didn't hesitate to say yes. Then I lost them in the pile of crap that is my desk, and when they resurfaced, I pulled them out over dinner. Oblige me to share a couple of funny selections:

My best friend had a dog and her name was Kristle. She was our other best friend. She died like one year ago. She got her eye cut out from cancer, and she got ran over by a truck. It was so sad and she lived.
—Tiffany
Mr. Jones is a good teacher. He eats candy in front of us though.
—Lisa

The week before the 5430, I swam for a relay team in Aurora, just outside of Denver. It was a long sprint, almost Olympic distance. I hopped out of the water (pun intended) after a one-thousand-meter swim and tagged Eric Wiehenmayer (the blind dude who climbed Everest) and his tandem bike pilot, who rode the twenty-mile bike course before handing the duties over to Trish Downing (paraplegic who wheeled the run.)

Trish was a tandem pilot for a blind woman when we met at the disabled cycling national championships in 1998. She was hit on her bike a couple of years ago by a woman who took a left turn when she shouldn't have. Trish wasted no time getting back into sports. She has already done a few triathlons and a couple of half marathons. Her beautiful smile is as bright as ever. And I think we won the relay division; never did hear the result.

I competed the prior Wednesday in a weeknight triathlon in Connecticut. The Pat Griscus Memorial Triathlon is the only weekday triathlon I know of. I'd raced it a couple of years back. The race's namesake was the first amputee (a fellow BK) to run the Boston Marathon back in the eighties, and then, in 1985, the first to do the Hawaiian Ironman. While training on the bike course just outside of Kona in 1987, a cement truck struck and killed him. With the utmost respect, thanks, Pat, for setting the stage for the rest of us.

The race was a sprint distance event (0.5-mile swim, 10.5-mile bike, 3.1-mile run). Happy to say I had a good race and finished in 1:06 thirty-eighth place overall out of six hundred competitors. I ran the 5k in twenty minutes—good for me. When I can run, I do pretty well, and as of late, I've had little to no leg problems, which helps my time tremendously.

The previous Sunday, I raced the Holliston sprint triathlon in Holliston, Massachusetts (0.5-mile swim, 15-mile bike, 5-mile run). My performance wasn't as strong as other recent races, but good enough for thirteenth of forty-one in the age group. I did this race with three other gimpy friends, all missing legs to some degree. We were all in town for the Amputee Coalition of America's annual meeting in Boston. The best part of this trip was the fireworks. Friggin' amazing! With the Boston Pops jammin' and the streets packed and crazy new fireworks I've never seen before. Sometimes I wish I still dropped acid. Not really. Well, sorta … well … no, not really.

I'm kinda running out of story telling steam here, but we're not quite done. Did a thirty-five-plus criterium bike race in Louisville, adjacent Boulder, and got spit out along with some others by the third lap of a fifteen-lap race. Then, on the last lap, I went screaming into this corner to avoid the shame of getting lapped with just a half mile to go, but I couldn't hold it and had to bunny hop the curb and go into the grass. I hit a rock and punctured my tire and cracked the rim of my five-hundred-dollar carbon front wheel … and ^)@($(%^#(@*&$#*&^#*!

And last but not least, I raced my first duathlon (run-bike-run) in Atlanta on June 22. The night before was my birthday (my first beer-free birthday in about twenty years). I was stoked to be able to run so relatively pain free. I gotta say "relatively" each and every time because it *always* hurts on the run; "pain free" refers to not having to stop and reboot.

I ran the opening 10k in forty-four minutes, biked the hilly, turny 40k bike in 1:09, and ran the closing 5k in just under twenty-three. I'd been having so much trouble with Stumpie in the recent past that these were the first runs, training or racing, that I didn't have to reboot since last August, nearly a year ago! Cool stuff.

I'm sure there's some other stuff to write about, but I'm all done. Is anyone still reading?

European Cycling Championships
September 2003

It's 5:00 AM here in Boulder. I'm still on Euro time, hoping to snap out of it before long. Got home last night about 8:00 PM and watched the Broncos spank the Raiders; it's good to be home.

The bike races in the past several days came with one major goal outside of winning: the events in the Czech Republic served as the first qualifier for next year's Paralympic Games in Athens, Greece. Those of us coming home with multiple medals would score an early invite to the Big Show.

We arrived on Wednesday, September 10, with a reasonable four days to acclimate to the time difference—eight hours from Colorado. The team had spent the previous two weeks sequestered at the Olympic Training Center in Colorado Springs. Being a Boulder boy, I was lucky to get away three or four times and be back in my own bed, something of a rarity these days.

Things opened up on Sunday, September 14 at the velodrome in Prague. The kilo (one-thousand-meter sprint) was the opening race. I went right to work on those qualifying medals and notched a bronze on day one with a time of 1:17.1—my slowest ever in international competition. But that was cool with me. It was a slow track, and my training has been a bit slack in that event, as I was traveling around trying to sell books and focusing on triathlon for the last couple of months. With four events left, I felt confident that I could squeak out another medal before the closing bell.

The next day was the qualifier for the 4k pursuit race. Of the fourteen LC2s (guys in my category—mainly below-knee amps), the top eight would move on to the semifinals. In the pursuit, competitors line up on opposite sides of the oval, on the straightaways. At the gun, you "pursue" each other. I pursued my guy, a Swiss rider, and caught him on the eighth or ninth lap of twelve. After passing him, I finished in a time of five minutes, twenty-one seconds. Also my slowest at an international event. My buddy Ron beat his guy, and together we qualified third and fourth, respectively. This meant that in the semis, I would go up against the sixth fastest guy, and Ron would face the fifth. The finals would pit the two fastest semi riders going for gold and the third and fourth fastest semi riders battling for the bronze.

The third day of competition started with the Olympic sprint in the morning before our pursuit semis later that afternoon.

The Olympic sprint is a team thing: Three riders lined up on one side, and like the pursuit, the competition—that day it was Team Australia—was 180 degrees away. The race is three laps, with the team's lead rider pulling out on each go-around. As you know, in bike racing, it's always easier to ride behind someone and benefit from his or her draft. Well, in this race, the first guy goes all out with his teammates in tow, and when he completes a lap, he gets out of the way as the remaining two continue. The second rider then busts his ass for a lap before pulling up and letting the closer do his thing.

Dan Nicholson, a rider with cerebral palsy, was our strong opener, and he put a couple of seconds' lead on the Aussie guy riding the first wheel. Ron then had to do battle with a CP rider with just a slight disabling affect from his condition and, hence, a strong cyclist. That lap left me with just a little over a second lead on yet another CP rider with only a slight disability—the guy who happened to have the fastest kilo of all riders with any disability in yesterday's event. We lost the race by 1.8 seconds. Kind of a bummer, but our two teams were the two fastest and had qualified for the final gold medal round! Silver at worst. Not so bad. This meant I had my second medal and Ron his first.

Ron and I each beat our guys in the pursuit semis later that afternoon, and again I was third and he was fourth. This meant that two good friends would be going head-to-head for the bronze the next day—not the most enviable position. Ron still had to earn another podium spot for an invite, while I had already secured mine. It was important for him to ride strong, so he was a little hungrier.

The fourth and final day on the track started again with the Olympic sprint finals. The Aussies got us by 1.5 seconds, despite Team USA knocking a half second off yesterday's time.

The afternoon's pursuit finals were kind to my good friend, and he crossed the line a half second ahead of me, giving us two medals each, qualifying us for Athens and taking off the edge. We were ready to tackle the time trial and road race without fear of results and consequences.

The road races were in another city called Teplice, about an hour's drive from Prague. It's near the German border. In Germany, prostitution is illegal. In Czech, it's not. *Why bring this up?* you ask. Well, on the drive over, we were informed that the Germans often came over to hire those in the world's oldest profession, and that we should be wary of overly friendly women, as their motives might not be so moral. Upon arrival at our half-star hotel, while one of our athletes was moving his things into his room, he turned around to see a woman standing there. She was in her midforties and, according to classically Oklahoman Brad, had "fallen out of the ugly tree and hit every branch on the way down." She said something in Czech, which of course he didn't understand but assumed had something to do with room maintenance.

"No. I'm fine," was his mild-mannered reply.

She then walked over to the door, shut it, moved to the bed, tapped the mattress, and gave him the two-fisted, elbows-bent-to-ninety-degrees pump signal to see if he'd care to take the edge off. Brad was married—happily, I might add—and he not so morally asked her to leave.

I know what you're thinking, and no, I didn't go there, despite the fact that I haven't seen "fireworks" since, coincidentally, the Fourth of July.

Back to business. On the fifth day of racing, we tackled a 14.2k time trial, comprised of two 7.1k laps. Relatively short, but long enough to be legit. Having won the time trial at world champs last year, I felt confident that I might get another podium finish. Twenty minutes and twenty-seven seconds later, and having been the last rider of twenty-five LC2s to give the course a go, I ended up with a bronze. My third medal. Cool.

A new cat on the block, from Romania, didn't race the track. He'd lost his leg a couple of years ago after, rumor has it, a successful career as a marathon inline skater. He came in fourth, a mere ten seconds behind me. I thought someone said his name was Carol, so I wasn't too worried about him at the start.

The next day, the last day, as Ron and I were getting ready for the road race—nine laps for a total of 63.9k—Coach Griffin informed us that he'd just learned Olympic sprint medals didn't count toward Athens qualifying, that only individual hardware would get us where we wanted to go. Ron was seriously pissed off. This was now a much more meaningful event against some serious competitors. Of the twenty-five racers out there, there were three or four teams of three riders apiece, while Ron and I were the only Americans. Fortunately, Jiri Jezek, the world's number one rider, who happens to hail from Prague, was without a teammate, as was the Romanian.

From the gun, one attack followed another. I covered most of them, the serious ones anyway, to help Ron conserve. I wanted him to medal almost as much as he did. At the closing of the fifth lap, Jiri covered a French attack, and the two of them stayed out front for a lap and a half, with Jiri doing most of the pulling, burning himself up. Early in the sixth lap, Roberto Alcaide, a strong Spaniard and time trial gold medalist, took off the front to catch Jiri, taking several riders with him, including Ron.

I was just about to go with them when I noticed that the strong young Norwegian, Morten Jahr, was on my wheel, and if I were to pull him to the front, I would be putting Ron in further jeopardy … and yes, I was a bit whipped at that point. I eased up, and Morton hesitated, and we let those six guys off the front chase the two farther up the road. Turns out that was the right thing to do.

Ron stayed with the pack that within two kilometers caught Jiri and Frenchie. Climbing the last hill, a short and steep one two hundred meters from the finish line, the Romanian went strong, followed by Roberto, Jiri, and Ron. Jiri buckled, cramping from overwork, and Ron took off with Roberto just behind him. Ron put on the afterburners, held off his chaser, but he couldn't catch his chasee. He ended up with a silver, and the flight home with him was much more pleasant than it otherwise would have been. I finished in tenth, also my worst finish in an international road race.

That's it. Race is over. Got up at 5:00 AM to catch the bus to the airport.

I'm gonna throw this out there now, just so that there's no confusion in a year or so. While I did qualify for the 2004 Paralympic Games in Athens next September, there remains a chance that I will forgo the opportunity. A little over a year ago, I made a big decision: I want to do something different. That particular something is to go back to school. To law school. And I've decided on the fall of 2004. Just so happens that the Paralympics start two weeks after school gets back in session. With the Games drawing nearer, I certainly have been thinking more about how cool it would be to win a medal—which I missed out on in Sydney—in the birthplace of the Olympic Games. The issue is this: if I opted for school in 2005, the moment I returned from Athens, I'd be wishing I were in school for the next eleven months. I just turned thirty-six; I have gray chest hairs and toe fungus. I'm damn close to being ready to focus on something else.

I'll be applying to schools soon, within the next month. If I get into the University of Colorado here in Boulder, by far my first choice, I'll immediately begin looking for a way to matriculate in the fall while heading to Athens too. It'll be tough but not impossible. We'll just have to wait and see what happens.

As I have said many times in the past, thanks for taking the time to share my experiences. I hope to see you all sometime soon and that all is well in your corner.

Peace.

🚲   🚲   🚲

You've probably noticed by now that there's some redundancy in these e-mails with regard to racecourse descriptions and the like. You've probably already figured out why that is, but just in case: these posts were delivered to an ever-growing list and so I had to continually educate the readers. Here's another one that hits this note a couple of times.

Half-and-Half

November 2003

October was without much athletic incident, but I was busy with trips to speak about whatever it is that I speak about. Early in the month, I spoke to students at Boston University, then at my alma mater high school—go Gardner High Wildcats!—and then another just north of Boston. On the way back to Boulder, I stopped in Cleveland—where I left my left foot—to address podiatry interns one day and bariatric patients the next. (Bariatrics is last-resort stomach surgery for those who need to lose some weight. I spoke at the dinner celebrating the weight reduction of ninety-five "graduates"—they lost a total of thirteen thousand pounds!) On another trip East, I spoke at the high school of my publisher's son, then with kids at a private K-8 school near Poughkeepsie, New York. Apparently, the thought of amputation was too much for a fourth grader, who got up, ran to the back room, and emptied his stomach behind the eighth grade girls! That was funny. All the shrieking and teacher panic ... while I'm trying not to laugh.

In between those two trips, I made my way to Ann Arbor, Michigan, for the season's opening camp of the U.S. Amputee Hockey Team. We have a couple of new freaks who are sure to improve our chances of winning the '04 World Champs against those pesty Canucks in April. The tournament will be in Prague, and last year's teams from the United States, Canada, Finland and Russia will be joined by new teams from Czech Republic and Sweden ... I think.

November was busy with a couple of half marathons in San Diego—running the relay for the San Diego Triathlon Challenge and the Silver Strand Half Marathon, which doubles as the leg amputee national championships—before a trip to Florida/Puerto Rico.

The first race was the first day of the month, right around the time of the big San Diego fire. Fortunately, La Jolla was without smoke or charred remains.

96

Take a second to thank Something.

The SDTC is a half Ironman: 1.2-mile swim, 56-mile bike, and a 13.1-mile run. I ran for Team Coldwell Banker. And swam just for fun. Ocean swimming is something we lack in Colorado, so when the opportunity arises, we landlocked triathletes go for it.

I ran a 1:40 and was very happy with that. (Particularly since I'd slept less than two hours the night before. Wasn't my fault.) I have no idea how our team did. It's more of an event than a race, and no one really cares how fast they go—it's all about raising money for the Challenged Athletes Foundation.

Two weeks later, however, it did matter. At the Silver Strand race, I lined up against four other below-knee runners. My direct competitors were Joel Sampson, Ivan Steber, Ray Viscome, and J. P. Theberge. There was rent money to be won and prestige to pin—and I'm sure it's no surprise to you that both are always welcome at my house.

Ivan took the pack out quickly; it didn't take long for things to settle in, and I was at the front a couple of minutes later. I was not taking these competitors lightly, particularly Ivan and Joel, and I held an aggressive pace: 6:20 at the first mile.

What the hell and I doing? I thought. *I barely run this fast in mile repeats on the track!*

I pulled back a bit, and the next mile was a 6:40. I felt a little better there. I probably slowed it down a bit over the next two miles since Stumpie was already aching, and he soon talked me into taking a quick ten-second break to dangle the prosthesis (gets the blood back in Stumpie—feels good). This was my first glance back at the competition, and Ivan was just thirty or forty meters behind me. I quickly got back on pace—I imagine that I was running just under seven-minute miles at that point. Two miles later, at mile 6, I stopped again for a dangle (fairly standard procedure for longer races) and saw that I'd put some more distance on Ivan. At mile 8, the hardware was a little loose, and a bit more painful than I like to put up with, so I pulled over to reboot. Ivan was more than one hundred meters back, and I began to feel as if I'd probably win. But of course, I hadn't yet, and I redonned the leg in a minute or so and hit the road once again.

At mile 10, I stopped to dangle, and as an able-bodied competitor approached, I asked about my nearest competition.

"At least two minutes back." Good to know.

Miles 10 to 12 make up an out-and-back section of the course, which gave me a good chance to see just how far I was ahead of the others. I reached the turnaround at mile 11 and took note of my watch. Two minutes and fifty seconds later, I saw Ivan about a half mile out and quickly deduced a 5:40 lead. Then, less than a minute later, there was Ray; then, a minute later, there was Joel; and still less behind was J. P. These guys had a serious battle going behind me!

It was around mile 9 or so that I did the math and recognized that I was hanging on to just under a sub-1:30 pace—somewhat of a long-term goal of mine. But I was fading at that point, and Stumpie wasn't exactly smiling, and I sincerely doubted my chances. Then, right about when I saw Ivan coming the other way, I felt a little surge of adrenaline when I realized it was still within reach, but just barely—I'd have to keep the pace around 6:45 for the remaining mile and a half. At the mile 12 marker, as I dangled, I saw that I had seven minutes and eight seconds available to get under 1:30. I dropped the hammer best I could.

The final stretch of the race is probably a third of a mile, straight and flat. I had two minutes left, with what looked like less than a quarter mile to go. Then, with a minute to go, I dropped the hammer a little harder. With about fifty meters to go, I checked my watch—I had twenty seconds. I crossed in 1:29:52!

Then, as I huffed and I puffed, I gimped over to a table, leaned on it ... and got all choked up. I just didn't think I had that in me.

Some of you may know what it feels like in most races: you do good or just okay and think about how you could have done better; or maybe it sucked altogether, and you're kinda bummed. But on occasion, you know you knocked the cover off the ball, and you get that rare feeling of being quite proud of your accomplishment. Well, this race provided me with the latter.

Seconds later, I was sitting on a bench, doffing the leg. I gingerly peeled off the liner and groaned as the blood hit the concrete. Yep, *niiiice* open blister. Was it worth it? Damn straight! New official national record and 750 big ones.

Then there are the intangible benefits, like the impression left on a young boy. Roderick Sewell is a double above-knee amputee who was there to watch and gain some perspective. He watched the other amps run across the finish line and was by my side when I took off my leg. His mom came up to me afterward and told me that Roderick had just witnessed something new: he'd never seen a bloody stump, and he asked his mom how I was able to run like that. His mom said to him, "Because he wanted to win." Seriously, I hope he understands what that means on all levels. And it's a huge honor to think that my race mattered to him.

Now, here it is, two and half weeks later, and Stumpie's just about healed. I was relegated to crutches for a couple of those days immediately following. I jumped on a plane to Orlando the following Wednesday, and Thursday I spoke to a group of Central Florida YMCA scholarship benefactors, gimping up on stage and not feeling too athletic. But fortunately, my twenty-minute spiel seemed to be well received, and they kindly paid me for my time. That afternoon, I spoke to an after-school

YMCA program for middle schoolers. You know, to keep out of trouble, to keep them from being like me ... when I was a younger man, that is.

I spent the next few days in San Juan with my sister Paty (yes, that's how she spells it), her family, and my mom, who came down from Massachusetts. One of Paty's clients gave her the keys to her condo on the beach for a week, and we enjoyed ourselves with tennis, Scrabble, and relaxation. A day later, I was playing hockey and cycling in Boulder, and a couple of days after that, skiing in Winter Park.

It's not bad work if you can get it.

I could say "Happy holidays" or something like that, but it seems so unoriginal. So ... umm ... ahh ... *I got nothin'*.

P.S. The law school apps are in. With that done, I'll almost certainly be in Athens!

🚲   🚲   🚲

Racing was replaced with off-season training. While there were no races to write up, something big did happen, which would forever affect the rest of my life: I met Sharon Wetherall. She's the most incredible creature ever to walk the planet. Less than two years later, she married me.

The scene was the Rio Grande in Boulder. It was December 23, 2003. She was hanging out with a friend in a booth. I was with some of my buddies, celebrating the holidays at an adjacent table. She'd taken a quick walk and upon returning, she offered a smile—within minutes, I requested permission to pull up a seat next to her.

Turns out we had a lot of the same friends; she was once a professional triathlete, currently spending her energy in medical school. We hit it off immediately. I almost left without getting her number, and that, my friends, would have been the biggest mistake of my life.

We went on a date a few days later, just a couple of beers on a Sunday night. That was fine with her, which, in turn, was huge with me. Two months later, I was in love and quite certain I'd spend the rest of my life with her. But as experience had taught me, love cannot be rushed. I waited six more months before asking her hand in marriage. She remains my best friend, mother of my children, bringer of happiness, joy, love, and all things sacred in my life.

The next several reports contain some sort of Sharon's commentary. Keep in mind that my upcoming successes on the racecourse were made possible with the support of this woman.

In transition to the bike at the 1997 ITU World Championships in
Perth, Australia.

The original "I...am...Ironman" pose at the finish line of the 1998
Hawaiian Ironman. The first of ten Ironman finish photos.

The camera puts on ten pounds!

It's convenient when someone is already on scene to clean your wounds.

Fielding questions at the 2001 Ironman Malaysia press conference.

Pegging my way to the bike moment after donning
the leg at the IM Malaysia swim exit.

A little repair on the prosthesis before heading out on another adventurous day at the 2001 Expedition BVI (British Virgin Islands).

This is how I felt after digging deeper than I've ever
gone before. Not fast, just didn't have it that day.

Feeling strong on the run at the 2004 Buffalo Springs Lake Triathlon.

Feeling no so strong a few miles later...

More often than not, I'm in a rather pleasant mood
when another Ironman is in the books.

This photo from the velodrome in Athens is straight from the 2007 United States Olympic Committee Calendar. Still blows me away that by some strange twist of fate I get to be Mr. June in an Olympic calendar! Photo by Brian Bahr/Getty Images.

The fastest one-legged Ironman finish to date at Ironman
Coeur d'Alene, 2005. Yeah, I was happy.

The rare swim photo at an Estes Park, CO sprint triathlon.

Jack's first triathlon finish at three
weeks old. NYC, 2006.

Sharon and Jack
(and Luke in-utero),
on Jack's first
birthday celebrating
another Ironman
Coeur d'Alene
finish in 2007.

Block Island Triathlon
August 4, 2007

I finished 2nd in my age group. The awards only
went to the top age-group finishers!

Skating Prague & Running Boston

May 2004

Just took down my housemate Ethan—best of three in foosball. Three overtime games at that: 11–9, 10–12, 11–9. I'm on top of the world.

I was on the other side of the world a couple of days ago. We—Team USA—skated in the 2nd Annual International Standing Ice Hockey World Championships. Cutting to the chase, the Canadians took it 8–1 in the final.

I was on this side of the world, but the other side of the country, a couple of weeks ago, running the Boston Marathon. I ran it with my sister Paty. Cutting to the chase once again—me 3:24, Paty 4:04. She once ran faster than I, when I had two legs and she didn't have two kids.

The stories go like this:

I returned from Prague yesterday, via Amsterdam. The final game was Friday afternoon, after which we ate a pig off a skewer and then went into town, drank beer, and played drums on the tables. Then Saturday we tooled around a bit and went to see an able-bodied world championship game (our tournament coincided with this one for, primarily, publicity's sake), but not before spending time in a tent. A true staple in European sporting culture: the beer tent. A band butchers classic rock, the Euros try to mouth the words that they don't know, and the Americans point fingers. We point fingers because we're jealous that they're all so fanatically fanatical about their hockey teams. And we're drinking Budweiser, by the way. Czech Budweiser, where it began sometime around the year 300. Much better than Bud at home; it has a little color.

It was Austria versus Germany. End of the second and Germany's up 3–1 (I think. I could be wrong; I have no idea, really). We're back at the beer stand, seven of us, athletes and staff, enjoying ourselves. All of a sudden—and it kept happening so suddenly—time for another round. I had neither the wherewithal nor the belly space to enjoy another, and I took advantage of the last round having come up one pint short, telling the boys I'd pass. Then some wisenheimer has to go and give me the "skirt" commentary. I flipped over a chair—kicked it, actually, with the good shin (stupid)—and then I flipped over a table, shouting, "You wanna piece of me!" All in good fun and jest and merriment, of course. But the yellow jackets, a.k.a. security, didn't see the humor. They saw the idiot. They tossed the idiot.

I made my way back to the via feet, train, bus, and feet about an hour and a half later.

That was Saturday night. Sunday night I spent in Amsterdam. Not on purpose, but it worked out okay. We were on layover there when the plane broke, and they didn't have a spare, so they put me up in a hotel with Captain Karl—one-armed team captain Karl. They fed us. Then they sent us to one of the most mysterious places I've ever been: the Red Light District. Tourists from all over the world, young and old alike, were laughing and commenting, looking and leering at prostitutes wearing lingerie a mere ten feet away, on the other side of red full-length neon-framed windows. Some not looking as good as others.

Then there are the pot cafes all over the place. The street pushers on every bridge—there're many little bridges over many little canals.

Now don't start thinking all kinds of outlandish thoughts—nothing illegal, nothing immoral. Strictly taking it all in. It's funny how the Olympic Committee keeps an eye on you—less than twenty-four hours after I got home Monday, the U.S. Anti-Doping Agency (USADA) showed up at my door—earlier today—to perform a random testing. No, not random like math or geography, but a test to see if I'm using performance-enhancing drugs like … whatever they are …

Some actual Gimpy Team USA hockey highlights included spanking the Finns, then the Russians, then getting spanked by the Canadians, then spanking the Czechs, all in round-robin opening rounds. That left the Finns facing the Russians for the bronze, and the Canadians versus the Americans for the gold.

With six minutes left in the third, the Russians erased a two-goal deficit and beat the Finns 4–3 … I think … something like that.

In our earlier game against the Czechs, one of their players suffered a heart attack moments before "The Star-Spangled Banner." It was followed by a major one, and he was in the ICU when we left; sadly, he had left the ice for the last time. Let's all take a moment to throw him a little …

Playing in that game was my good friend Jiri Jezek, the world's best BK cyclist on both the road and the track—typically one/two/three spots ahead of me. He wasn't much of a goalie, but they needed a body and the publicity he could bring (he's on the country's Web site). Nonetheless, every shot I took, he stopped, and I took a lot of 'em. There was a coach mandate for my line mates to get me the puck to score on my cycling nemesis. I handled the puck more than I had in any game *ever*. But nothin' doin'. After the game, he told me that his wife, Sonya—both of them good friends of mine—mandated he not let *me* score on *him*. They do have power, those better halves.

In that Canadian game, the final one, the one we lost 8–1, we did a few things right. Our goalie, Mike Ginal, stopped many, many shots and was voted the tourney's best goalie. We kept them from reaching the back of the net on a five on three. My line scored the one goal—on the one shift that I sat out.

I recently spent a couple of weeks at a U.S. Paralympic Cycling Team camp in San Diego. Two weeks of lots of riding, one five-mile run. Not the best approach for a marathon, but not the worst. I had put in a few good long runs in the weeks preceding this camp, even running twenty miles once without taking off my leg. New record.

Bill Beiswenger of Abilities Unlimited did a little work on the run leg. You might remember the last race report, a half marathon had me bleeding and bumming at the end. He took out one inconspicuous bump inside the socket and *boom*! Perfect fit.

I arrived in Boston a few days before the race, visited the family, etc. The goal, once again, was to break that national record of 3:18. A 7:33 minute-mile pace. Keeping in mind this course goes downhill for the majority of the first fifteen miles, I ran my first 5k—3.1 miles—in 22.19, 10k in 44:47, 15k in 1:08, and half at 1:35:59. I was running a 7:19 pace. I was starting to think about that record. To make things more exciting, the Sox were in town for a stint with the Yankees. I was asking for and getting game updates on the course. Sox were down by three somewhere around mile 13.

I reached the 25k mark at 1:54:08, the 30k at 2:17:49, and then the 35k at 2:22:59. Seven point two kilometers to go. The Sox were down by one.

It wasn't so much going up Heartbreak Hill that hurt, but coming down. The jarring of the guts. Almost killed me in '01. The damn bellyaches got me again, the kind that make it too hard to breathe, to get enough oxygen to fuel the muscles, the kind that made me stop running for a spell. Somewhere in there, I ran back-to-back ten-minute miles before kicking it in again for the last couple. In the midst of this kick, the Sox won 5–4, and hearing this brought a good feeling. That is to say, I felt horrible to a lesser degree. I finished in 3:24:42 and was very, very happy. And that's with seven reboots.

The heat (high eighties) made for much sweat and, hence, much slop when running for an extended length of time, particularly with a lotta downhill thrown in there. I finished 1,554 of 16,743. Well within the top 10 percent.

Being gimpy has its rewards and Paty and I were welcomed at the VIP finish corral adjacent the finish line—no need to walk what seems like an eternity to get your bag of clothes. We then showered across the street from the VIP tent, at the Copley Fairmont Hotel (my friend Cheri Blauet, last year's wheelchair winner, accommodated us with her room). From there, we made our way a couple of blocks to Dick's Last Resort, residing under the Prudential Center, where we met our parents, sister, aunt, cousin, and four drunk high school friends who were all at the Sox game. I convinced everybody it was tradition to "shoot the boot." Yep, that's right, all eleven of us drank from the wholly socket—the run leg. Got pictures to prove it.

Let's see, it's now Tuesday night. That means I've got a whole four days here in Boulder before heading to Japan on Saturday to promote the publication of *One Man's Leg* in their native tongue. Should be fun. Two and a half weeks. Sharon's meeting me there for nine days. Sharon's my girlfriend.

Japan

May 2004

It's been a long time on the road. After a long stint in San Diego in March, and likewise in Boston and Prague in April, I headed to Japan in May for a couple of weeks. I was there to promote the Japanese translation of *One Man's Leg*. It's nothing short of a huge honor to be published in another language. In Japanese, at that, with pages that go the wrong way.

Let me just tell you a little about that trip. I arrived on a Monday night and spent the first week at the Madarao Resort just outside of Nagano—site of the 1998 Winter Olympic Games. This time was spent mostly training, as one of the early book-signing appearances was canceled. I was there, specifically, because it was the home of my host, the honorable Raisuke Kotaki—he's the head ski instructor at the resort and recently founded an adaptive skiing clinic there, which ultimately connected us. (A big thanks to Hal O'Learly from the National Sports Center for the Disabled in Winter Park, Colorado. Without his friendship, the Japanese version of the book wouldn't have happened.)

It rains quite a bit in Japan in May, and much of the time on the bike was spent rather damp. The first ride had me zipping downhill in a cheek-stinging downpour. I didn't mind it—once you're wet, as long as you're warm, it's not a big deal. I got in several rides, runs, and swims that week, before we headed to Tokyo for the Tokyo City Road Race—a 10k. The race was a personal best but could have been faster. They put me in the *back* of five thousand people (no option to self-seed and get closer to the front), running with the twelve-minute milers on an extremely crowded road. I was held at around nine-minute miles for the first fifteen minutes before the race took a left-hand turn onto a much wider street, breaking things up. I turned it on there and felt good in the light rain and cool temps. With that early hindrance, I didn't know how well I was doing (the course wasn't marked much). I was shooting for one of those longtime elusive goals: the sub-forty-two-minute 10k. At the "1k to go" sign, I saw it would be close, and I really turned it on before entering Tokyo Stadium—site of the 1964 Olympic Games—for the final four hundred meters. I hit the line at 42:00 flat on my watch. Never saw the official results. For all I know, it might have been 41:59. If anyone can translate the results on the Web, please let me know.

Sharon, she's my girlfriend, joined me in Nagano, and spent a week with me. She stopped in en route to America from Australia, her homeland, where she'd been visiting her family for seven weeks—she hadn't been back for two and a half years. This was her last big hurrah before graduating from medical school and starting her job as a resident surgeon *today*. First day and she's on a thirty-hour shift! Baby, I'm so proud of you!

We were invited to meet two senators while in Tokyo. Both pleasant and interested in what we were up to. One of them gave us a mug with his picture on it. Funny stuff. We also got a chance to check out a little sumo wrestling while in town (sumo wrestlers on little bikes, also quite comical). Apparently, we got lucky since it only happens at certain times of the year in certain cities. Not the most exciting stuff, to be honest with you. Interesting rituals. Fat men. Funny outfits. With all due respect, if it's not too late.

Then we flew to whatever that island is called, just south of the main island where we'd been, to Oita City. I spoke to a junior high school and to students and staff at Oita University. Tough assignments, I must say—speaking to a group through a translator, trying to be funny with everyone being Japanese, even the twelve-year olds. Picture me rattling on for a minute or two in the energetic way that I do, then trying to contain myself as the translator translates with hands clasped in the front, without facial or body expressions, the audience behaving ever so politely, not smiling much and not catching my translated humor (for the sake of the story, let's assume that I'm funny). Not easy. The second presentation to the university folks went a bit smoother with the experience gained from the first. I even met Yoko Ono at the latter talk. Not *that* Yoko Ono.

I decided to test the translatability of one of my favorite jokes on Hiro Harakawa, a new friend who spent most of the trip with us, as we drove by Tokyo Disneyland. "*Did you hear Mickey and Minnie Mouse were getting a divorce? Yeah, it's true. But the judge said to Mickey, 'I can't grant you a divorce on the grounds that you think your wife is a bit silly.' To which Mickey replied, 'I didn't say she was silly. I said she's fucking Goofy!'"*

He didn't get it.

We then headed to a rice-producing little city called Itako for an Olympic distance triathlon. This race also happened to be the Collegiate National Championship. Schools over there accept students on a slightly different scale, primarily based on their personalities. Not a shocker that I discovered one of the schools with a strong triathlon squad came from the popular Kinki University.

The race itself was as flat as a rice paddy, which, not surprisingly, we actually rode through for 40k, with forty-five, yes, *forty-five,* ninety-degree turns! Not a fast bike: 1:09; but a fast run: 42:03. And I'm happy to say, a personal best for me off the bike. (Thankfully, I didn't feel the blistered Stumpie until the race was over.) At the awards that night, I found out that I had reached another milestone. I finally stood on the age-group podium of an Olympic distance triathlon, third place of twenty-eight athletes in the 35-39s More happiness. After the podium appearance, the folks in the crowd came by the table we had set up to sign and sell books. We moved sixty books, with the proceeds going to the Japanese Special Olympics.

I got home a few days later, after spending four hours in a chair being interviewed on film for a Japanese television show called *Unbelievable.* It'll air Thursday night, July 8, if you happen to be there.

Thanks a million times over to Mr. Kotaki and Mr. Harakawa for taking such wonderful care of Sharon and me. They're cool. Japan is cool. You should check it out.

May your travels be safe and fun all at the same time.

P.S. So much sushi, so little time …

The Fastest Half

June 2004

I've had this goal for several years now (one of an elusive many): to bust a sub-five-hour half Ironman. I raced at Buffalo Springs Lake Triathlon last weekend with this goal once again seemingly within reach. Sharon came with me. She's my girlfriend. Up and over from Australia for her graduation, her parents came too!

We arrived Friday night for the Sunday morning race and camped at the lake. This added a little something. This something came in the form of wind, rain, lightning and thunder. Minutes before nature's fury, the local radio station interrupted our relaxing time by the fire with a warning of the coming storm. All was calm ... then ... *wham!* We sat up in the tent with our refreshments and watched the sky light up. A couple of hours of this, and the dampness inevitably seeped into the feet of our sleeping bags. Her parents were in the adjacent tent, adjacent the truck. Mom needed to be near it in case she had to head for last-minute shelter from the Mega-Giga volt, eight-inch chords of electric death that flirted with her. She toughed it out.

The storm let up after a couple of hours, and we managed a few hours of sleep. In the morning, we ate camp food and registered for the race. It was tuna and pasta over the Coleman for dinner before retiring to a few s'mores. I slept all right despite the surrounding campsites' battling ethnic music. Got up at 5:00 ... 5:05, actually. Then couldn't find my sandal anywhere. Ate cold oatmeal and a spot o' campfire coffee before heading off at 5:50, late from the get-go for my 6:40 AM race start.

Got there a bit rushed and didn't have much time to get all ready to go. At the last minute, Sharon scored me a chair for leg changing in transition. At 6:30, I got in the water with my foggy and scratched backup goggles—I'd misplaced the preferred ones—and swam the 1.2 miles in thirty-two minutes, about average for me.

Onto the bike after a 1:36 transition, and as I started up the first big hill, which is an out-of-the-saddle granny-gear grind, I was downshifting and struggling and thinking how I must not have quite recovered from the two-plus weeks spent hammering at a Paralympic bike camp in Colorado Springs. Then I saw that my rear derailleur wasn't doing anything; the shifter cable had loosened.

I hopped off, inspected, cursed, jumped on the bike, and reversed course down the hill against traffic, 250 meters back, grabbed an Allen wrench from the bag (and this is precisely why we carry them), reset my cable connection, and went.

Once out there, I felt good on the bike. My back hurt (nothing new), the wind blew steady, and I passed many riders.

On a separate note, I must say once again that I'm diggin' racing without a watch these days. There's just less pressure. There's no constant nagging in the brain of "I'm not going as fast as I should be!" No negativity.

I got off the bike in two hours, forty-one minutes, including the mishap. Then a decent second transition: 2:36—slow, but I'm trying this new tape for added suspension on the run leg and it's a *bee*-atch to put on in a hurry, I'd just learned.

The typical gut cramps came early in the run, not as bad as I usually get, ran them off by mile 2.5, and fell into a groove. I came upon struggling friend and ex-housemate Ivy Koger, who was hampered by a sciatic nerve that numbed his left leg. I made a passing wise-ass comment about being faster than he was and kept going.

I hit what's called the Energy Lab II (the original Energy Lab is a notorious section of the Hawaiian Ironman) and was pleasantly comforted by the lack of the usual baking hot temps and humidity. The Lab was kind and I ran. I hit the turnaround feeling fresh and kept on keeping on. I zipped down the steep hills with my typical can't-run-any-slower-on-this-carbon-leg out-of-controlness.

On the flatter stuff nearing the finish, I paced my stride off the sound of the slapping feet just behind me, able to hold steady through all but the last quarter mile. Still pushing, I neared the finish line and saw the clock: 5:19:59! Which meant that since my age-group wave started twenty minutes after the clock started, I was about to come up seconds short on the sub-five goal ... But *so* close! *How to feel?! Happy for a fast race? Sad I just missed it? That blasted mechanical failure early on the bike stole my thunder! So close!* Then happy. Then bummin'. Then happy. Then bummin'. Then happy for real.

Right after the race, we jumped back in the car for the ten-hour drive back home to Colorado. I called Sarah Reinertsen, an AK who had raced that day, to see if she had validated her invitation to the Hawaiian Ironman. She finished with twelve minutes to spare and has sealed the deal to suffer on the third Saturday of October 2004. Congrats.

She said, "Nice race. Four fifty-nine."

"What did you say?!"

"Yeah, that's what they said at awards."

"Four fifty-nine!!! Four fifty-nine!!! Four fifty-nine!!!" I yelled it repeatedly from the passenger's seat of Black Betty—my '89 Pathfinder. I was so happy. Just so *happy!* That got me to thinking. I've PRed in the last five races I've done: half marathon (1:29:52), marathon (3:24:42), 10k (42:00), 10k off the bike at an Olympic distance triathlon (42:03), half Ironman (4:59:31). Happy.

The next day was my birthday, and Sharon threw me a not-so-secret party at The Southern Sun. I was utterly content with life.

So that's the latest. Next on the agenda is a sprint race in Estes Park, Colorado, on July 11 before heading to Lake Placid, New York, on July 25 for Ironman USA.

A Great Day

July 2004

It was a great day at Ironman USA Lake Placid. I'm tickled pink to say that last Sunday's 10:30:50 finish time was another personal record for me; they're coming out of my butt these days! I've actually just started using that new PR toilet paper. Kinda rough but leaves you feeling quite fresh.

Wednesday's arrival was accompanied by decent weather: overcast, seventies. Thursday was the same. With last year's crazy downpours, which I was not there to experience, we were all a bit concerned about what Mother Nature might dish out for us this year. Then on Friday, the rains came. And they went. Saturday was kinda nice. Sunday ... was perfect.

It was excellent right from the beginning. Got up at 4:30 with Sharon by my side. I'll digress for a moment here. She worked an on-call shift at the hospital on Friday in Denver, going to work at 6:00 AM and getting out at 6:00 AM on Saturday morning. She then flew to Newark, New Jersey, got a car, and drove five hours to Lake Placid, arriving at 7:30 PM. She was sleeping at 9:30, got up with me to go watch the race (and while I was swimming, she met for the first time, and hung all day with, my mom, sisters, and four nieces, sans protection), caught my finish, then drove back to New York City for business on Monday morning. She's a stud, and she's my girlfriend.

I got to the race around 5:45 AM, got body marked, and set up my drinks and food on the Griffen Vulcan rocket ship, which had been racked the night before. At 6:50, I jumped in the water and moved into a more aggressive spot in the swim start than is typical for me: about fifteen feet back from the start line and twenty feet inside the corner. This put me right up front of the nineteen hundred athletes getting ready to scramble for space. This was unquestionably the right thing to do. The gun went off, and for the first two hundred meters, I experienced far less head bashing than in my previous Ironman races. The slugging came soon after but subsided quickly.

This swim course has one distinction many of us were able to take advantage of and appreciate. The course buoys are literally lined with a rope about six to eight feet underwater, which, with Mirror Lake's clarity, you can see throughout the entire swim, allowing those athletes who choose to "swim the rope" to focus on swimming without the typical need to sight. (The rope is set up for rowing competitions.) I was on the rope the whole time, to the point of headbutting many of the buoys as I came through.

The real benefit experienced by those who line up near the front is the fast water. The lead swimmers are obviously faster, and faster swimmers drag faster water along with them; therefore, swimming in their wake makes for a more efficient swim.

The course is two 1.2-mile loops, each loop comprised of a 0.6-mile stretch out to the turnaround, with about a fifty-yard lateral swim to the return leg. After the first loop, swimmers cross a land bridge about twenty meters wide and reenter the water. My first lap was twenty-six minutes (I'd later learned since I now race without a watch), and while I didn't know my elapsed time, I knew I was swimming well. Rounding the final turn buoy, I still felt good and pushed hard to stay on the feet in front of me. On a couple of occasions I lost focus and the feet I followed were suddenly ten feet away. I went hard to regain contact, each time feeling the benefit of the draft once I got there. Also, at that last turn buoy, my cap, which had slowly been sliding off my bald head (yes, *bald* bald[1]), popped off and now resides in the murk at the bottom of Mirror Lake.

I hopped out of the water to grab a seat on the chair Sharon had scored for me while I swam. I attempted to sit, but the dizziness of the swim and the unipod base had me sliding off the plastic and onto my ass in seconds. Back on, I stripped the suit and put on my run leg for the quarter-mile run to the bike transition. I crossed the timing mat just after donning the leg at 59:15, 205th overall, which means I came out in fifty-eight-plus minutes, besting my previous swim PR by five minutes. *Can you spare a square?*[2]

I was riding the bike a few minutes later, taking on the 112 miles of beautiful, hilly terrain. This course just might be *the* most beautiful of all the Ironman races.

---

1   *Seinfeld* reference.
2   *Seinfeld* reference.

Early in the ride, I was feeling a bit heavy-legged, more than I'm used to. I thought back to the previous Sunday, when I rode in a 5430 half Ironman relay team back in Boulder. I'd felt sluggish early in that ride too, but I managed a two-hour, twenty-two-minute fifty-six-mile ride, and that included a five-minute flat change. This relaxed my head a bit, knowing that the heavy legs would lighten up before too long. And sure enough, they did, and soon I found myself riding in the midst of some fast guys, one of which was a friend from Boulder, Armando Galarraga. We exchanged relative leads, along with a few other guys (no, not drafting) for the next sixty miles. Along the way, I was pleasantly surprised to find myself passing Heather Fuhr, former Hawaiian Ironman world champ, who has won this race four of the last five years. Then I saw her husband, Roch Frey, whose coaching program I followed for my first IM finish in '98, and said to him, as I climbed the the four percent grade, "I'll never forget the race I passed your wife on the bike." Not sure if he appreciated that one ...

I'd already passed Melissa Spooner and before long Andrea Fisher, former and current Ironman USA champions, respectively. Not surprisingly, I was feeling good about my ride and my race and kept on it. Upon entering town, preparing for the run transition, the energy from the crowd reminded me of how much I missed the Ironman, two years removed.

I hopped off the bike in 5:26:00 with Sharon's leg-swapping assistance. It was the seventy-sixth fastest ride; I was in sixty-fifth place at the start of the run. And I was ready to run.

The run started a little stiff in the back and more cramped in the gut than I'm used to in the longer races, but experience has taught me that each of these discomforts would pass. Right out of the gate in the town of Lake Placid, runners descend a rather steep section of about one hundred meters, getting steeper as it goes. I opted to run most of it backward, which I do quite often on steep stuff in training runs, but I'd never done in a race. It eliminates a lot of pounding on both Stumpie and on the good leg, which does all the braking, de facto.

As I ran downhill, glancing occasionally backward in search of obstacles, I witnessed Heather Fuhr coming at me. Apparently, I hadn't put any time on her in that entire second lap on the bike. She passed me just as I turned to a forward stride at the bottom of the hill, and I watched her as the crowd cheered for this Canadian, the locals' favorite, now in third behind an Aussie and a Kiwi, respectively. A poignant moment, indeed.

As mentioned, the weather was near perfection for race day: mostly overcast, around seventy for most of the bike, and nary a noticeable breeze. It was a bit chilly early on the bike (I wore arm warmers on the entire ride). This made for a drippy nose, and consequent farmer blows and snot abound. One of the benefits of the arm warmers was the built-in handkerchief. While I did manage to mop up most of it, much of it landed on my legs, along with a lot of energy drink. The point of this being that early on the run, my suspension sleeve was quite sloppy since its interface with my skin was compromised with gooey stuff. I had to stop twice in the first two miles to reboot. At the second stop, an aid station, I scored a towel and cleaned it all up, and the Flex-Sprint stayed in place much better for the rest of the run.

Stumpie himself was in rather good shape to start the day, although I was having some issues in the days leading up to the event and had ambulated via crutches for much of my stay in town prior to Sunday morning. I'm so glad I brought the sticks with me, something I never do.

The cramps subsided, the back loosened up, and the run progressed without much notable incidence. At the first turnaround at mile 5.5, a volunteer informed me that I was the 105th male (there were now four females in front of me), meaning I'd been passed by around forty runners so far. Not unreasonable. I just kept plugging away, opting to walk pretty much all the aid stations, gathering food and drink to keep the energy stores intact. This was something I'd decided upon ahead of time to address the late-run energy loss I've experienced in every Ironman I've tackled. I ran the first of two 13.1-mile laps in 1:54. Several times along the way, I also incorporated the ever-so-pleasant ice-watering of Stumpie. Feels so good, makes him so happy—a bonding experience between a man and his stump.

Early on the second lap, the legs were getting lead-like and I wondered if the sub-eleven goal (that's always the goal) would be attainable. Around the seventeen-mile mark, having eaten an energy gel at each of the last several aid stations and coming out of my funk, I saw my good friend Katie Jereza coming from the turnaround I was headed toward. She was smiling and happy to be tackling her first Ironman along with her sister, Monette.

Katie is pretty much the reason I was racing here to begin with. She was a friend of mine from my corporate days just out of college, fellow trainees at the Lincoln Electric Company. Back then, she and I, as well as the other "rookies," spent a lot of time together and became quite close. She was there when I lost my leg. She visited me most every day in the hospital both before and after amputation. I became a little more energized seeing her run so strong—neither of us having the least of triathlon ambitions when we'd become friends. (Katie scored nine of us the killer townhouse near the race start.)

I was feeling good and turned up the heat a bit, pushing what felt like eight-minute miles. I continued to walk all the aid stations to take in fuel. Soon I was no longer looking around, looking for friends and distractions from the grind. It was time to focus on my stride and forward motion. My eyes and head stayed forward and the encouraging comments from the crowd went unanswered, save the occasional finger wag.

With less than three miles to go, I was actually running faster each mile, knowing that I wasn't going to bonk. The focus got more intense, as did the crowd. Climbing the last hill, the one I'd been running backward down, still running (I'd walked it the second lap in 2002), the crowd was throwing lots of support my way. I felt good. Perhaps I'd beat my previous PR of 10:41:43, set on a much easier course in Roth, Germany, three years earlier. Without the watch, I didn't know. After the hill, still climbing but at a much lesser grade, I came upon the race clock near the finish: 10:15 with about 1.75 miles to go. *Holy Shit! A possible 10:30 race.*

I gave it all I had, and in the midst of the thick crowd, the energy poured in ... and I ran. Probably 7:30s at this point. The final turnaround left the athletes with less than a mile to go with a slight downhill grade. I kept pushing, and the crowd kept helping. I entered the finish track—the 1980 Olympic speed skating oval—feeling strong and proud. I saw the clock in the final stretch: 10:30:34 ... *Nice!*

The crowd carried me through the finish with a smile to wrap up my PR 3:57:08 run. I completed it in 10:30:50 and was 141st overall, 31st of 344 in the 35-39s. I couldn't have been happier. (The fourteen Hawaiian Ironman qualification spots in our age group rolled to twenty-sixth, to a time of 10:26. I came so close to qualifying as an age grouper!) Then Mike Reilly, "The Voice of Ironman," called across the PA: "Do it, Paul, do it!" I turned back toward the crowd, reached down and doffed the leg, held it over my head, and proclaimed, once again, *"I ... am ... Ironman!"*

Thanks again for taking the time to read about it. I wish all of you the best of everything and peak experiences that leave you feeling on top of the world.

At heart, I was more of a triathlete than a cyclist. While the U.S. Cycling Team coach wasn't so thrilled about it, he had conceded that there was no stopping me from swimming and running while I trained for cycling at the Athens Games. I did hang up the goggles and run shoes for a solid eight weeks in preparation for the Paralympics.

Back from Athens

September 2004

Hey race fans,

Here's the rundown on my experience in Athens. I took this off my Web site, on which I kept a journal. It's prit' darn long so warm up your coffee.

Just in case you don't have much time, or more likely, interest, to read all of this, I'll cut to the chase. I won a couple of medals. But you'll have to read to find out which ones!

Happily not riding my bike for a few more days ...

Sunday, September 12

Got in yesterday and slept lots to make up for the sleep that never happened on the nine-hour flight from D.C. Got up around 4:30 AM and read some before heading over to the 24/7 cafeteria to down some fish, olives, artichokes, and bad coffee. Spun around the Paralympic Village for an hour-plus. Now I gotta go get a massage. So far so good.

I'm back. The massage was good.

This afternoon we hit the velodrome—the track, and a very cool track indeed—for an hour just to get a feel for it. I, like everyone else, was still quite tight from the two days of traveling, and so, as we will do tomorrow, we rode easy. Just enough to shake the legs out.

Monday, September 13

We rode the time trial and road racecourses today, which are nearly the same, the road race being a bit longer, and each being a certain number of laps. Not so sure of the distances at the moment, but the TT is something like a 5k course that we do three times and the RR around 7k that we do nine times.

The fifteen-mile trip from the village to the course (along the ocean's edge) was the most polluted experience of my life. My system takes a hit pretty well, but I had a headache and burning eyes from the not-so-sterile air. We were trying to do the fresh air-cooling thing with the windows down but were forced to return to man-made lack of freshness. We got a bit lost on the way, but eventually we made it to a genuinely beautiful coastline road. A couple of hours later, and ten laps down, we had the course well scouted before heading home. Winds had cleared the air somewhat, which made the Parthenon clearer in the distance than it was on the way out. (I hope to get up close and personal to this and other touristy sights when things are said and the medals are won.)

Back at the ranch, I got another massage.

Then we hit the velodrome once again in the afternoon, where the go-sticks (legs) were starting to come to life.

Tuesday, September 14

First the good news: I'm fine; so is my bike. Logically following is the bad news: I crashed today. Nothing big. It all went down while descending a short little 15 percent grade into a flat ninety-degree right turn. We were warned, "The roads are slick and turns are tight so *be careful*!" Coach wasn't kidding. Kinda glad I crashed, to be honest. Seriously. The reasons are that (1) I got it out of the way; (2) I was relatively injury free—the right hip raspberry will remain a nice little memento; (3) I know now to take that 180-degree downhill to an uphill turn in the road race on September 27 a bit more conservatively than otherwise anticipated.

Today was our first real deal workout since arrival. Hitting it felt good—the workout, that is, not so much the pavement.

My massage therapist blew me off to go food shopping ...

The afternoon track workout was mostly good. We did a 2k effort that was a tad slower than coach prescribed. Why didn't I just go faster, you ask? Doesn't really work that way. Hip felt great, though—sports medicine is a good thing. Thanks, Julie.

The massage therapist made good after dinner.

Wednesday, September 15

A nice little rest day. Rode around the village for an hour, taking it easy. Sports med worked on my miraculously healed and pain-free hip (I'm truly amazed!). I hung by the pool and read, got yet another massage, ate a third meal, chewed the rag with some old and new friends—the fruits of labor.

Some kids from around the United States put together care packets for us athletes. These bags were dispersed last evening via the USOC; I'm the proud owner of new floss and a toothbrush. My red, white, and blue friendship bracelet graces my right wrist. Thank you, sixth graders from Winter Garden, Florida!

Thursday, September 16

Team photo was this morning. Reminiscent of lining up in Sydney. I secretly swelled with pride as I stood representing the USA for a second time in front of the camera. All fifteen of us, and the three tandem pilots we've endearingly termed "tools," are happy to be here, properly trained and ready to rock! This was confirmed this morning, when we all popped out some fast times training on the track.

Friday, September 17

Opening ceremonies are going on as I type. I think they're up to the Bs. Bulgaria, perhaps. Or maybe Belarus. We, the majority of the U.S. Cycling Team, are not there, as we are far better served, as is our country, to sit and watch by the light of television, that technological wonder of the 1920s.

You see, we have these legs that prefer sitting to standing, eating to hurry-up-and-waiting, sleeping to commuting … to the tune of eight hours at the ceremony. We race tomorrow morning, or at least some of us do. Me at 11:45ish, Hellenic time. The pursuit qualifier. Four kilometers of pain. If I place in the top eight—out of, *ahem*, ten—I move on to semifinals the following day. At that stage, the fastest qualifier races the eighth fastest, and the second races the seventh fastest, and so forth and so on. Of these match-ups, the fastest two winners go for the gold later in the day (that loser gets a silver), and the slowest two winners chase the bronze.

I think I hear Cameroon … or is that Cambodia?

Saturday, September 18

The butterflies were under control today as I prepared to knock the socks off myself. Experience helped tone down the emotions in this morning's four-kilometer pursuit qualifier. In Sydney, the thoughts in the starting gate were excited and jumpy. Today I settled into my saddle and thanked all the people, places, and things that put me there on the Paralympic velodrome.

Karmic forces or otherwise, something worked in my favor, and I finished third of ten; my buddy Ron Williams took fifth. The top eight move on to tomorrow's semifinals.

I had the advantage of a higher ranking than most, riding in the third of four match-ups, and so I was able to gauge what effort level was critical to move on to the next round within the top four positions. In the pursuit, you line up against another rider on the opposite side on the track—in this case, as with most international races, on a 250-meter oval with forty-two-degree banked corners. Kinda cool. Ideally, by the standards of most experts out there, you want to be as consistent with your lap splits as possible, conserving energy easily spent in the early laps for the treacherous final few.

Ron rode the heat before me, and there was one more ride after mine. Ron's time of 5:17 was just behind his match-up, Germany's Gottfried Muller, who rode 5:14. The latter time I had to be sure to beat. Coach Craig Griffin had me follow a "schedule" of around 19.1 seconds per lap. He said the German came out in 18.5 and then slowly bled each lap. Griff said I might benefit by doing the same if it came to it. And it did.

My opening lap time, from a standing start with a fixed gear, mind you, was 23.8 seconds. Then 18.3. Then 18.4. Then 18.5. Then 18.6. Then 18.7. Then 18.8. Then 19.0. Then 19.2. Then 19.1. (I could be off a little, so don't quote me.) Then something like a couple of 19.5s and a 20.0 thrown in near the end as I started to run out of juice. At the line in five minutes, 11-point-something seconds.

This means that tomorrow I'll race the number six guy, a young buck from Norway by the name of Morten Jahr. He's a good man. I've known him for a couple of years, and I should be able to handle him readily. He finished a soft twenty seconds behind me with a 5:31. The top dog today was Spaniard Roberto Al Caide Garcia—whom I rode against and who, to my dismay, passed me in the final lap (of sixteen) and now owns the title of "First man to ever catch Paul Martin in the pursuit." Not much of a title, I suppose. Something of a bummer for me, but I'm still very much in the medal hunt. He rode a commanding five minutes flat. Number two today is number one ranked Jiri Jezek, who rode a 5:06.

Ron has to face the German again tomorrow since they finished fifth and fourth, respectively. If Ron wins—sure, that's a good thing—there's going to be an issue. Because if I win (yes, I expect to, with all due humility), I'll have to face a good friend for a bronze medal, as has happened in the past, and it's a bit of a bummer. However, I suppose I shouldn't sell myself, or Ron, short here. We just might have the rides of our lives and face each other for the gold.

Hold your bets.

Other team news. Katie Compton and Karissa Whitsell, the former a sighted pilot for the latter visually impaired rider, took silver in the kilo. (I'll race the kilo on Monday.)

Sunday, September 19

This is good. This is very good. Things went down just about as expected. Ron put together a great race and beat the German by 0.4 seconds. He was down for the first ten or twelve laps of sixteen and then slowly peeled away for the win—an exciting race to watch.

I was seated adjacent the track, preparing for my own race as they went at it. I was a bit emotionally mixed, as I mentioned yesterday, not knowing whom I'd rather race for a medal.

In either case, I still had to beat the Norwegian rider first if I was going to be racing either of them. Happily, my plan came together: I rode out hard for the first few laps, until I saw him within reach—sixty meters in front of me—then I held a steady, easy pace, taking the win without killing myself. I rode a 5:26. Ron had to kill *himself* to take the win, riding a personal best 5:10. Congrats on digging deep, buddy.

We lined up a couple of hours later for our mutually respected battle. I did not for a second believe that the race was mine to take. Granted, he had probably not fully recovered from his earlier effort, while mine didn't take much out of me, but he had his wife in the crowd, and he surely wasn't going to lie down in front of her ... so to speak.

In the end, the poor sucker couldn't hold up to the likes of me, and I took it to him hard, passing him in the fourteenth lap! (Your beer will never be as cold as your friends, Ronny boy!) Yep, a bronze medal for me. My first Paralympic medal. Happiness.

On the podium, the former ten-year head of the International Olympic Committee, Juan Antonio Samaranch, presented us our medals and flowers and placed the olive wreaths on our heads. When they raised the respective countries' flags (Roberto the Spaniard won, and Jiri the Czech took second), I saw Old Glory reaching for the ceiling, well aware that I facilitated the moment. I welled up, as I hope to do a couple of more times this trip.

Monday, September 20

Today not so good. Not so bad, really, but not so good. Finished seventeenth in the kilo. Now, I have to explain. Women's events and men's handcycling events were added to this year's Games, which is certainly a good thing. Unfortunately, the International Paralympic Committee (IPC) has a limited number of medals that they are allowed to award, per some agreement with the IOC. So, the concession was to whittle away a few. In this case, by combining the four "amputee" divisions of the kilo into one.

By God, how could you have a leg guy racing against an arm guy? you ask. Well, the higher-ups agreed on a system whereby each competitor races against his own class's world record.

It just so happens, for whatever reason, that those with greater disabilities—a guy missing an arm and a leg, or, say, someone having two messed up legs, or someone who rides with just one leg, sans prosthetic—have been getting faster than the guys in my class or those missing a hand.

This led all of us to believe that a rider from one of these classes would take the win. Sure enough, a single-leg athlete won it. The world record in my class of 1:10:65, set by American Dory Sellinger in 1998, wasn't close to being matched, nor has it been since. (Since I first wrote these words, that is. More on the new record later.)

So while my 1:14:14 (0:01 seconds off my personal best) would have landed me a bronze had I raced only guys in my class ... it landed me in seventeenth place.

Tuesday, September 21

First the good news: we set a Paralympic record in the qualification round of the team sprint!

Then the bad news: it lasted about five minutes. The Austentatious Aussies laid it down in the next heat and took it away. Bummer.

The team sprint goes down like this: three riders from each country line up on opposite sides of the track, 180 degrees apart. At the gun, the riders fall in a single file line: 1, 2, 3. At the completion of one lap, the first rider pulls up (gets out of the way), in this case, teammate Dan Nicholson. Then Ron, the second rider, gives it his all for a lap with the third rider, me, in tow, and I let it all hang out for the final lap.

Our best time in training was 57 seconds. We were hoping to go 56 today. We went 55.4! We raced the second to the last ride of four pairings. At the finish line, we were numero uno. Fastest Paralympic team ever! Then, as mentioned, Team Australia went and knocked us clear off the pedestal, riding a 53.4.

The semifinals work just as they did in the pursuit seedings a couple of days ago: number one races number eight, number two races number seven, and so on. Then, ninety minutes later, the two fastest winners race for the gold, and the two slowest winners race for the bronze. The good part is that the third, fourth, and fifth fastest teams were all in the fifty-sevens. So it does look like it'll be the USA versus Australia in the finals.

The relatively bad part is that the Aussies are basically too fast for us to catch. You might be thinking that we should just ride a little faster. Well, in this sport, 0.5 seconds is a huge gap to close. So expect us to be dressed in silver tomorrow. The Creator willing.

Wednesday, September 22

Short on time here, so I'll be brief: Silver medal in the team sprint!

Thursday, September 23

Nice relaxing day. Didn't even ride the bike, save the trip to the cafeteria for some grub, including, of course, a tasty ice cream bar at lunch … and another at dinner. Even got into the city today for a little gift shopping. Ron and I went in and met his wife, Brookums, and her mom, Babs, at the base of the Acropolis, in the section of town called the Plaka. (Or is it La Placa? I've only heard it and not seen it. Spelled, that is. Or is it *spelt*?)

We had ourselves a sit-down at a nice cafe and ordered a round of the popular local coffee drink: the frappé. Not the kind you get at Friendly's, but tasty nonetheless. It's Nescafé (popular in Europe) with some more hot water thrown in along with some milk. Then they whip it into a frothy frenzy and sprinkle some sugar on top. Yummy.

And now some details from yesterday's race: In the semifinal round, we were to have raced the Italians, but for some reason they bailed. It's funny how focused I'd gotten out there—I didn't even notice that we were riding alone until the race was over! (I had pulled up track—ridden to the top—after completing my lap as third wheel, wondering when the second gunshot would go off, signifying their finish, and saw no one.)

We finished a tad slower than the day before, with a time of 55.68 seconds. Fastest of the day so far. The Aussies were up next and smoked the Canadians' bacon: 53.96 to the Northerners' 1:08.80. (They do play some good hockey, doing them absolutely no good here in Athens.)

So there it was: a guaranteed silver medal with a shot at the gold. For the finals, I proposed to Coach Griffin that we swap things around a little, as we had nothing to lose. Up until now, I'd been riding last in line, which obviously wasn't going to get us the top spot. Therefore, Ron and I traded spots for the gold medal ride, hoping that I might be able to drop him off at a faster speed, and that maybe, just maybe, he could muster up enough mustard to beat them to the line.

That didn't work either. We rode virtually the same ride—55.60 seconds.

On the podium, being presented my silver medal along with my good friends Ron and Dan, we three resonated with pride, each a part of the others' reward.

Friday, September 24

Another easy day. Ron and I headed out of the village for a spin in the nearby countryside. About forty minutes into it, we stopped for another frappé … just because we could.

Tomorrow's the road race. Monday's the time trial. These two events will be combined for the final cycling medal of the Games. I'm feeling rather confident going into these races, having put two pieces of hardware in the bank already. In 2002, I won the time trial at world championships; the road race here is fairly flat—good for a thicker, heavier rider like myself.

Ronnie's feeling ready too. He's a road racer—that's what he does, and does well, receiving a silver at worlds and also at last year's European champs. The team sprint silver took the monkey off his back, so he'll be feeling light and ready.

To top it off, rumor has it that rain's on the way. That'd make for an interesting couple of days.

Saturday, September 25

Road race today. Eighth place. Not so happy. Just got back and it's kinda late. Details tomorrow—a rest day.

Sunday, September 26

Feeling better about botching yesterday's road race, despite last night's earthquake, which I slept through. Kinda bummin' I missed it. I'm told it was a 4.3.

Before I get into the details of the race itself, let me start by saying that the strategy was patience: not to go too hard too early, expending precious energy that would likely be needed in the final laps of the race. A 63k race comprised of nine 7k laps. Griff warned us that in the day's previous races, all the early attacks came back to the pack. *Patience, that was my MO.*

Right from the gun, Carol Eduard Novak, the strong and teammateless Romanian, took off hard and the entire group—twelve of us, teeny for a road race—fell in line. The remainder of that first lap was high tempo, but nothing killer. Near the start/finish line, about one hundred meters into a three-hundred-meter climb, the course crested a hill before dropping another three-hundred meters. There, Patrice Ceria of France and Roberto of Spain created a slight gap, with me sitting at the front of the peloton, thirty feet behind them, not thinking much of this early, seemingly harmless little surge.

Then Ron and the dominating Czech, Jiri, attacked from the back, and suddenly there were four of the best road racers in the world off the front. In the second lap of the race, it was pretty much all over. With a teammate in the break, all I could do was watch the gap get bigger and bigger and bigger.

In the chase pack with me, which did absolutely no chasing, were another Frenchie and Spaniard, both of whom shared my situation, choosing not to chase. The Romanian, winner of last year's European Championships did nothing, telling me after the race that his early surge left him nothing to go with when the chips fell. Gotty Mueller of Germany did next to nothing, while Morten Jahr of Norway kept attacking in an effort to get the field to react, but no one was biting. (What he should've done was communicate an organized chase.) Along with us were David Kuster of Slovakia and Rivaldo Martins (my Brazilian friend and triathlon nemesis), who each did little as far as pushing the pace was concerned.

The course was an out-and-back with a direct twenty-five-mile per hour headwind going out and, obviously, a big tailwind on the return. That's why the breaks in the earlier races weren't sticking. No one wants to lead the charge into a strong wind. The same went for us. And I mean *no one* was putting any effort into the wind, whereas the four-man breakaway knew they had a job to do and each, I would have to assume, did his or her part to ensure the break would stick.

As we rode by the coaches and feed zone each consecutive lap, just past the start/finish line, Griff told me that I was doing great, exactly what I should be doing in the current race situation: sitting third wheel, not working, not taking any pulls, letting Ron get away. This provided some consolation, but it didn't change that fact that my hopes for a gold medal were all but gone.

Nothing much changed until the seventh lap, when Griff gave me the literal thumbs-up to do whatever I felt I needed to do. He could see I had lots of energy and wished to do something with it. I hadn't planned to empty my tank just yet, but moments later, the Norwegian attacked, and we all took chase, myself at the back, with hopes the field might let up when it caught him.

That it did, and I attacked from the back like a gold medal depended on it.

I instantly had a fifty-meter gap. Then it occurred to me that I'd just made my second mistake of the day, the same mistake Morten made, by not ensuring a partner or two would come with me. (The first was thinking nothing of that little gap early on.) I soloed the next lap and a half, with the first half being straight into that wind. I rode all-out to the turnaround atop the steepest climb of the course—not all that steep and only two hundred meters long. As I made my descent, I had a twenty-five-second lead or so. I hammered it out, hoping they wouldn't bother organizing a chase.

I came back to the line with the twenty-five-second lead and the coaches and staff saying, "Keep it going" and "Great job, Paul." I rode hard down the back side, while popping a PowerBar Gel for some energy insurance. Unfortunately, it literally popped, and I soon had gooey, slimy, soon-to-be-very-sticky stuff all over my right hand and handlebar. Clearly not something that would affect my race, but enough for me to cuss a bit.

I got out of the saddle for the three-hundred-meter climb (thanks Griff, for those one-thousand-meter out-of-the-saddle climbs up Gold Camp!), and put a much bigger gap on them when I crested. But then it was straight into the wind for

3k, which, by myself, was a huge assignment. I made it to the top of the opposite end's climb with my lead whittled down to less than twenty seconds and far less in the tank than I started with. I pushed the descent into the left-handed S turn at the bottom, the most "fun" part of the course, just to see if I could make something happen with a good tailwind.

Nada.

They reeled me in, and by the time we reached the line for the final lap, I was sitting third wheel again.

Now it was back to the same pack and an imminent sprint for fifth place. The pace remained conservative for that entire lap. Up to 1k to go when the German started winding things up, followed by the Romanian, the Frenchman, me, and the Norwegian. Not sure what the others were doing behind me.

At five-hundred meters, I started getting ready to go; I wanted to be first off at two-hundred marker, knowing well that I'm one of the strongest road sprinters in the field. Those three-hundred meters went by much faster than expected and the sprint began before I had my head together. (My lack of road racing experience reared its ugly head.) I think it was Rivaldo who came around the right side (I was on the left), with the Norwegian behind him.

I was instantly two or three bike lengths behind. I wound it up and gave it all I had, closing in on the leaders as we approached the line. But the line came twenty meters too soon. The Norwegian won the sprint, followed, right to left, by the Romanian by half a wheel, followed by the Frenchie by a few inches, followed by me by an inch or two.

Eighth place. Out of the medals—even a time trial win tomorrow won't do it. All because I waited a second too long. That's bike racing.

Surfing today's racing news, I found more consolation in the race report from USOCpressbox.org:

Ron Williams (Birmingham, Ala.) placed third in the Men's LC2 Bicycle General Class Individual Road Race. Paul Martin (Boulder, Colo.) finished eighth back in the pack. "Ron rode a great race," says Coach Craig Griffin (Colorado Springs, Colo.). "He picked the best guys to go with and rode a smart race. Paul had a good race. He did not try to bridge the gap when the group went away. He could have gotten there, but he let them go so Ron could get away. He played the role of a good teammate."

Monday, September 27

Happy birthday to my sister, Paty!

Well, today was the time trial, and it went as bad as it could have. I had a front wheel mechanical (a problem) that ultimately led to my inability to ride in any real capacity. I'm the reigning world champ … and I came in last!

Since I'd blown Saturday's road race, I wasn't in the running for a medal today (the road race and time trial were combined for one medal), so my only motivation was to win this thing and save a little face, stroke a little ego. With nothing truly having been lost with today's result, I am honestly not too upset.

Something good did happen today. Ron Williams placed fourth, which, combined with Saturday's third place finish in the road race, landed him a bronze medal. Congrats, Ronny, and thanks for what you've done for me with friendship and more.

In the end, I'm a two-time Athens Paralympic medalist! Life is good!

Tuesday, September 28

Finally made it to the Acropolis and shopped for some olive oil and ouzo for some friends at home. (Yes, Sharon, got a couple of surprises for you!) Closing ceremonies tonight, then onto the chartered flight back to the good ol' US of A tomorrow evening.

Thanks to all of you who have helped me get here. Thanks to all of you who have helped me bring home some hardware. Thanks to all of you for tuning in … and to all a good night!

Upon returning to Boulder it didn't take long to get back into run mode. I had begun to miss it, and I also needed some money! I set off once again to earn a few bucks running as fast as I could.

First Loser

November 2004

The Silver Strand Half Marathon was run on Sunday, November 14. Officially, it's the Open Air MRI Silver Strand Half Marathon. It's also officially the national championships at this distance for leg amputees: BKs, AKs, Symes, hip disartics, bilaterals, AK/BKs, though-knees, you name it—it's their nationals. But this year, nothin' but BKs. I've always thought they were the coolest cut-ups anyway.

There were five men and four women racing for the five-thousand-dollar purse. My biggest personal sponsor to date, Össur, had put up the moola. The race started in Coronado, the near island just across from downtown San Diego, and went to Imperial Beach, the town just north of Tijuana. Flat as a pancake and billed as one of America's fastest half marathons.

En route to the race, I stopped in Fresno for a night. Wawona Middle School had invited me to share some time with the students. (Can you call it "sharing time" when you're getting paid?) The presentations were scheduled just after a local Fox TV spot, and I arrived with minutes to spare. (Fodder for funny story comes in nicely here.)

I was up at 6:45 AM for my 7:45 arrival at a station ten minutes down the road—scheduled to be on at 8:20. No problem so far. I was unlocking the rental car at 7:15, just outside my Days Inn room, gathering things in the trunk, feeling well rested, chipper, and happy. An EC individual (economically challenged) came up and started on a story about running out of gas, blah, blah, blah. I've literally heard this story before. But being the happy-go-lucky guy that I am, always looking for an opportunity to grow my karmic value, I put down my keys, pulled out my wallet, and

142

flipped him a couple of bucks. He said thanks as I was shutting the trunk. *With my keys inside it! Aarrgghh …*

Try to be nice and … breathe …

Okay. No need to panic, but the legs are in the trunk. Need them for TV. That's how I get paid from Össur—no leggie on TV, no checkie. Need them for the school too … sorta. Kids love 'em. They were locked in the trunk, and I had to go. *Shit!* I quickly called a towing company that employs those guys that easily break into cars, and he was there at 8:00 sharp. Car was open, and the bill was paid by 8:05. I made it to the station at 8:15. On TV at 8:20.

At the school at 9:30. Knocked off two talks. Sold some books. The teacher took me to lunch at Applebee's with three lucky students (4.0 students, not so much lucky as hard working) who got to have lunch with a Paralympian. *Ooohh … Aaahh …* They all ordered the bacon cheeseburger, I ordered a salad (race coming up). I was at the airport and airborne by 2:30. Like buttah!

The half marathon brought in a bunch of newbies, one of which came all the way from Wales to beat me. Seriously, I read a Web site several months ago that had this guy claiming he wanted to beat "the American, Paul Martin." The dude might have been stocky and hairy, but he sure could run. At the gun, he took the lead with this other new guy, C. J. Howard. C. J. was on the heels of the Welsh, whom we'll call "Andrew Palmer." I hung onto C. J.'s heels for maybe a quarter of a mile, then intentionally began to fall off pace. I felt good, but they must've felt a bit better. As they passed the mile 1 marker, I understood why I couldn't hang. They hit it at 6:10! Sorry, I don't run that fast. I hit it at 6:17.

At mile 2, "Andrew" was still leading, and C. J. was right there. Another 6:10. A 6:25 for me. (I'd struggled to pop off 6:25s on the track in training!) Miles 3 and 4 were about the same—I was off by about thirty seconds. Soon they slowed a bit as I ran steady; the gap stopped growing. I was back there buying time, feeling confident that at least the hairball would frizz out and just maybe C. J. would too, who, by the way, also came to beat me, which was becoming increasingly clear. At mile 5, C. J. said, "Later" to "Andrew," who replied, "Bloody hell …"

At around mile 6, on the overpass (the *only* hill on the course), "Andrew" stopped for water at an aid station, while I ran past him thinking he was probably toast. His ego took offense, and he turned it on and caught me on the little downhill, commenting, "You snuck up on me." Yeah, that's right.[3]

We were then running side by side. I don't much care for racing side by side, particularly when it's accompanied by idle chitchat. First, I stopped responding. Then I faded back just a little, maybe two feet. Then he faded back, and I took that as a sign that it was time for me to turn up the heat a bit. I said, "Later," to which he replied, "Bloody hell …"

I kept it turned up for most of the remainder of the race. I couldn't have run any faster. (I did have to stop around mile 10 for a quick reboot to restore Stumpie circulation.) C. J., on the other hand, could run faster … and did. There's an out-and-back turnaround on the course at around mile 11. As I approached it, C. J. had reached it nearly two minutes before, and he looked strong and confident. *Second place. Gotta hold onto second place.*

At this point, I'm thinking "Andrew" is probably thirty to forty-five seconds behind me. I hit the turnaround and ran for nearly a minute before I saw him, which meant I had him by a couple of minutes. I kept it up, ensuring a second place, hoping for a PR—previous was last year's 1:29:52. A couple of miles later, I reached the finish line in 1:28:04. A rather hefty PR at that. Happy being the first loser. A 6:44 pace. Happy. My $750 check made me even happier. C. J. "The Rocket" Howard finished in 1:23:59! And he took home $1,250 in the process. He was very happy. He lost his leg eighteen months ago!

In December 2002, the doctors had diagnosed him with bone cancer. When he asked his dad about the prognosis, his dad had said, "Below-knee amputation in a few months." C. J. said, "Why not sooner? Let's get on with it. I want to do some research and see who the fast runners are and get to work on beating them!"

How cool is that?

He wanted a carrot to chase, and it turns out that carrot was me. C. J. soon e-mailed me for some prosthetic advice (our kind sticks together). I said, "Buy the book and we'll talk!"

Just kiddin'. He'd already gotten his hands on the book somehow. (At the finish line, his mom thanked me for writing the book, for what it did for her son. *The absolute biggest compliment I could ever hope for!*)

The bottom line here is that there's a new carrot in town. His name's C. J. Howard. Congrats, my friend. And to "Andrew," Gilberto, Clint, and the women as well, nice work.

---

3   *Seinfeld* reference.

There's one more story from the race, a tragic and inspiring story. A man had a heart attack at the finish line and died ... but right behind him crossed a cardiologist, who brought him back to life! The stricken man was there at the race by himself, so when the ambulance brought him to the hospital, two fellow competitors, total strangers, accompanied him. Again, *how cool is that?*

If you've read any of these ramblings of mine, this year you may have seen a pattern of PRs. Yes, it's truly been a blessed year racing: PRs—in all distances; medals—from Athens; prosthetics—relatively issueless. Been a good year in other ways too: I'm engaged and have a record income from speaking and sponsors. The racing stuff has even garnered me an award. I'm not so sure I'm supposed to divulge the info just yet, but it's from a prestigious, honorable, and highly admirable committee in the endurance sports world. The award itself is $250,000. Pretty cool stuff.

Well, that's a wrap. I'm looking forward to next year, a year with a new focus. And that's just it—focus, something I've lacked to some degree in the past. I've left the U.S. Amputee Hockey Team to free up some time and energy to pursue a specific goal, hopefully within the next two years: the sub-ten Ironman. Hefty indeed, and one I'm not wholly convinced I'll attain, but I'll try. Last July's 10:30 at Lake Placid with less-than-total focus—and that indescribable finish line high—brought with it a renewed appreciation for the sport and lifestyle I love so much. Law school's gonna have to wait. I have work to do.

All the best to all of you.

P.S. Just messin' with you with the quarter of a million dollars. I'll get a plaque and be grateful.

Two Companies, One Award

February 2005

Last November, while riding my bike along the fabled Morgul-Bismark bike course in Superior, Colorado, I had a thought. (In and of itself, something quite remarkable.) I've noticed in recent months that people in the triathlon community are starting to recognize my name. At first, I thought it was probably just because Canada's prime minister has been in the news quite a bit lately—his name is Paul Martin. Then it occurred to me that triathletes don't watch the news, so it must have been me they'd heard about. And it's probably not the Paul Martin who plays defense for the NHL's New Jersey Devils, with the league on lockout and all.

The thought was this: there must be something I can do to cash in, so to speak, on this name before it fades into obscurity amongst the many folks who share these ever-so-popular first and last names. Let's take a look: I don't have a real job—i.e., I have some time; I've been racing triathlon for ten years—i.e., I have a pretty good idea what I'm doing; and I've inspired people, so they tell me, to take on some challenges they might not otherwise have ventured into—i.e., I'm full of myself.

Maybe I could … start a coaching company. Yeah, yeah, that's it! And I'll call it … ummm … Amplitude Sumthin'-or-other. ("Amplitude" came to mind through the training philosophy of *periodization*—part of which is training hard, then resting. In other words, it's reaching a specific peak of effort, or *amplitude*, before returning to the valley to rest. It sounded scientific enough and kinda hip.) And the selling point will be … ummm … *If we can help Paul Martin go 10:30 in an Ironman, what can Amplitude Sumthin'-or-other. do for you!* That was it. I went home and called my friend Allison Seymour, the super-talented graphic artist, to make me a logo. That's exactly what happened.

As I was telling Allison the company's name, she said, "Cool. Amputee. Attitude. I like it."

"Uh, yeah, that's it …" That had never even crossed my mind. At least not on a conscious level. I suppose some things are just out of our control.

Then I called webmaster Jen Forsyth, whom I met in Perth, Australia, at ITU Triathlon World Championships. I also met Donny Forsyth there. I introduced one to the other, and now they have a cool little kid named Gibbs. Not that I'm a credit monger or anything.

The original idea was for me to basically be the testimonial guy and remain behind the scenes, drumming up the business. I'd have some friends doing the coaching, and I'd take a slice of the monthly pie. One of these coach friends then made it quite clear that I know enough about training for and racing triathlon—and that I could get boned up on the coaching aspect—to go ahead and coach athletes myself. I listened and now, three books later, I'm getting up to speed and am currently pending official certification in triathlon and cycling. However, I will still have some other coaches working with me once the client list grows a bit.

The company officially opened for business, in an unofficial manner, on February 1, 2005. A couple of nights ago, I received a request for my services via e-mail from a man in Sylvania, Ohio, and will soon have my first little piece of company income. And while the papers have yet to be signed, I can say with relative certainty that Amplitude Multisport LLC will be the official coach of the Challenged Athletes Foundation, which should bring in several clients to get the company up and running.

That's one company. The next is The Hartford. This nearly two-century-old organization is the founding sponsor of U.S. Paralympics. I'm quite fortunate to have aligned with them awhile back; part of their deal with USP provides Paralympic athletes the opportunity to speak at various functions around the country on behalf of The Hartford. These engagements pay quite well. And they can be fun. Last Thursday, I skied Squaw Valley with employees and clients, then spoke at dinner. The next morning I flew to Salt Lake City, spoke at lunch, then skied Snowbird. Then flew home around dinnertime.

The next morning I flew to San Diego with my lovely fiancée (that would be Sharon, for those of you whom may be new to these passages). The occasion was the 13th Annual Competitor Endurance Awards held at

Sea World. This gala was established to honor those athletes who typically get little fanfare: endurance athletes. Being honored that night was Bob Roll, of the Versus Channel's Tour "day" France fame; Greg Welch, winner of the 1994 Hawaiian Ironman World Championship and, at one time or another, winner of Olympic distance, long course, and duathlon world championships; Deena Castor, bronze medalist in the marathon in Athens; Meb Keflezighi, silver medalist in the marathon in Athens; and many others.

I was the GOY—Gimp of the Year. Technically, the Challenged Athlete of the Year. Quite an honor, indeed. This is something I'm proud of, humbled by, and do not take for granted.

Thanks for taking the time. Go out there and make the most of it.

Kaizen

March 2005

I have a new laptop. This makes me happy, in a productive kind of way. I'm on a flight from Boston to Denver, seat 23C. I got lucky with an earlier standby flight: I'll be home for dinner instead of the scheduled 1:00 AM. This, too, makes me happy.

Earlier today, I ran in Boston's inaugural Run to Remember half marathon—an event staged in honor of the 280 police officers killed in the line of duty throughout the city's historic past. I approached this C-priority race with relative disregard, not tapering, not expecting much of a result, using it as preparation for next month's Boston Marathon. Perhaps it seems a bit odd that I'd head all the way to Boston for a training race, when, say, I could've run the half in Moab, UT this weekend, with everyone else from Greater Boulder. Well, I gotta tell ya—I'm almost giddy about it—this was the first race anyone has ever paid me to be in! It does thrill my amateur self.

But alas, a free lunch is rarely free. Yesterday, in stark contrast to what I would consider proper race preparation, I stood on my feet all day, on concrete, at the race expo, promoting my new coaching company and my book. ("Hey, you like to read? Can I tell you about a really good book?" That's the typical opener to the unsuspecting passersby.) I ran twenty miles on Monday, swam and rode on Tuesday, traveled on Wednesday, drove all over western Massachusetts and spoke to a couple of schools on Thursday, and ran nine miles on Friday, including 3x10-minutes tempo with ten minutes of recovery after each effort. Again, "training through" the event.

I manned my booth up until the last minute, sold a few more books, then walked out to the starting line—right outside the door of Boston's World Trade Center—with all the other slackers and ended up farther back in the self-seeded pack than I should have. The gun went off shortly thereafter, and I was immediately bobbing and weaving up the right side of the seventy-five hundred other registered runners. In my head, I was still treating it as a noncompetitive event, just looking for a good, hard workout. I noted an 8:30 pace at mile 2—just plain crowded conditions. Things started to open up by mile 4, and I was able to run the expected 7:15 pace.

By mile 8, I noticed how great I was feeling, despite the lack of a taper. (However, I did get in a great eight-hour sleep.) Then it happened: that competitive thing came out. I picked it up to a pace I thought might tap my abilities. Next thing you know, I'm running a couple of 6:20s and feeling great.

At mile 12, I decided to lay it down: I wrapped up the last 1.1 miles in 6:44. A 1:31:42 half marathon that included two pee stops (when am I gonna learn not to drink so much on forty-degree days?) and one hug-the-family-members/sip-sister's-coffee-for-no-particular-reason stop at the halfway point.

In the last few feel-good miles, I pondered how I could be performing at this level. I concluded that *kaizen* deserved all the credit.

I've recently learned of the Japanese concept of *kaizen*. The term represents a notion that skills are best developed through a series of ongoing incremental, barely noticeable changes over an extended period. In other words: practicing consistency and patience in effort to acquire a certain trait or ability. I would imagine that this is not an entirely new concept to you.

I've been running, cycling, and racing triathlons for eleven years. In this time, I've not only gradually learned more and more about the sports, but I have also gradually grown more and more committed to them. I started with the "Can I finish?" mind-set. I then moved to one of "Can I be competitive?" I've recently entered the realm of "How fast can I really go?" While over the past ten years, I've claimed to be "committed" to being an athlete, I've recently realized that I was committed, primarily, to the lifestyle–with no regrets whatsoever, I might add.

I believe this new commitment, the one that is truly testing my abilities right now, could only have arrived in such a proper capacity through *kaizen*. The reason I'm racing faster is because I have *gradually* added skills, *gradually* added physiological adaptations, and *gradually* added knowledge (tactics, techniques, and awareness of various physiological states), all the while avoiding burnout and injury.

This is comforting for me, but more importantly, this is a critical lesson for the novice endurance athlete with expectations. Allow your skills and abilities to build. Be patient and dedicated in all aspects of your life. Understand that the reasonable results you desire in athletics and elsewhere will come if you stay the course while pushing the envelope ever so slightly.

Yes, it is sometimes necessary to go harder than you thought you could—just be careful when you do.

Challenges
April 2005

Every now and then, an experienced athlete can be well served by a disappointing race. Such was the case last Monday for me at the Boston Marathon, which came with a lion's share of challenges. This was my third running of The Race, and as with the previous two, I'd told too many people that the mission was to break the American record. Last year I came up short in 3:24; in 2001, 3:38.

Things were looking good just five weeks ago. All signs pointed toward a solid race: I'd run a 1:28 half marathon in November and a 1:31 half just last month, at the end of a three-week training block. There was no reason to believe I'd be running anything less than fast in Boston.

Superstition has no place in my world, but it is interesting to note that following the 1:31 race, I'd written about the benefits of incrementally progressive increases in training load, one of which is the avoidance of injury—I've been competing in the long stuff injury free for ten years. That race was March 13. On a March 19 long run, I was suffering from some sort of hip flexor pain, and I struggled to make it sixteen miles.

A week later, I covered eight miles before the pain set in, but I squeaked out a couple of more miles before calling it quits. This was a mile from any real civilization, along a newly built road north of my home in Broomfield, Colorado, a new road with no homes or traffic. I was running with my dog Roman. I was limping and bumming and hoping that for some reason, someone would be taking a Sunday drive along this deserted stretch. That someone turned out to be a police officer, and he opted to bend the rules to pick up a hitchhiker and his best friend.

"We're not allowed to have dogs in the cruiser," he said, "but get in." Roman only weighs twelve pounds.

It was a slow day for the officer, and he hadn't much else to do, so he brought us right to our doorstep—eight miles down the road. We chatted about this and that. I asked him what days are the busiest. "We make the most arrests on holidays," he said. "Thanksgiving's the busiest. Uncle Joe has too much to drink and starts at it with the in-laws, and next thing you know, we're getting a call from the neighbors."

A couple of days later I flew to San Diego to train with the U.S. Paralympic Cycling Team. We had our annual March camp at the Olympic Training Center in Chula Vista. I got in 312 miles in five days that week, many of which were hard efforts. To wrap up the week, we did an eight-mile uphill time trial to test our fitness against previous years. I crossed the line in 33:14, taking a minute off last year's time. Coach put himself out there and said he'd buy a Starbucks for anyone who could better his previous best. I never got my coffee. Then again, he never got that twelve-pack I owed him from the golf game just before Athens.

So I was feeling good on the bike; the hip flexor, oddly, didn't affect my riding, and vice versa. With a week of relative rest (I only ran once while in San Diego, and a pain free run at that) and some specific hip flexor stretching routines from the folks at USOC Sports Med, my hopes were up for a healthy marathon.

I flew home on Sunday, April 3. On Monday, I ran fifteen miles before the hip started to bother me. I bagged the run and walked home another couple of miles. (At a reasonable clip on that traditional run near home, a couple of miles out seems so close. With a tender leg—on a hitchhiker-picker-upper-less trail—it seems so far.)

I got a deep massage and opted for lots of rest, ibuprofen, and an exaggerated taper for the next two weeks. I swam more than usual and rode easy. When I got to Boston a few days before the race, I had Reiki performed on me by a practicing aunt. She and I both felt the heat generated as she passed her hands over my hip.

While on the Reiki table, I started feeling a little scratchy in my throat. This type of healing is known for exorcising toxins stored within, so I immediately contributed the discomfort to this. When I got off the table, I felt strong and mentally jacked and ready to go.

I had also told my cousin T-Paul about the hip flexor tendonitis. He proceeded to tell me about the magic of bee stings. (Big family back home ... into all kinds of crazy stuff.) He told me about how he developed tendonitis in his elbow from swinging his hammer years ago (he's a home builder when he's not flipping eggs at his diner), and that bee sting therapy fixed him right up. When it returned eight years later, bee stings again returned him to good health.

"All right, bee stings it is," I said. On Saturday, the day after Reiki, I held a honeybee in a pair of T-Paul's daughter's eyebrow-plucking tweezers, holding his posterior stinger inches from my member, rooting him on for a successful assault. (Just so happens a mutual friend's mom raises honeybees!)

That took about a second. I pulled him off and he flew away, leaving a pulsating poison pouch behind. Rumor has it they die after they sting, but I'm not sure how long that takes. He seemed just fine tooling around the kitchen. And it didn't hurt too much. The next four stings hurt even less after the original numbing.

That was Saturday afternoon. By Saturday night, I was very tired. Since arriving in town on Wednesday night, I had also spoken at a breakfast and two luncheons on behalf of our Paralympic sponsor, The Hartford, and had spent hours driving around Greater Boston in search of a suitable, affordable, proximal neighborhood Sharon and I might like to live in when we move to Boston this coming December. (She landed an anesthesiology residency at Boston's Brigham and Women's Hospital—the Harvard Medical School hospital. She's wicked fucking smaht.)

I blew off the wedding and reception I was to have attended on Saturday night, opting to spend an hour with my grandmother, who lives across the hall from my mom, and to get some couch time. After all, I told too many people that I was going to run a fast marathon on Monday, and I wasn't feeling so swift.

On Sunday, I took up an offer to attend an altogether different reception at Fenway Park—in honor of the wheelchair division winners of last year's race. With this came a seat in the grandstands to witness said wheelers throw out the opening pitches and to watch Tim Wakefield hurl his knuckleballs at the whiffing Tampa Bay Rays. Sox won 3–1. Unfortunately, I didn't see the final out. By the sixth inning, I was starting to feel ill, on top of the stuffy head/scratchy throat thing that had been growing ever since Friday's ironic healing table.

I left the game and headed to a friend's house in nearby Holliston. He lives just minutes from the start of the race, and I've had the pleasure of staying with him for my previous two starts in Hopkinton. The spaghetti and meatball dinner his wife prepared went down well. To my chagrin, I continued to go down as well.

I was weak. My head was fully congested. Coughing hurt. Each of the accompanying loogies, with its distinctive dirty green hue, had a form of its own. The kind Cliff Clavin would claim look like any one of our former presidents. I probably could have sold a couple of them on eBay.

Then a rough night's sleep. Up every hour, blowing and coughing.

At the starting line, I had myself nearly convinced that I felt good; I felt okay at best. My throat hurt, but not terribly. My nose was a bit clearer than expected. I was still there to break the 3:18 mark. That remained the goal.

The race opened up with a congestion of its own. I was held to an 8:30 pace for the first mile and a half before the opportunity arose to hit a 7:30 pace. For those of you who can relate to marathoning, you know how you typically feel great for the first eight to ten miles of a marathon? Well, I didn't have that pleasure. I felt like ass the whole time.

But I was on a mission, and I pushed on, hoping the moment would arrive when the sickness in me would give up the fight, bow to its opponent, and grant me the energy to run strong and long.

At mile 6, my hip started hurting.

At mile 7, I considered bailing out—that is, if the hip pain got any worse. No need to do any real damage.

At mile 10, the hip remained a dull pain, and I continued to run 7:30s or less. However, I was forced to pull over and reboot the leg twice already due to Stumpie cramps, adding a couple of minutes to my time. I was behind schedule, I felt horrible, and the thought of bailing continued to plague me. Along with the shame of not finishing, the unpleasant logistics of getting to the finish line kept me running.

At the halfway point, I was two minutes behind record pace. I had to keep running. The hip was bothersome but not debilitating. My throat longed for the aid station water and Gatorade. I ate many orange slices from the crowd because they felt so good going down. I kept up the pace.

At mile 18, into the Newton Hills, approaching Heartbreak, I was still just a couple of minutes off pace, despite a couple of more reboots.

At mile 22, past Heartbreak Hill, I was toast. Burned toast. Done. I continued to shuffle, throat dry as a bone, coughing on occasion, wincing from the pain, longing for the next orange. Up until then, I had been passing people far more than being passed, but now the backs of competitors were getting smaller instead of larger. I wondered if I'd be able to finish.

Four point two miles later, some of which I walked—and I would have walked more, but oddly my hip hurt less while running than walking—I crossed the finish line with a total time of 3:39:27, my worst Boston finish. But the key word here is "finish." No DNF. No shame. Part of me is proud. Part of me is disappointed with what could have been. I understand the pointlessness of the latter. It won't last long, I promise.

Monday night was the worst night of sleep in a long time. I woke up at one point drenched in cold sweat. Soaked. I was sore all over, and it took some amount of work to edge over to the dry side of the bed, where there was some semblance of comfort. With that, I was over the hump. The fever was working its way out of me.

Today I'm feeling all right, hoping I'll be good enough in a day or two to get back at it. In preparation for June's Ironman in Idaho, I've laid out a heavy training load for the next month. Let's hope the hip's up for it.

So how will this experience serve me well? First, I'm further convinced that I can deal with whatever comes my way. Second, while I might not hit the intended target, I'm humbled in the knowledge that I'm human, and that failing is far different from losing. Humility is a good thing; we could all use a little more, myself included.

Incidentally, the words on the back of one runner's jersey that I somehow memorized on Monday come to mind (actually, I almost memorized them, and then I just did a Google search for the rest):

The miracle isn't that I finished. The miracle is that I had the courage to start.
—The Penguin Running Club credo

Lastly, I'm already looking forward to my next marathon. I know I have a fast one in me. Maybe I'll pick an easier one than Boston next time ... One of these days, it's all going to come together. The anticipation is awfully exciting!

You may have gotten the gist by now that I'm madly in love with Sharon; I'd do anything for her. Since committing my life to her—and this happened some time before I proposed marriage—life itself has become sweeter, even on the salty taste buds. Time away from her is time of a lesser quality. I'd been traveling a great deal the last couple of months (March and April), and this was tough on both of us. Frankly, tougher for her. This is not because she misses me more than I miss her, but because she was in her tenth month of her twelve-month surgical internship—stress sans sleep. My absence brought further distress, and for that, Sharon, I apologize.

Three weeks after running Boston, I was to have raced at the Gulf Coast Triathlon, a half Ironman in Panama City. I bailed out on the event, despite the race director's generosity in offering me a complimentary entry. I couldn't do that to Sharon. I was starting to think more and more about somebody else besides myself. I'd been putting myself first since the moment I embarked on this athletic journey, and to some degree, my whole life. That's not to say that I've been selfish, just self-centered. There's an astounding difference: the former shows disregard for others, the latter refers to basing the vast majority of your actions on what's best for you; athletes must be self-centered if they are to reach a significant level of achievement—otherwise they'll end up out of shape and off the podium.

I still don't "automatically" think about Sharon with every decision I make. Often, I find myself coming to some conclusion before considering the effect it has on her (or my dogs!), but rarely does the plan go into action before being corrected.

I missed that race, which, in turn, probably led to being plenty rested for a 5k I ran a week later in Boulder, notching my fastest cross-country 5k ever—a 19:14 on the out-and-back trail adjacent Boulder Reservoir on a windy Tuesday evening. Boulder's good for both wind and Tuesday night races.

That accomplishment brought a tinge of redemption from my performance in Boston. But the 10k Bolder Boulder a couple of weeks later brought even more. So I titled the e-mail accordingly.

Redemption
June 2005

You might recall my piece on April's shortcomings at the Boston Marathon. Well, I'm happy to say that while my marathon goal of 3:15 remains unreached, another longtime goal was reached on Memorial Day. On the streets of Boulder, Colorado, at the twenty-seventh running of the Bolder Boulder, I ran my first sub-forty-minute 10k!

I'd come close once or twice before, but this time I did it with a degree of authority—39:18 on my watch, 39:38 officially. How our watches so often disagree with those of the officials is beyond me. But I'm certainly not here to complain. I'm friggin' ecstatic, to be honest with you! The preparation for this C-priority race left me downright sore and tired when I toed the line, which, of course, left an even sweeter taste on the buds as I crossed the finish line.

As with most events in my life, I showed up later than expected, with a certain degree of anxiety as to whether I would even get there before the gun went off. Sharon and I parked a couple of miles away from the start, near the finish line at the Folsom Field, the University of Colorado stadium, where the Buffaloes roam.

As we climbed out of the car with twenty-five minutes to spare before that start, I figured I'd be in good shape to use the two-mile jaunt up 30th Street as the perfect twenty-minute warm-up. As soon as I got out of the car, I had to go number two. Again. For the third time before 7:00 AM on race morning. All you endurance athletes know what I'm talking about.

There happened to be a Starbucks right there on 30th, so I pooped in—er, popped in—to take care of business. There was one guy in line in front of me. An old guy. An old guy who took *sooooo* long when his turn came up. I was standing there jumping around, cursing the sexagenarian under my breath, straining in both a physical and emotional sense.

He finally exited. I entered and exited in less than thirty seconds. I am seasoned.

With more than a mile to the start, but not really sure just how far, and just under eleven minutes to spare, I handed Sharon my jacket and took off at a hardy clip. I was soon running on the sidewalk adjacent the racecourse, and I saw the wheelchair racers coming toward me and the start banner a quarter mile up the road. Three minutes to go time.

I reached the start line just as the first wave of five hundred (of fifty thousand) runners took off. I was in the second wave, scheduled to go in one minute. But the start chute was lined with six-foot fences and no breaks for who knows how far up the road. So I hopped the fence. As I was going over, two other guys follow my lead, and as my leg breached the barrier, a security guy said, "No hopping the fence!" I said, "Uh, sorry, too late," and the three of us hopped over in unison. In mid leap, I heard, "Way to go, Paul!" It was Dave Scott (name drop), a couple of waves behind me. I was feeling good already.

We wiggled our way along the fence and past the third wave to the back of our pack. I took two or three deep breaths, and the gun fired.

I fell into a good, comfortable pace right off the bat—the perfect warm-up, apparently. The first live band of many came up on our right-hand side within a quarter mile. A right-hand turn onto Pearl took us under the one mile banner. The watch told me I was coming out a bit hot at a 6:22 opening mile. (Wore it to get where I was going on time.) I kept the effort steady as the course gained a 1 or 2 percent elevation.

An extremely fit woman running next to me gave me some encouraging words, and I returned the sentiment. At that moment, I knew she was the one I'd look to beat, for no particular reason, solely for the sake of friendly competition.

At the 2 mile marker, after the infamous Bellies Dancers (as in multiple rolls), I was at 12:55—slowing up some, but the slight ascent called for it.

A few minutes later, as I made a mental note of my fresh-feeling legs along Glenwood Street, Michael Lovato (name drop) called out, "Go, Paul!"

Next thing I knew, the 5k banner was overhead, and the watch told me I was at 20:07 at the halfway mark, with just a bit more climbing before the long, steady, easy descent. *Huh. I think I can negative split this thing. It'll be close; the sub-forty is teasing me right now.*

Up and over the high point at Casey Hill, fifty meters past the four-mile mark, I turned up the heat on the downhill (the prosthesis *loves* easy downhills.) I was feeling great and incrementally increased the pace as I headed east on Pearl Street.

With 1.2 miles to go, just before the turn onto Folsom Avenue, I was where I needed to be. The pace continued to pick up as I picked off lots of runners. I passed under the 9k banner at thirty-five-plus minutes. I gave it all I had, aware that my then current pace was below four minutes per kilometer, and that as long as I didn't blow, the goal was scored.

At that moment, I thought about the response I'd received from Gale Bernhardt (name drop) last week at the USA Triathlon Level 1 coaching certification class I attended (credential drop) when I asked her why it is that I'm able to race so far above my lab tested lactate threshold. She said, "It's because you're competitive."

I was competing primarily with myself at that moment and laid it all out, entering Folsom Field with less than two hundred meters to go and a minute and a half to spare.

I crossed the finish line carrying a big fat bowl of pride mixed with contentment. Then I looked up at the jumbo screen to see the extremely fit woman I chose to race entering the stadium ...

The next day, in preparation for Ironman Coeur d'Alene on June 26, I rode 110 miles on a beautiful day, feeling fresher than I had on any of my recent long rides. (And the morning after that, at the rink, I scored a few goals in pickup hockey, with softer hands than I'm used to.) This is where the redemption part comes into play so fittingly. I now know that my fitness is where I need it to be. I know that my base miles in January and February are paying off. I know that the speed work I've done the last couple of months is working. I know that my relatively poor performance at the marathon will not affect my performance in Idaho.

In between racing the Bolder Boulder and Ironman Coeur d'Alene, I did a couple of more races—not age-old peak performance wisdom, that's for sure. I wouldn't have recommended it to my athletes, and more than one seasoned triathlete widened their eyes when I told them of my plans.

The first of these two races was a sprint triathlon in Boulder, Colorado. Motivation to race just seven days before Ironman came on many levels: (1) It was the first in a three-race series in town that I hoped to do well in; (2) I wished to shake out the triathlon rust on a less important race than Ironman; (3) I had just dropped nine hundred dollars on a new rear disc (that's with a big discount!), and I wanted to make sure that thing was working—you never go into a big race with untested equipment; and (4) a race of just a little over an hour at high intensity might be exactly the type of last-minute tune-up the body needed.

The race proved positive. I had my fastest ever half-mile swim, in around eleven minutes. I rode an average speed of 24.4 miles per hour along the seventeen-mile course, a PR, I believe. But during the run I had gnarly stomach cramps, the kind I experience in nearly every shorter distance race I've ever been in. (Diagnosed—by Sharon, of course—as a possible result of blood shunting: When riding hard on the bike, as I do on shorter courses, blood not imminently needed in my gut goes to my legs to power the ride. When I dismount and get vertical to run, blood returns to my abdomen, causing acute pain. The solution, as I'll test in races later this summer, could be to ease up late in the bike—mentally, very difficult—and maybe pop an Imodium AD or Pepto-Bismol tablet late in the ride. Such a test is next to impossible outside of actual race conditions.)

I finished eleventh of over two hundred in my age group. Yeah, I was a bit peeved since I had legs that wanted to run but a gut that wouldn't allow me to breath, which cost me a top ten.

The second race was a time trial on the bike. My only motivation for this one was obligation. It was the U.S. Paralympic nationals, which doubled as a European championship qualifier for those interested in breaking onto the scene. This race was Tuesday, two days after the triathlon. So on Monday, I packed up, flew into Salt Lake City, raced on Tuesday morning, June 21 (my birthday!), came in second to a blind tandem, earned $250, and was home in time for dinner with Sharon—filet mignon, Alaskan king crab legs, a couple of healthy sides, and a bottle of wine in the privacy of our own home, dogs at our side!

And apparently the lead-up strategy worked.

How the Race Was Won

June 2005

The 2005 Ironman Coeur d'Alene will not soon be forgotten, at least not by me. The entire trip was something quite remarkable, with the highest of highs and the lowest of lows. The trip began on the Wednesday preceding the Sunday, June 26 race. That day alone was a big one for our household (Sharon, me, and the dogs–Roman and Maggie): Sharon completed her internship year in general surgery just three hours before we piled into the Subie at 4:00 PM for the eleven-hundred-mile road trip!

En route, somewhere in Wyoming, I received word that I'd been nominated for an ESPY, the Grammys/Oscars of the sports world, formed by ESPN some dozen-plus years ago. Many thanks to all of you who voted for me already, and to those who will.

Not long after that phone call, we pitched a tent and camped that night a few miles short of Montana, reaching our Idaho destination on Thursday night.

This is where the low part comes in. On Friday morning, Sharon received word that her father's kidneys had failed (he's been battling pancreatic cancer since January). The next phone call on Friday afternoon brought sadder news: he only had three or four days to live. After many tears and many phone calls, we arranged a Saturday morning flight to get her to Melbourne, Australia, where she grew up and her family still resides. Her mother then asked if I could race for her dad, which, of course, I did.

The high point lasted pretty much the entire day on Sunday. The forecast called for showers in the morning, yet it was as perfect a daybreak as one could have hoped for. And daybreak comes early at this time of year in that part of the world. The dogs woke me up at 4:20, and I climbed out of bed at 4:30, with the sky already turning blue. Oatmeal with raisins, a banana, and a cup of coffee later (with Mr. Wetherall in my thoughts), I was ready to go.

I arrived at the course at 5:30, and despite the bike being set up the night before, I still wasn't completely ready until 6:50, ten minutes before cannon blast.

The swim took place in Lake Coeur d'Alene, on whose sandy banks stood nearly nineteen hundred athletes ready to rock 'n' roll. I took advantage of my physical impairment and was granted an in-water start, some ten feet off the shore in the shallow water. I learned at last year's Ironman Lake Placid that I'm fast enough to be up front, and that being even just a third of the way back makes for a more difficult swim when struggling for position.

The gun went off, and as I stood and dove, the front line immediately swarmed me in the run to deeper waters. I found my groove early on, not needing to throw too many elbows to hold my spot. However, I did catch one just seconds into the swim, dislodging my right goggle, requiring a quick head-up fix. In the middle of the short lateral section of the elongated triangle of the two-loop swim, I caught another hard elbow in the left temple, which left me a bit dizzy. This passed, and I swam on.

The first-loop exit required just a few hops under the arch before diving in for another 1.2-mile swim. Coming into the stretch, I caught a heel to the face, which dislodged my goggles once again, this time the left. Without too many people around late in the swim, the head-up goggle fix was a breeze. The swim passed by faster than any of my previous Ironman openers, an indication of fitness, I'm happy to say. Since I race watchless, I didn't know my time, but I felt it must have been somewhere under an hour.

With crutches waiting, I hobbled along the mushy red carpet, out of the steep and soft sand, to where my bike leg was set up. Donned and ready to go, I skipped along through T1, where the wetsuit-stripping volunteers assisted the athletes on a patch of grass. As I came through, immediately after a left-hand corner, one man slipped on the wet greenery and dropped like a rock right in front of me—I went down with him, prosthetic getting all twisted in the process. I believe I said the F-word and used the Lord's name in vain ... Please forgive me.

Back up in seconds, I grabbed my transition bag, which contained my bike shoe and helmet, ran into the change tent, donned those, stopped ever so briefly at the marvelously efficient sunscreen application station, and went for the bike. As I hobbled along, I found the leg had loosened a bit too much from the spill on the grass to ride 112 miles, so I opted to reboot. All said, a relatively slow five-plus-minute transition. I later learned that I'd swum 1:00:36 (176th overall)—since I was hoping for a combined swim/ T1 of one hour, I was now five minutes behind my sub-ten-hour goal. But since I wasn't wearing a watch, I didn't know this, and I continued on, ignorantly thinking I was kicking ass!

Early in the ride, on the return trip through downtown, at mile 13 or so, disaster nearly struck. A family of five, kids first, darted out into the road in front of me. I grabbed for the brakes, but fortunately, I saw that I had enough space (two seconds less, and I think I would've clipped that last kid) and rode it through, again dropping the F-bomb and using the Lord's name in vain in the process ... Please forgive me.

Another lesson I've learned through experience (and the use of a PowerTap power meter) is that in the past, I've gone out too hard on the bike, and I consistently fade harder than I should near the end of the ride. I opted to ease into it, which paid off, as I felt good nearly the entire ride, save a few miles around mile 90 or so.

The ride took us through the hills at the start of the first lap, with some fairly steep stuff, but not as nasty as Lake Placid—as steep but not as long. On the back side of those hills are some fun descents with some sharp switchbacks. This is where the bike skills came in handy, and I made time on many of those around me, who, in my opinion, ride their brakes too much. I know, safety is paramount; remind me again in my next life.

I shared a lot of the ride with Spence, some random dude who was either ahead or behind me by no more than fifty meters for close to five hours. He dropped me during that low section ninety miles in ...

Five hours and nineteen minutes later (91st overall), a personal best, I was off the bike. About a quarter mile from the bike finish, as I rode past a bank, their digital clock told me it was 1:22 PM. That's around 6:22 into the race. That meant I had to run something like a 3:30 to reach the goal. I was damn sure that wasn't going to happen.

Yet, I felt awfully fresh the moment I started running.

The run has been treating me well this year, when I've been healthy. I felt mentally and physically strong. This was going to be a good run.

The crowd along the streets of downtown Coeur d'Alene, two or three miles into the run, cheered as I came through, as I'm sure they did for every athlete. The run was also much flatter than Lake Placid, which added to the positive outlook I carried.

Like marathons of the past, I stopped several times to cool off Stumpie with a few cups of ice water. It just feels *sooo* good. At the third icing, around mile 12, upon rebooting, I couldn't find either of my two stump socks. I became frantic and hopped about looking all around the area—I'd sat on an aid station table—but nothin'! (The volunteers helping with ice water said they didn't see anything but the liner when I took it all off.) Another second and I might have started freaking out. I was having a great run thus far, and the thought of blowing it because of something so silly would've killed me. Just then, one of the volunteers asked me if I'd like the socks off his feet.

"Yes, please."

Surprisingly, it didn't stink, and it fit and felt great! Back on the run.

In the past, if I haven't started to waver by now, the half marathon point brings the hurt, and with it more walking than I'd like … and some passing thoughts of *Can I do this?*

Not on Sunday. I remained in good spirits and good shape, and I kept running. The crowd acknowledged what they were witnessing, and much energy came my way. Out to the last turnaround, a short steep section around mile 21, I knew I had enough in me to pick up the pace a bit and finish strong, and just maybe break ten hours. I was forced to take one more ice-down break, but other than that, I ran.

At mile 25, I asked a spectator for the time of day. "Five o'clock," he said.

"Damn!" Short of the goal, but also well aware that I'd soon PR by nearly twenty minutes, and with a little more effort, I could break the WR for leg amps: 10:10:30, set by Rivaldo Martins at the 2001 Ironman Europe, now the Quelle Challenge. (I was at that race and went 10:41, and I was certain he was untouchable.) Whether or not I broke the record, I felt confident a Hawaii slot was coming my way, which, in the end, didn't happen.

A smile broke out as I rounded the last corner onto Sherman Street, which brings you in toward the finish for a quarter mile on a slight downgrade. The adrenaline was pumping, the descent was welcome, and the clock in front of me read 10:0 … *Is that an eight or a nine?* I was beginning to fly. As I closed in on the finish line, I saw the ticker click over to 10:09, with just meters to go, and the world record was mine. I was on top of the world! (I'd run 3:42, 109th fastest run, which put me at the finish line 89th overall.)

The finish line brought much emotion, pride, and cheers. There was no one in sight behind me, so Mike Reilly, "The Voice of Ironman," brought me back out to the chute for an encore.

I doffed the hardware and did my thing: "*I … am … Ironman!*"

Throughout the race, I consistently thought about the suffering of Mr. Wetherall, Sharon, and their family. My suffering on the course paled in comparison, and that thought brought with it enormous energy. Mr. Wetherall gets mountains of credit for helping me race fast on Sunday, and I thank him for that. And he knows it. He can hear me, and he can read these words. David Wetherall's soul moved onto the greater plane this morning, Wednesday, June 29, 2005 at approximately 3:00 AM MST.

I spent little time with him but loved him nonetheless. His was the kindest of spirits, still is, and always will be.

Extremes

July 2005

Sharon and I stood on the top floor, overlooking the swarms of people in the atrium below us. We had just left the 2005 ESPY Awards show, held at the Kodak Theater in Hollywood, the same theater recently built for the Academy Awards. We were directed up the escalator and to the VIP entrance to The Highlands, the swanky bar where the post party was being held.

"How did we get from down there to up here?" we simultaneously asked each other.

We were at the show because I was honored with a nomination for "Best Male Athlete with a Disability." I should begin by saying that this nomination alone was a supreme honor, and to those of you who voted for me, thank you very much.

The entire ESPY experience was surreal. The hour-long bus ride on Monday to the ESPN Celebrity Golf Tournament was interesting in itself, sitting beside Joe Theisman in the back row—"Joe's row"—absorbing his wedding advice (married four times, he must know something). They put us up at the Mondrian Hotel, a swanky place in Hollywood. The weekend before, I was in New York City, staying at the YMCA on a bunk bed, with community bathrooms down the hall; the following weekend we camped in Colorado Springs, cheaper than a motel. (Sharon ran a twelve-mile trail run halfway up Pikes Peak in preparation for her marathon there next month—she's a stud.)

At the Tuesday night party at the Playboy Mansion, I was awed by the likes of Peyton Manning, Sugar Ray Leonard, and, of course, Hef.

I was itching for pics with some of these folks, being the common man that I am, but I was much too timid to approach. Sharon, on the other hand, was not so timid and didn't even know who Peyton Manning was. And told him so.

"Hi. I don't know who you are, apparently a footballer. We play Aussie Rules Footy at home, much tougher. Anyway, my fiancée would like a picture with you. What da ya say?"

I was mortified, yet a moment later, his expressionless face was briefly replaced by a feigned smile as he put his arm around me for a quick pic. *Yes!* (I'm giddy to say that photos with Theisman, Brendan Shanahan, and Ben Rothlisberger were borne from actual conversation.)

Seeing my lovely fiancée dolled up on Wednesday before the show, after four hours of professional hair, makeup, wardrobe, etc., was a real treat. Her loaned jewelry alone was worth thirty thousand dollars. The day before, Sharon had tried on the very same ten-thousand-dollar dress that Danica Patrick wore on stage.

The walk down the red carpet, right in front of Curt Schilling, alongside Natalie Coughlin, was a total trip. While the NFL, NBA, and MLB athletes were getting nearly all the attention, photographers were still yelling "Over here!" to get our attention for a clear photo. The one interviewer who did pose a question asked, "Who are you wearing?"

"A watch by Elini, a shirt by Boswell, and a suit by Men's Wearhouse," I said. Laughter followed, and I didn't make the tabloids.

Outside of swimming and, to some degree, Olympic fanatics, nobody really knows who Natalie Coughlin is (2004 Olympic backstroke gold medalist), and so she was getting about as much attention as I was. She and I watched in amusement as reporters fought for Terrell Owens' next quote. Nonetheless, we both smiled, absorbing the wonder of it all.

When I took my seat alongside Sharon at the ESPYs—I deeply hoped the aisle seat meant that I'd won, which, I soon learned, it didn't—I pondered the path I'd traveled. I marveled at the fortune that's come to my life. I smiled at the woman who, in six weeks, would be my wife.

You see, it wasn't so long ago—1982 really isn't all that long ago—that I spent a few days not knowing where I was going to sleep that night, mooching off friends' couches in transition from parental home to foster home.

It wasn't so long ago—1992 is definitely not all that long ago—that I lay in the hospital bed checking out the stump that once had a leg attached to it, wondering if I'd be able to have any type of active life whatsoever.

It wasn't so long ago—1999 is like yesterday—that I took advantage of "The Paul Martin Factor," the additional percentage each of the friends I dined with would have to pay to make up for my lack of funds.

Sharon and I understand how we got here—I was an ESPY nominee, and she was headed to Harvard in the fall for an anesthesiology residency. We worked hard. We were blessed with opportunities, and we took advantage of them. I sincerely believe that nearly everyone born to freedom in an industrialized nation can one day perch above the gallery if he or she puts his or her heart into it.

Eleventh

August 2005

A couple Sundays ago, I raced the 5430 Long Course—a half-Ironman distance triathlon—at the Boulder Reservoir. The race was aptly named for the number of bong hits the average University of Colorado trustafarian does in his or her five years as an undergrad. The race director says it's because of the altitude of the host city, but I suspect otherwise.

This race was the third of three in a new triathlon series that included the 5430 Sprint and the Boulder Peak. As you might expect, I had a goal going into the series: top ten.

Before going into details of the Long Course, I'll bring you up to speed a bit.

If you're even a freshman of triathlon, you probably know that Boulder, Colorado, is a focal city in our sport, and that competition here rivals that of any place on planet Earth. (Call the city nestled up against the fabulous Flatirons "Planet Triathlon.")

So, *Top Ten*? What the hell was I thinking?

Well, I was thinking that with a great coach (myself), some great legs (made of carbon fiber), and some serious mileage since pre-Christmas, I'd have a chance. And that's all any of us can ever ask for, isn't it? A chance.

I'd written earlier about the Sprint distance race that opened up the series on June 19, the race I strategically used as a tapering event for Ironman Heart of an Awl (Coeur d'Alene). It was at this race that the lovely Dr. Sharon Wetherall (if you're sick of me extolling her virtues, too bad, get used it) diagnosed the blood shunting issue.

The strategy for the next triathlon then became to ease off on the bike with about two miles to go. In addition, I popped an Imodium AD to assist with a buffering coat of the stomach. At the New York City Triathlon three weeks later (two weeks after Ironman), I staked an off-the-bike PR on the 10k run: 40:36. No cramps, no worries. Nirvana.

On June 24, I showed up for the Boulder Peak Triathlon, the second of the three in the aforementioned series. The competition the Peak draws would undoubtedly make this one the toughest of the three in the series.

This was my sixth Peak performance. At each of the previous five, I'd bested my prior time. I pretty much knew this wasn't going to happen this time around. You see, I was tired. All this racing and the EPSYs shenanigans had taken their toll. Not to mention that at thirty-eight years of age, some of the *boing* has been reduced to *bing*.

Nevertheless, the swim has somehow become a strength of mine this year (high elbows?), and I came out of the water in sixth. On the infamous Old Stage climb, where I've become accustomed to reducing my competitors, I found myself reduced. My bike split was four minutes slower than last year.

The run further depleted my stores, and at the finish line, I crumpled up on the grass, all blank and weak, where the doctor, Roman, and Maggie helped lick my wounds—the former figuratively, the latter two literally.

The two weeks between the Peak and the Long were spent primarily resting, traveling a bit to earn some speaking dollars, planning a wedding, and playing a little hockey. Race day morning was chill and emotionless, and I was ready to get this block of racing over with.

We were blessed with beautiful weather the morning of the race—a slight chill in the air was warmly welcomed, as it's been hot as balls lately here in Colorado, sympathies to the Northeast.

Again, fifth out of the water in the swim before a carpet-meltingly quick T1 got me on the bike to ride the backhand-familiar roads we train on year-round. The two guys with whom I shared the Sprint and Peak bike courses also shared the Long course with me; the three of us swim about the same times. These two guys were right behind me after one lap of the two-lap course. My buddy Scott was one of them, and he reeled me in before too long; Bill had a flat and never recouped his loss. *C'est la tri.*

Without question, despite the altitude (actually, due to the altitude), this is a fast bike course: great roads, lots of long gradual downhills and easy corners. With it came a good split, 2:29, considering I was still feeling flat.

The run course isn't too fast: all dirt with little rocks and a few ups and downs, not to mention that it was starting to get hot. A few years ago when I did this race, the run took me over two hours.

This time, I just kept plugging along at eight-minute miles, feeling good and holding her steady, up until the last couple, where I faded hard while Stumpie screamed. I managed to clock a 1:46 on the run and land myself a PR at the half IM distance: 4:51:47. Good enough for, you guessed it, *eleventh* of eighty-four in the 35-39s.

I did what I could in the series. I came up short of the goal but landed a PR in the process. I guess I should just thank my lucky stars that I never got caught up in all that Mother Nature stuff back in college. No, wait a minute, I mean high school ... or was that middle school? I can't remember.

AWADs in Honolulu

October 2005

Someone just called me an "a-wad." I haven't heard that one in awhile. Or was it "butt wad" that used to offend me? Fortunately, it's been too long. As derogatory as it sounds, that's the title we below-knee amputees and the other physically challenged athletes at this year's ITU Age-Group World Championships were given: Athletes with a Disability—AWADs.

Our division competed with the other non-pros in Honolulu, swimming in the waters just off Waikiki Beach, riding the effectual Honolulu Marathon course and running (some wheeling) the fast and flat two-looper adjacent the start/finish of the inaugural and legendary 1978 Ironman.

Thirty AWADs comprised this year's field of competitors, each of us hoping for a podium finish, perhaps leaving the island with a top honor. Fourteen gold medals were up for grabs: seven disability classes, two genders.

There were the above- and below-knee amputees (AKs and BKs, a.k.a. hoppers); the above- and below-elbow amps (AEs and BEs, a.k.a. wingers); visually impaired athletes (blinkies—don't worry, they're cool with that) who race with a guide; the "les autres" class (French for "the others," who as of yet have no cool nickname), made up of athletes whose parts are all there and don't use a wheeled device of any sort, such as those with cerebral palsy, muscular sclerosis, muscular dystrophy, brain injury, etc. And then there's the popular wheelchair athletes (wheelies, of course), divided further into two classifications—those able to ride a bike but unable to run, who therefore race the run course in a push-rim wheelchair, and those who race a handcycle and also use a push-rim for the run.

This was an average number of challenged athletes for a world championship event—less than we've had at some championships in the past, more than we've had at others. American Jon Beeson, head of the ITU AWAD division and a below-elbow triathlete has worked tirelessly to get the word out globally in an effort to create awareness of our division, recognition of the world-class competition within, and to establish triathlon as a Paralympic sport.

Les McDonald, head of the ITU, did his part at the award ceremony, emphatically stating his commitment to our mission. He will personally do what he can to see a race in Beijing, 2008. Hats off to you, Les. We greatly appreciate your dedication.

Because we're special, we were the first wave to go off on Sunday morning, 6:15 AM, before the wind and the heat became an issue.

All AWAD classifications started on the same gun. While this has been the case in each of the previous four world championships I've raced, this was the first time my elbow found the hard surface of a *woman's* head in the frenzied "go-time" waters. I felt sorry for doing so, but in the end, I was glad I had an elbow to throw to begin with!

The swim course was two laps parallel to shore, which created a side-to-side current that made for relatively slow splits. Sophomore superstar American Akian "A. J." Aleong, a bilateral AK/BK (one above- and one below-knee amputation due to a motorcycle accident), who competes in the handcycle/wheelchair division, reached the shore first in just over twenty-three minutes. Behind him came Canadian AK Grant Darby, followed closely by Frenchman Cedric Delescluse, stricken with, I believe, cerebral palsy. Next out of the water was yours truly, just in front of Frenchman Yannick Bourseauz, whose left arm is completely paralyzed, racing in the AE class. American BEs Beeson and Tommy Knapp were right on our heels en route to T1 (yeah, I know, I only have one heel … very funny.)

Bourseauz passed me on the bike before I even had my one foot in its shoe (my bike prosthesis has a Look cleat mounted directly to the carbon platform surface). I'm strong on the bike, so, ya know, I enjoy the challenge when someone throws down the glove. I held the gap for a couple of kilometers, about as long as it took me to realize I couldn't hang with this guy. Through the tops of my Rudy Projects, I watched him ride away before I reached the first of two climbs.

There was a slight headwind heading east past Diamond Head, the volcanic crater that frames the eastern edge of Waikiki. The stretch down Kalanianaole Highway was straight and rather flat into a ten- to fifteen-mile-per-hour breeze. Near the end of the main section of the bike course, I saw the French colors in front of me at the same moment I came upon A. J. flying along in his brand-spankin' new handcycle, *ten* pounds lighter than his last one.

Making time on Bourseauz, I was surprised how fast he fizzled. I continued closing in as we approached the turnaround, situated on the back side of a short but steep pitch.

I had broken one rule of triathlon basics already; I failed to preview the bike course in the days preceding. Halfway up the hill I asked a police officer monitoring an intersection how much farther to the summit.

"Oh, just keep goin'," I was told.

"Thanks."

Another couple of hundred meters and I was there. As I crested the hill, Bourseauz was coming up the other side, so I figured I must be close. But unbeknownst to me, there was still another rider to catch—Frenchman Delescluse, whose identical race kit I had been keying on, while Bourseauz did indeed continue to increase his lead. Delescluse was a bit more manageable, and several miles later, I reeled him in.

With T2 in sight, Bourseauz came flying out on the run a good thirty seconds before I crossed the mat. I swapped legs as efficiently as possible, with high hopes not only of catching up with the leader but also of holding off A. J. who, with wheels under him on the run, is extremely fast. (While the athletes aforementioned were all racing in separate categories, we're still competitors at heart and strive to be the first to the line.)

As I exited transition, hampered by abdominal cramps (despite the easing off at the end of the bike and the Imodium ADs) and a tight lower back, Delescluse came by and soon had a twenty-meter lead on me to start the run. At the one-kilometer mark, my gut had settled, the back pain had subsided, and I was able to get in stride. I soon caught Delescluse, and at that moment was subsequently caught by yet another Frenchman, Jose Rodriquez (yes, French), a visually impaired athlete and his guide. (Unlike any other country represented, France is remarkably supportive of their AWADs, despite the acronym, and covers 100 percent of the costs associated with the world championships; therefore, loads of athletes represent each year.)

The three of us ran together for less than a kilometer before Delescluse dropped off. At the 2k out-and-back, still side by side with Rodriquez, we saw Brazilian Roberto Carlos Silva, an AE, some fifty meters back. For the next couple of kilometers, it was Rodriquez and me up front. At the 5k point, the start of the second lap, I picked it up and got a small gap that was soon rebutted by Rodriquez, who then had me by two or three meters.

We then came upon a sharp left-hander, which I used to jump inside and reestablish the gap, taking advantage, cheekily, of his inability to sight a tough corner.

I turned it up a bit to bite him both physically and mentally. At the 7k turnaround, I was still five meters up as Silva closed in slightly to forty meters back.

This was a new experience for me in the sport of triathlon. Never before had I battled nearly the entire run side by side with a competitor. Typically, I get a good gap on the bike, followed by one of three scenarios: (1) In AWAD races, I run alone before getting passed by American AE Willie Stewart, who didn't race this year; (2) I chase (have yet to catch) Rivaldo Martins, Brazilian and fellow BK, also unable to make this year's trip, who regularly knocks off twenty-minute swims; or (3) In able-bodied races, I slowly get eaten up by the two-legged freaks.

The competitive fires were licking at my soles, and I found myself running nearly stump-pain free—it's all relative, Stumpie always hurts to some degree on the run. This day, all I felt was the lactic burn. I pushed to keep my lead.

At the 9k turnaround, I saw both the pain in Rodriguez's face and the gap on Silva down to twenty meters. I picked it up another notch, running around a 6:00 minute-mile pace—that's fast for me. Through the final fifty meters in the finish chute, I glanced several times over my right shoulder to see my lead holding steady on the French athlete, but slowly deteriorating to the Brazilian.

If you've never fought for the line, let me tell you, the feeling is magnificent! I crossed the line third overall, with a time of 2:21:31. Bourseauz took the overall honors in 2:13:15 with a 38:39 run. A. J., who'd passed me at around 8.5k, wrapped up his race in 2:18:11.

Silva finished second in his class, just two seconds behind me, and got the edge on Rodriquez, who took the win for visually impaired males, another two seconds back.

This year's event was a milestone for our division. "We made a huge breakthrough at this year's world championships," said Beeson. "Both ITU and USAT have made a real, tangible commitment to seeing triathlon into the Paralympics. We are on the way."

Our sport does wonders for the average age grouper who finds a new outlet. You can imagine what it does for someone with a disability when he or she discovers what he or she is capable of accomplishing. Amy Winters, a BK mother of two and a welder from Pennsylvania, put it like this: "I guess I'm overwhelmed with a sense of accomplishment, and I know that I have set an example for my children: anything is possible as long as you try! I just know that the more I accomplish, the easier it will be for them to believe in themselves and what they want to do."

People are taking more and more notice, so … AWADs of the world unite! We're here to stay, and, if I may, I think the triathlon world is better off because of it.

It's Only Natural

March 2006

Race season is almost upon us. It landed on me last Sunday, a little heavier than expected. Boston's 2nd Annual Run to Remember, an event created to help memorialize the city's 280-plus police officers slain in the line of duty since the city became a city way back when, has both a five-miler and a half marathon. The race organizer and I met a couple of years ago at Ironman Lake Placid. He told me about this new event he was putting together and asked if I'd like to be a part of it. The race has a good-sized prerace and postrace expo at Boston's World Trade Center, and he offered not only a free booth but a little cash incentive to boot. I took him up on that offer again this year and manned the booth, joined by The Lovely Dr. Sharon Wetherall, peddling copies of *One Man's Leg* (still "selling" the book, but it's getting a bit old, frankly), showing off the Athens medals (not getting old), and promoting the coaching company, Amplitude Multisport.

I had intended to race the shorter race but ended up going long. As often happens—and this is fine with me—the race went a bit better than expected. I hadn't put a lot of faith in myself for one simple reason: lack of training. Yeah, I know what you're thinking: *What else does he have to do?* As of late, plenty.

Some of you are aware that The Lovely and I are remodeling a house in Boston. This undertaking has taken up most of my time and energy since late October.

Projects have included (and continue to include) a complete stripping of the entire kitchen, down to the studs, before putting in a new one. Looks good. Proud of that one. Did 90 percent of the work myself but did receive some help from family and friends. I hired professionals for the rough plumbing and electrical work. Dad put in the sink. Thanks, Old Man. (I don't think he reads these …)

I tore down a three-story chimney that once resided in the middle of the house, by hand, and cleaned and saved—at least attempted to—all the bricks. That was fun—can't wait to do that again. Patching the roof was easy.

Put in a new laminate floor. Nintey-seven cents a square foot at The Home Cheapo.

I stripped two thirty-year layers of shingles off a section of the roof before installing two big skylights (thank God for printed directions). That *was* kinda fun, putting in the skylights. I hadn't been on a roof since "one-legged" became part of my vernacular. It wasn't all that difficult. The difficult part came in when all that funny twisting and carrying and suspension sleeve ripping resulted in a whole lotta pain! Stumpie hadn't seen that many cases of folliculitis (infected hair follicles) and other strange bumps and blisters in quite some time. I hadn't spent as much time on crutches in the past ten years combined as I have in the last four months.

Stripped the vertical wood siding and the asbestos shingles (while holding my breath) on the front of the house and re-sided it with cedar clapboard. Still needs paint.

With all that energy being spent getting this little house of ours livable, I spent relatively little time on the bike (although the stationary rollers, the TV, and I spent some quality time in February), and far less on the run. I stared at the black line on the bottom of the pool a few days in early January, but nothin' since.

Last year, I learned a very important lesson with regard to Ironman training: winter base miles make for fast times in the summer. Not that I didn't know that before; I just didn't truly practice this tenet as well as I could have, but I did last season.

Since the base training, which was to provide the foundation for a solid Ironman Japan on May 28, never materialized this off-season, I've decided not to race triathlon of any significant distance this summer. I'll probably pop off a sprint or two, and at least one Olympic distance event, but no Ironman or half IMs.

This decision was further gusseted by the notion of becoming a better bike racer by doing more bike racing. This September, I hope to be on the line in Switzerland for Gimpy Cycling World Champs. I happen to be the reigning world champ in the time trial (won four years ago), and I would like to defend that jersey successfully.

A second factor swaying me out of the long, tough stuff this summer was a decision made by others. Now, I honestly don't hold a grudge toward these people, but I was led to believe—not guaranteed, by any means, but given a strong impression—that I would be a member of a well-funded Ironman Triathlon team this coming summer. Well, that never happened. I didn't get all bent out of shape about it, as I've come to learn, in multiple classrooms, that things happen for a reason. Had I signed with this team, I think other aspects of life would've been trickier to handle than what might be considered healthy. (If they offer next year, I'm on it and dedicated. I have every intention of breaking that ten-hour Ironman barrier in the near future.)

Other aspects being, for starters, remodeling the house. A large financial commitment from aforementioned party would have required me to put Ironman success ahead of all other energy expenditures. You gotta do what they pay you to do, no matter what field you're in.

So, to back up a little, it only follows that as one gets married and buys a house in his, er, late thirties, that one considers st … sta … starting a … *a family*! There, I said it …

I'm only kidding here. I've wanted to be husband and father longer and more deeply than anybody knows. The time has finally come, with the aspects of responsible parenthood all lined up, to procreate. I think most of you already know—I'm gonna be a daddy. And yes, Sharon's on the docket to be the mommy. "Cornbread" is due June 21—my birthday! The baby probably won't actually greet the world that very day to show an impatient grandma what type of equipment its packing, but wouldn't that be a cool present? Next year, babe, I want twins!

(Oh yeah, in Cornbread's room we stripped the shag rug and painted the floor, scraped the *Puff the Magic Dragon*–era wall paper, painted the upper halves of the walls yellow and the lower halves a darker yellowish-brownish color, and tore down the ratty acoustical ceiling, which we then drywalled. *Mémère* is making the curtains.)

Today is Wednesday, three days since I raced. There was once a time when there were far fewer things demanding my time, and I could scribe the details of my race on Monday mornings. Well, I've been coaching some of my Operation Rebound athletes (the Challenged Athletes Foundation sponsors injured veterans from Iraq and Afghanistan to be coached by me in triathlon, running, or cycling), and have been coaching a few of my other athletes, working on the entirely new upstairs bathroom (just got done texturing the walls and ceiling up there). I'm now sitting here in my underwear with the TRUST ME, I'M FAMOUS print with joint compound stuck in my hair and drying in my cuticles, knocking off this report before I go toss a steak on the grill and mash soft cubes of yellow squash for my forty-inch-waisted wife.

It's only natural, really, that racing gets trumped by life. Someone else's life at that. Trumped by the American dream of homeownership. Trumped by the need to earn a buck. There's still plenty of racing in me, I know it. I just gotta figure out how to make it all work. After all, there are plenty of folks out there who put it all together. I'm still learning.

So how'd the race turn out, you ask?

I went out easy, not knowing what to expect, not knowing if Stumpie would bitch about the transpiring events or if the engine had been given enough maintenance to hold up under pressure. I started with the self-seeded 8:30 minute-mile pace runners for no real good reason and was forced to bob and weave through the crowd on the three-hundred-year-old streets of the financial district. I caught the official 7:30 pace runner with the bright yellow shirt with bold black letters proclaiming his official status at about mile 4, on Memorial Drive, alongside the river Charles.

I eased ahead and found myself feeling kinda spunky at the six-mile turnaround of the mostly out-and-back course. I opted for the Porta-Potty just 'cause it was there and it felt good, telling myself that when I exited the blue box, I'd turn up the heat some. I did just that and picked off a bunch of people who were probably left wondering how they just got picked off by person of less-than-perfect composition, and I posted a 1:30:56, 69th of 708 in the 30-39s, a couple of seconds under a seven-minute pace.

Training be damned!

Bad Luck or Stupidity?

May 2006

Oooh, this could be a funny one, you're thinking. *What does he do this time?*

Throughout my travels, whether en route to a race, at a training camp, or maybe even during the race itself, I've had some bad luck. I've missed flights, forgotten to pack a run shoe, left my laptop on the security screening belt, affixed my left forefinger to the adjacent middle finger with a nail gun (previous career, or lack thereof). Sure, these things seem to fall into the "stupid" category, completely bypassing the bad luck line. Yet these things happen to many people, many upstanding successful individuals, save the nail gun incident.

I consider myself, despite opinions of some, a rather successful person. My checklist has checks on it next to the following: (1) write a book—a decent one, for that matter; (2) earn a college degree—a hard one, for that matter; (3) win Olympic medals—in Athens, for that matter; (4) complete an Ironman triathlon—set an unofficial world record, for that matter; (5) walk the red carpet—in Hollywood, for that matter; (6) marry a doctor—a beautiful Aussie, for that matter; (7) buy a house with my own credit—without a job, for that matter (Sharon's name wasn't even on the mortgage!).

Clearly, I'm not stupid.

There was a time when my confidence was a few notches lower, when I didn't know why the sky was blue, or what made ocean waves wave, when I considered ten dollars a lot of money, when I didn't know how to introduce myself to a girl. That was more ignorance and naïveté, I suppose, than stupidity. Innocence. Inexperience. Nonetheless, I often felt stupid back then. That wasn't all that long ago.

Nevertheless, I believe I have graduated to another level. *Worldly* might be a bit of a stretch, but I have seen a good part of this planet, more than most. I've witnessed how uneducated certain populations can be. I feel blessed with education. I feel smart. So when these unfortunate occurrences show up in my life, I'm hard-pressed to view them as anything other than bad luck. I mean, smart people don't do stupid things, do they? Successful people are successful because they're smart, no?

As you may recall, the house we bought is a fixer-upper. The remodeling that I've been doing without a whole lotta experience or help is coming out quite well. The brand-spankin' new bathroom that I've installed looks sharp. Sharon calls it the "bed-and-breakfast bathroom." Plumbed the vanity all by myself. No leaks. I'm smart.

Sharon's 36.5 weeks pregnant and her mother arrives this Friday, all the way up and over from Australia to live with us for a couple of months, to help out and do mother-in-law stuff. I'm currently on a flight to Colorado Springs to train with the U.S. Paralympic Cycling Team. This comes on the heels of six weeks of intensive remodel focus. The winter project was the kitchen/dining room/living room/baby room. The latest was getting the master bedroom and attached aforementioned bathroom and guest room for Nanny up to snuff, so that when I return from camp, all my focus can be on family and bicycle. Smart. I've timed everything just perfectly.

Woven into this project has indeed been some time spent riding and a couple of races to sharpen things up. The first bike race of the season was with my new team, Union Velo Masters—me and bunch of other old guys. I hadn't done a road race in a while and, frankly, was a bit concerned about my abilities to hang on, to not get dropped. However, I was feeling a bit cheeky, and so I attacked and created a break that was soon swallowed up. I sat in a good portion the remainder of the race and finished with the pack. Smart racing.

The following Saturday, I swindled my Uncle Errie into coming up and cutting down two huge pine trees that were swallowing up all the sun to the house. With these down, our home is now bathed in sunlight and the backyard is ready for a garden. Perfect.

All that tree removal and immediate burning of nearly all the branches and resident needles that come with two sixty-five-foot trees takes a lot a work. I was fried at the end of the day, which came at the end of a very long week, and I knew that the following day's race would best be approached as another "work" day, with little hope of shining among the others. So that's what I did. I attacked and covered breaks and quickly got back on my bike and back into the mix after the crash immediately in front of me sent me ever so slightly off the road—upright but unclipped at a complete stop. The plan was to go hard until I blew and see how far that would get me. That's exactly what I did, and on a long, steady climb, shortly after a failed attack into the wind to try to cover a break, I was off the back. And only a couple of miles from my car. Exactly as planned. I'm a genius. Home in time for dinner.

After a weekend trip to earn enough money speaking to pay all the monthly bills and then some (this is when I feel *very* smart), followed by another to Brooks Army Medical Center in San Antonio to take part in a weekend of helping physical therapists and prosthetists help amputees from Afghanistan and Iraq (honored and lucky in this instance), I was headed to another bike race just outside of Newport, Rhode Island, feeling all hungry and anxious.

En route to the race, as we pulled over for some lunch, bad luck stepped in. With my three-thousand-dollar bike mounted on the roof of the car, I pulled into a parking garage …

The carbon fiber fork broke. The Dura Ace ten-speed derailleur broke. My spirit remained intact. Sharon, the dogs, and I took advantage of the free time and enjoyed an afternoon in Newport, eating some kick-ass fish 'n' chips on a windy dock, driving the scenic coast, and walking along the shoreline rocks. Unlucky … but somehow a successful afternoon. And Griffen, my wonderful bike sponsor, is sending new stuff this week. In the meantime, I'm riding my time trial bike, also a Griffen machine.

Five days after the gaffe in Rhode Island, I went to get my car inspected to fulfill my Registry of Motor Vehicles obligation. I drove into the garage with my forty-five-hundred-dollar time trial bike on top. This confirms just how incredibly stupid I am …

P.S. The TT bike is fine; the wooden garage door trim gave way to the superbly constructed boron carbide Griffen Vulcan rocket ship. Stupidity still rules the day.

Wild Turkey

August 2006

I'm sitting at Starbucks, just inside the security gate of Boston's Logan Airport, which sits inside another Starbucks, en route to gate C19, en route to Denver's DIA, en route to Colorado Springs, Colorado. The foiled bombing plot of U.S.-bound London airliners several days ago has us travelers exceptionally weary of long lines once again, so I reached the airport an atypical two hours before my departure. Fifteen minutes later, I cleared security … Someone's doing his or her job, and thankfully I'm chillin'.

In Colorado Springs, several other gimps and I, being well compensated for our time and energy to do so, will be representing the Paralympic athletes at an event called the Paralympic Experience, hosted by The Hartford. Customers and field salespeeps from around the country come to the Olympic Training Center to take part in Paralympic sports like sitting volleyball, wheelchair sprints, and wheelchair basketball. Then a bunch of us go play golf on a killer course nestled under Pikes Peak. As I've said before, it's not a bad gig!

This event overlaps a national bike team training camp I'll be at until August 31. We'll put in time on the road and track preparing for September's world championships, held in Switzerland. I'm proud to say that I still hold the WC title for the individual road time trial earned in 2002, but not so vain to say that keeping it will be a cinch. Not so sure I'd bet on me, to be honest with you.

I've been riding far less than I have in the past—and not swimming or running much at all, as you may have read in my writings this season. To reiterate: fixer-upper house, Stumpie issues, and general lack of motivation (yeah, that's kinda new and not so cool) top the list. PBJ (Perfect Baby Jack) is not to blame.

I have been putting in just enough miles to keep an edge, however. Things I've done right since May:

Solid work logged at Gimp Team training camp in Colorado Springs, early June. In the middle of this camp, I flew to Japan, where I was invited to speak. I did so, again, through a translator. They just stared at me … again.

Qualified for the worlds team on a Tuesday in central Pennsylvania by landing second at the National Time Trial Champs, mid-June. Um, perhaps due to some degree of poor planning, I wasn't registered when I got there and was told I couldn't race the next day. At 5:20 PM the next day, strings were pulled on my behalf. At 5:52 PM, I raced. Shocking to all of you, I know.

Won my fourth national championship in triathlon at the New York City Triathlon the following Sunday (somewhat ashamed to say this was my first swim since February and something like my fifth run since March). To highlight another athlete, let me say that no other below-knee amp triathlete from the U.S. has ever come close to beating me. That changed in New York City, where seven other guys and a couple of women showed up. I nabbed this one by a mere sixty seconds. Amy Winters, who recently ran a 3:25 marathon—a mere sixty seconds slower than my best time—is the one I know I'll need to train harder to beat next time. Hats off to you, young lady!

Raced well at the Attleboro, Massachusetts Crit, just outside of Providence, Rhode Island, which brings all the best locals. I must learn to stay up front when I get up front. Twice I was there and let myself drift back, which, with a few laps to go, means "will not win."

The days I did get out to ride, my prescribed efforts were indeed honest and hard-driven.

Learned to change a diaper.

I put in some good efforts and sharpened the pack skills at the local training crit and group rides.

Hit a ball off the tee—275 yards!

Built a cool island that perfectly matches the rest of the kitchen. Stools bought on the Internet should be in next week.

Avoided being pecked to death by huge wild turkeys when I got off the bike to take cell phone pictures. Never been so scared of fowl in my life.

In late July, I threw it down, at least early in the Cyclonauts Road Race, in South Central, Massachusetts. I went off the front in a four-man breakaway starting at mile 0.5, which, somewhat surprisingly, lasted not much more than a half hour, despite the hard pace—a pace that truly tested me, and I questioned my ability to hang with these guys. Then two other riders bridged up to us—one a teammate—and the heat turned up for a few more minutes. I was on the verge of popping moments before the peloton caught us. This often means things cool off for a moment or two. Well, we were headed uphill when they came upon us, which invariably means more power *now*, and I was forced farther into oxygen debt (think: breathe really, really hard with lactic acid eating away at your legs—fun stuff!). There, at mile 12, I thought I was about to drop out of the race. Then the course proceeded down a long, easy descent, and I was able to recover (think: get my shit back together). Another fifteen to twenty miles amid the draft of the peloton, and I felt good. This was before the steep section. On the fourth of four steep pitches, giving it all I had to stay in touch with the leaders, I popped. Cracked. Blew up. Done for the day.

Or so I thought. The first chase pack went by me, and I showed no interest in getting on. Then the second chase pack went by just as I crested the hill … and I got on. We rode in a quasi-organized pace line for about forty-five minutes. I had to tell some of these guys how to pace intelligently. These were the same guys who left me behind on the next bump of a hill. Truly done for the day. I rode the final ten miles solo, nursing my energy drink, appreciating the good workout.

Wish us luck in Europe. These races directly impact the size of Team USA at the Beijing Paralympics in 2008. That is indeed the next big thing for me.

If I make the team.

Be your best. If, for some reason, you can't do that (talking to self), I hope you're better than your competition.

2006 Disabled Cycling World Championships

September 2006

The Disabled Cycling World Championships wrapped up in Switzerland last week, sending several of us humbled riders home with a renewed motivation for training. This is often the response when performances fail to meet expectations and personal standards.

Other than the women's tandem team that has been dominating for several years, the U.S. squad did not claim the medal count we've become somewhat accustomed to in the past. My performances were among those left off the podium.

The racing got under way September 11, on the track. The guys in my category got things rolling with the four-kilometer pursuit. The top four finishers moved on to the finals later that day. I was fifth. I've been in the finals, the bronze medal round, each of my last three international events, so as you might surmise, I wasn't too happy about that. I did, however, ride about as fast as I'd expected: a 5:14 and change. Fourth place, a Chinese rider, rode a 5:13. That particular Chinese rider has no hands, nor did his teammate. You might think a guy with two legs and no hands may have the upper on us apparatus-wearing leg amputees. Not so much the case—guys like me still win the races. Unfortunately for me, I'd told the Chinaman I'd wipe his backside for him if he beat me ...

The race was won by Spaniard Roberto Alcaide. As I may have mentioned in the past, he's built for this business. At age twenty, he lost his foot descending a hill on race day, crashing into a guardrail that claimed his pod. He was racing for the Spanish national development team; his

188

father was an Olympic cyclist. Roberto broke his own world record by posting a 4:43. Next was Jiri Jezek, the great Czech rider, then a new guy from Belgium, Jan Boyen.

The next day's event, the kilo—a thousand-meter time trial—gave me what it always gives me: a 1:14 point something—1:14.689 to be specific. I rode a half second slower than my best. Again, about what I'd expected. But several of the other vets had gotten faster, and the new guy from Britain, Jody Cundy, set a new world record of 1:10:57. I finished up in sixth—my worst kilo place to date.

Next up was the road time trial, the event in which, as previously mentioned, I've held world champion status for the last four years. I told myself that I felt good, and I almost meant it. But once I left the ramp and started down the 24k course, the go-sticks provided not the power necessary to repeat, and I felt like a Chevy in Mexico: No*va*. I finished eleventh, six minutes (10 percent) off the day's best racer. I was down and out in the Swiss Alps. And humbled. The need to train to win was crystal clear—at this level, no one wins without paying his or her dues.

The final competition, the road race, did provide some redemption. It was a not-soon-to-be-forgotten rain-soaked day, where the wheel in front of you provided both shelter and a hosing of rooster tail road water. A rainy road race typically calls for at least one crash. In this case, it was the guys we warned rookie teammate Sam Kavanaugh to look out for: the two Chinese guys, with not a single hand between them, took each other out! (Sam lost his leg eighteen months ago in a Montana avalanche, spending forty-eight hours in the mountains with a compound fractured tib-fib. Amazing guy.)

I rode well and did some honest work in an effort to put my good friend Ron Williams in position to medal. We were confident as a team, being the only country fielding three riders, and we expected some good work out of Sam, who had done well in the TT and on the track. Unfortunately, he was out after a couple of laps due to a lost contact lens by way of the rooster tail.

On the fourth of six laps of a seven-mile course, with ten of twenty-five starters left in the peloton, I flew off the front and took a couple of guys with me. Unfortunately, Ron got worked shortly thereafter by the number one and number two riders in the world, the Czech and the Spaniard, and was left for dead. I had just completed a big pull and was presently falling back, seeking assistance from those formerly on my wheel, the Belgian and Romanian, Carol Eduard Novak. They were right in front of me, and as the request for cohesion left my lips, I saw them glance over their shoulders, past mine, and get off their saddles. In that moment, Jiri, Roberto, and a couple of others then zipped past me as Jan and Eduard got on those fast wheels and held on. I did my damndest but got dropped; I then held up a tad to hook up with a couple of other stragglers, neither of which was a teammate of mine. The three of us then made a solid attempt to get back up to the leaders, but no luck.

We then rolled the final lap at a decent pace, picked up another guy previously dropped by faster riders, and headed to the finish line. I took second in that pack sprint, for a respectable soaking-wet eighth-place finish.

I strolled home that day not feeling like the loser I felt like after the time trial. I felt like I wanted to be in the shape I was four years ago. Heck, the shape I was in a year ago.

To get there, the answer is obvious: I'll return to training. I'm thinking, on top of caring for Jack many hours per week, I'll run Boston. I'm thinking Ironman Austria. I'm thinking I'll keep up the bike racing too. I'll be busy, so busy that this weekend we excavated large holes to start building a two-car garage with a large great room above it and the extension off the back of the house for a nice big living room.

I'll be hiring help.

And I'll be back.

A Cool Marathon
May 2007

They were predicting "the worst April nor'easter" in New England's recorded history. The media was all over it. The *Today Show* showed up. *The Weather Channel* had their peeps in Hopkinton. The start of the 2007 Boston Marathon was certainly a wet and cold one, but the ferocity of the storm peaked at about 4:00 AM, saving many of us from experiencing an experience most would not warmly welcome.

I was dressed for the worst: two layers of Nike high-tech jerseys, a waterproof Nike shell, a cozy Nike ear-hugging cap, and to keep the legs comfortable, those unmanly Nike tights. (I have a new sponsor, can you tell?)

A friend from Boulder was in town to run the race, and we both agreed that the worst thing about the weather would not be the running but the waiting in the weather to do the running. Alas, every now and again, being gimpy has its advantages (it also helps to buy Red Sox socks for people in high places), and we were invited to hang in the race director's office at the start line.

It was a little drizzly at the start but nothing truly uncomfortable. The masses started down Route 135, and I stuck to my plan to go out easy. The early descents on this course are notorious for tearing up the quads, which competitors wish they had more of around mile 23, as has happened to me on my previous three outings here. For the first time, I had no specific time goal. In the past, it's always been sub-3:18, which is the standing American male record. That time became somewhat moot last October, when indomitable Amy Winters went 3:04 in Chicago. I wasn't about to go faster than that, and with my limited training, I figured a good goal would be to not fall apart before reaching the grandstands. She was also lined up yesterday so for me to be the first of the amputees—this is always one of the goals and after many years of this business, somewhat expected—was now a huge challenge.

Regarding the limited training, Stumpie has again been a bear this off-season. A little bit due to the never-ending home remodeling (starting in September, we've added one thousand square feet of living space and a garage so big and manly that it takes some of the bite out of wearing those tights). The time spent on my feet, climbing the ladder and carrying things twelve times my body weight, has been tough on the little guy.

There's also been another little medical challenge to deal with. Short story is I have this bacteria in my body that the doc tells me about two percent of the population shares. Mine just happen to colonize, creating incredibly painful boils on random parts of my body, mostly on my lower half and the most recent, in February, on the lateral condyle (outside bony part of the knee) of Stumpie, making the run an incredibly painful experience and hence somewhat nonexistent. That one did clear enough to allow consecutive weekend runs of fourteen, seventeen, nineteen, and eight miles on the weekends leading up to the race, with little to no runs in between to allow for further healing. Fortunately, I was able to get on my bike through this, and I got in many good rides. Docs are working on a solution.

So, as I said, I eased into the run. I felt good in those opening miles, sweetened by the anticipation of meeting Jack at mile 8. Our part-time nanny had him for the day as I ran and Sharon worked, and since we live just off the course, she was able to bring him down to share Daddy's day. A quick hello and a kiss, and I was back at it.

By the halfway point, things were still feeling good while running a bit under a pace that would nearly match my marathon PR of 3:24—I was running about eight-minute miles, including a leg reboot and a few circulation-restoring stop-and-dangles. However, I was well aware that holding the pace through and past the upcoming hills was a pipe dream. But the fact that all systems were go was fabulous.

The hat had come off, and I considered losing the jacket at around mile 9. The nanny had just mentioned a mile back that the temps were expected to drop around noontime. I heeded the warning, left the coat on, and patted myself on the back for the decision when the wind picked up and things got chilly around mile 14, where the hat went back on.

I still felt pretty good when I started the hills at mile 17—beginning to feel the wear but doing well considering the distance. Up the hills I went with the help of mental imagery, repeating to self, *I'm light. I'm light. I'm light.* I passed quite a few competitors on the three successive rises through mile 21 and Heartbreak Hill. On the back side of the last famous hill, the belly cramps that have hindered me in the previous three races came back, but thankfully not as bad as the past. Those cramps, along with just plain running out of steam, forced me to slow considerably, knocking off three ten-minute miles that included another reboot and more dangles.

Temps went up in those latter miles, and once more the hat came off. The finish line approached, and like the good little sponsoree that I am, I donned the headgear to let everyone know that I'm proud to sport the "Swoosh." Good thing I did. Mom saw me at the finish line on the 6:00 PM news, flashing a difficult smile as I crossed the line in 3:35:13, first of the mobility-impaired athletes and 6,782nd of 22,000-plus runners. Amy Winters was ahead of me through the halfway point but bad luck stepped in and she stepped on an aid-station water cup with her prosthesis, causing her to spill, twist her good ankle, and whack her gimp-side knee. And she still managed to finish about ten minutes behind me.

A marathon finish line is always an accomplishment, and I'm glad to have competed. Yet this race was on the schedule as good motivation for good training to prepare me for Ironman Coeur d'Alene, Idaho, on June 24—Jack's first birthday and three days after my fortieth. It'll be my tenth attempt at the Big Distance. I'll be the youngest guy in my new age group, I imagine, which is supposed to be a good thing.

I'd venture to guess that I'll be back out there next year; however, training will once again have its challenges. Deuce, our second child, is due in October!

How Cigarettes Saved My Race
June 2007

The trials and tribulations continue in life and racing. Ups and downs. Highs and lows. Same ol', same ol'. What's new are the things I do that make me laugh at myself, right after I'm through cursing. The latest challenge I've brought upon my mind/body/spirit was Sunday's EagleMan 70.3 half Ironman. The race itself, as was Boston's famed marathon a couple months back, was part of the preparatory process for Ironman Coeur d'Alene, up there in the panhandle of Idaho.

I'd say that my overall training has been good, having logged a half dozen century rides and eight or nine good long runs in the recent past. My swim stroke keeps improving too.

I needed a strong swim on Sunday to make up for my latest race day blunder: just minutes before the 6:50 AM swim start, as I scrambled to find my timing chip (the little thing you strap to your ankle that records your start time, end time, and all the swim/bike/run splits in between), it occurred to me that it must have fallen out of my race bag into the back of the Subie wagon as I scrambled to find my race suit the night before. Fortunately—there's always a "fortunately"—Gerry the handler, assigned to me by the race staff to take care of my every need, ran to get me a new one from the timing peeps and met me at the swim start. By the time I rechipped, my wave of physically challenged competitors (Major Dave Rozelle and myself) and the fifty-five-plus men and fifty-plus women (about one hundred of them in total) had already started this leg of the race some one hundred meters offshore. I jumped in and heard the race director bark over the PA, "Let's go, Paul!"

I was thinking, *Sharon's laughing at me right now.*

Sharon, Jack, and the dogs joined me for this trip. I picked her up at 6:30 PM on Friday after her shift improving the lives of little ones at Children's Hospital Boston. We drove straight to Annapolis, arriving at 2:30 AM.

This same crew drove up to Acadia National Park—five hours northeast of Boston—a couple of weeks before for a Memorial Day weekend of camping and trail running. As we made our way back home on Monday, clipping away at sixty miles per hour in the slow lane, with the Subie packed to the gills and the baby jogger riding on the huge cooler, which itself rode on the roof rack, tragedy struck. We heard a little thump from above just as the couple passing us pointed emphatically and mouthed something indecipherable. I was pretty sure I knew what happened.

The baby jogger remained, dangling, off the back of the roof, and the cooler lay on the grassy embankment some three hundred yards back. "Shit! There goes all the Bud Light!" I threw it in reverse, hazards a-flashin', reached Ground Zero, and witnessed something quite inspiring: the beers were all there in a little circle, the ice remained in the bags, the hot dogs, polish sausage, buns, green pepper, lettuce, eggs-already-deshelled-in-a-screw-top-container, and soft drinks were all there adjacent the cooler, which incurred no damage outside of the broken lid hinges. The lettuce was in the breakdown lane. All we lost was an onion. I propose that many a spouse would let the cargo packer know just how unacceptable it is to strap so shabbily. I'm happy to say Sharon merely laughed at me and my onion as we reconfigured the strapping situation before continuing our journey.

With this setback out of the way, I was confident my race preparation would go smoothly henceforth.

Sure, the swim started out a bit rocky, but despite starting a good minute or two behind everyone else (without the benefit of properly drafting off some of the faster masters), I got out of the water in thirty minutes. I popped on my run leg for the 250-yard haul to the transition.

The EagleMan, I was told, can be a miserably hot and windy experience. Flat as a pancake, but the elements can be trying. The athletes were lucky this year, with a five- to ten-mile-per-hour breeze on the bike and mostly overcast skies all day, with the temps hovering around seventy-five to eighty degrees.

To start things off on the ride, I was pleased to have a fifty-five-year-old rabbit going hard as he held a fifty-meter lead on me until mile 18 or so. Then he tossed out his anchor and began fading back, never to be heard from again. (That is, until he flew by me on the run.)

I picked off a few more of those faster grand masters before coming up on a female pro. I was both stunned and impressed to learn from the number on her calf that she was not a pro but a fifty-one-year-old age grouper!

After a couple more older guys, I caught another female; this one had a *P* on her calf: "Pro." (Their wave opened the race five minutes before ours.)

The flat course made it easy to keep it in the big ring with the occasional shift up or down a click or two from the fifteen cog I kept it in most of the ride. I'm happy to report that the legs kept up the power. The thirty-minute repeats at 210 watts on my long rides may even have helped me to negative split the bike.

I passed another female pro and a couple more grand masters, and with about ten miles to go, I had a new specific goal for the bike portion of this event: to hold off all the 40-44 guys that started fifteen minutes behind me.

With just a quarter of a mile to go, that goal was all but lost. He passed me at a marginally faster pace, and I stuck to the legal gap. Lucky for me, he apparently has yet to master the quick dismount, and we ended up crossing the transition mat together ... close enough to check that one off in the green column. A two-hour, twenty-five-minute ride, averaging 23.2 miles per hour. Not my fastest, but one of 'em.

I had the best rack in the house, directly across the mat from the T2 arch. As I racked the Griffen Vulcan rocket ship, Mr. Griffen himself, Tony Free (founder and president of Griffen Bikes) unknowingly stood nearly adjacent to Sharon and Jack, who stood adjacent to the arch, and all gave me some props on the good ride. (The only thing physically separating my wife from my bike sponsor was a Porta-Potty. I wonder what meaning lies there ...)

I ran unmatched for maybe a mile before that latter female pro passed me. It was less than a half mile later that Stumpie started bummin'. I pulled over to reboot. The leg was slipping some ... but nothing drastic. (Last month I received new walk/run/biking legs from A Step Ahead—a Long Island, New York, prosthetic facility, where the fastest American male and female marathoners have their work done.) There's merit in the theory that changing up years-proven prostheses just weeks before an Ironman proves reckless. Yet I have enough faith in the guys at ASA, and if you've read any of these writings of mine recently, you know that Stumpie's been suffering enough as of late to warrant something new. (Logistics being the only reason I haven't done so earlier.)

Just days after I received the new runner, I took ten minutes off my local fifteen-mile training loop. A week later, I ran a local 5k. The first mile was covered in 5:57, faster than I've ever opened a race. Unfortunately, the bugs have yet to be worked out of this new apparatus, and with the help of pouring rain and high humidity during the race, my leg suspension was severely compromised, and it kept getting too loose to continue running. Over the next 1.5 miles, I had to stop three times to reboot. I managed to cross the finish in 19:37, while the guys I was running with in that first fast mile, running at a pace I felt I could hold, finished in 18:11 and 18:12. My PR remains 18:47 on a track in 2001. Perhaps needless to say, but I feel the new prosthesis is worth sticking with.

Back to Sunday's run. Soon after I rebooted and got back to it, the first female pro I passed on the bike overtook me. By mile 3, Stumpie was starting to bum, and I was forced to reboot again. This time, I noticed a nice juicy blister on the anterior distal tibia (the front of the bottom). I surmised I was not wearing enough plies—not thick enough stump socks. I got out there again, keeping my eyes peeled for something on the side of the road to stuff into my socket to lift me off the bottom. That thing turned out to be a freshly discarded pack of Marlboros. I silently thanked the littering smoker, flattened out the box, and stuffed it along the front area, between my stump sock and the socket wall.

This worked well enough for the next three miles, and probably saved my race as well as my upcoming Ironman, but I still needed more lift. At the turnaround of the out-and-back run, I recalled a trick I'd picked up at my last Ironman: I requested the sock off the foot of the volunteer manning the timing mat. He quickly obliged, and I was once again back out there, running more comfortably. The damage, however, was already done. Stump pain held me back a bit, and I rebooted another three or four times before reaching the finish line. With less than 150 meters left in the race, I couldn't/wouldn't allow myself to reboot, but the pain forced me to stop and dangle twice en route to the finish line.

I reached it in a total of four hours, forty-one minutes, and forty-four seconds.

This race is one of, I believe, two remaining half-Ironman distance qualifiers for the Hawaiian Ironman World Championships. This race, therefore, brings many, if not most, of the East Coast's fast guys and gals in search of the Golden Ticket to Kona. My time put me 44th of 227 in a very competitive 35-39 field and 184th of 1,200 male finishers. A personal best by eleven minutes, mostly from the one-hour, forty-minute run. This makes me happy.

I FedExed the bike and run legs to Long Island last night for some last-minute tweaking. It's 4:00 PM on Tuesday, and the hardware is already en route back to me, scheduled to arrive by 10:30 AM tomorrow morning. A couple of more swims, bikes, and runs, and I'll be ready for Ironman Coeur d'Alene a week from Sunday, on Jack's first birthday, June 24.

I've granted Stumpie a couple of rest days. I'm presently chillin' in the living room, writing this piece, taking care of Mr. Jack. Life is good. There's always, in my opinion, more ups than downs. Today's an "up" day here in the Martin household. I hope you can say the same.

The Stumpie Blues

June 2007

There's a long-held standard in endurance racing: don't race with new equipment—you need to know what works, not hope this bright white pair of shoes or theoretical bike fit will give you the advantage. At Ironman Coeur d'Alene a couple of Sundays ago, it could be argued that the new prosthetic legs I wore added close to forty-five minutes to my finish time.

My old bike and run legs were working okay, but each of them had caused me enough frustration over time that I felt a change was justified. Despite the credo, I believe the change was, at minimum, fairly well timed. I started riding and running on the new legs six weeks before race day, having success in training runs and knocking off my fastest half Ironman ever. I was confident we'd work out the bugs, particularly since they were feeling good right out of the box.

Some issues arose. The hardware was FedExed to the leg shop on Long Island, twice each, in the first few weeks. Stepping into the sockets left me with a warm, fuzzy feeling—they both felt so comfy ... before the miles got to them.

Before jumping too far ahead, let's talk about the swim. Lake Coeur d'Alene is a big beautiful clear lake up in the panhandle of Idaho. We arrived (husband, wife, son) at the race on Wednesday, eager to swim on Thursday morning. The water was cold and choppy; same on Friday, Saturday, and, of course, Sunday. So choppy that the race director offered the option of skipping the swim altogether to those athletes who might not be so confident in their aquatic skills. I'm told about fifty competitors took him up on that offer.

I lined up right up front, on the inside, ready for action, ready to throw elbows and get pulled along with the fast guys. The gun went off, and I went out hard … hyperventilated … freaked out some … got all scared by the waves crashing in my face … the arms clubbing me … the inability to control my breathing … and scrambled for an outlet to compose myself. Felt like a rookie. My tenth Ironman. Haven't learned a damn thing.

Without question, this was the most unorganized group of twenty-two hundred swimmers I've ever been a part of. The waves made it difficult to sight the upcoming buoys, and we were all swimming zigzag. Every time I looked up, there was at least one person breast-stroking, trying to get his or her bearings. I was not exempt in this triathletically unacceptable behavior, even after I got my head back together.

The first left-turn buoy was complete madness, which is typical in most Ironman races when you're in the thick of the swimmers. I came in from the left side and thus was pinched at the turn and opted for going around underwater—not recommended …

From there, things got much more manageable, and I began, as did all the others, to find my stroke on the return 0.9 miles with the current behind me. A quick hop out of the water, across the timing mat, and right back in for a second round into the chop. With the crowd well dispersed, the repeat trip brought far less commotion.

I finished in 1:11, 322nd in the swim—about ten minutes slower than expected—pretty much how everyone fared.

It was relatively cold, around sixty degrees, when we departed on the bike, so I opted for the Nike skintight technical jersey that worked out perfectly the entire ride.

What didn't work was the fake bike leg. It's a strange problem we're dealing with. The leg feels so comfortable when I step into it, more comfy than the previous prosthesis. And it continues to feel great for thirty to thirty-five miles. Then, in a matter of minutes, I suffer an incredible ache in the majority of my remaining calf muscle. Starting at mile 40, I pulled over every five miles or so to pull my leg off; doing so allowed for the cramp to subside after forty-five to sixty seconds. (As I complete this final edit in January 2010, it's been discovered just a few weeks ago that my popliteal artery, the one that carries blood to my lower leg, ends behind my knee on the prosthetic side. The only blood supply Stumpie receives is through a network of capillaries. This find answers the fifteen-year mystery of why Stumpie cramps so much on the run, sometimes the bike and often simply walking—and it seems to be getting worse. It's a relief to have the answer, but, unfortunately, an answer that has no solution. I'm told surgery has a slim chance of providing better circulation, and could very well land me in a new class as an above-knee amputee. Looks like I'll have to deal with what I've got.)

I was basically leapfrogging backward—each time I got back on the bike, I passed a slew of people who'd just passed me on the side of the road, but I'd never get all of them. Twelve of these reboots later, and I was more than a little frustrated. This problem had reared its head some during training, but it was nothing major and nothing I hadn't experienced similarly with the old leg(s).

I felt strong while riding the marginally hilly, considerably technical, and relatively windy course. My first lap was completed at over 21 miles per hour, including a couple of those reboots. I ended up averaging 19.4 miles per hour. Not so good by today's standards. My bike split of 5:46 was twenty-five to thirty minutes slower than expected.

Bob Prieto, the famed Leg Handler Extraordinaire, was there with the run leg in hand as I crossed into the bike/run transition. I was in and out in less than three minutes, off on the run.

The crowd on the run elevates me so in every triathlon I race. There's no question that the advantage challenged athletes receive is real. The energy thrown our way so enthusiastically picks us up and carries us along. Through the first two miles of the run, the crowd brought a smile to my face. The stump pains I typically experience on the run—one type similar and the other distinctly different than that on the bike—hadn't set in yet.

By mile 3, I was rebooting. The pain was more of a distinct discomfort at that point. The big blister Stumpie received two weeks prior at Eagleman had healed, but the skin there was thin; I didn't want to push the issue when I felt something not so funny.

This problem arose every couple of miles, wherein I rebooted nearly ten times on the run. Like the bike, when I was running—save a chunk of miles in the middle of the marathon—I was running strong, but too much stopping killed my run split. The lofty goal (one I'd given myself, say, ten to one odds) was a sub-ten-hour race. I crossed in 11:03:56 (3:56 marathon). Sorta kinda happy. Not as thrilled at the line as I've been in the past.

Of course, I pulled off the leg and "*I ... am ... Ironman!*" came out with sincere gusto. I was disappointed, but (here we go with the sappy stuff) Jack and Sharon were right there at the finish line, and I was smiling and happy in no time.

Regardless of the finish time, there's one major aspect of this race that brings tremendous satisfaction: I've completed ten Ironman triathlons. Never woulda thought. Ten years ago, I would have called you crazy if you said one day I'd have that many notches. There are a handful of accomplishments in my life that I'm truly proud of. This one's right up there.

I'm sitting on the couch nearly two weeks after the race, unable to wear my leg. Stumpie felt relatively good the morning after the race, despite a couple of nice blisters on the bottom. I was up at 3:45 AM that day to drive Sharon and Jack to the airport in Spokane. I got on a flight to Colorado Springs for a three-day Hartford sponsor event that included a round of golf. Got home at 2:30 AM on Thursday morning, before a three-day all-out assault on the backyard, preparing for Jack's first birthday party cookout blowout.

Come party time, with fifty guests and duty on the grill, I was limping, self-medicating with MGDs, and anticipating the upcoming rest. (Watching Jack attack the chocolate cake with both hands was a welcomed respite.)

By 7:00 PM, enjoying a tub alongside the birthday boy, I began to shiver uncontrollably. The fever that came over me stemmed from the return of the cellulitis I've been battling for over a year now. The sore on Stumpie was one of those infections I hadn't had since March. Apparently, the stress I'd put myself through in the preceding week left my immune system a bit compromised. The fever broke that night (I went from wearing a ski hat in bed to sweating and sheetless in a matter of minutes), but it returned two days later. That was three days ago, and I'm happy to say the antibiotics are working, and things are looking up. With any luck, we'll get the infections and the legs under control in the near future.

My next race is July 22—the New York City Triathlon, which doubles as the PC national championships. I believe I can be there and be ready. You see, there's another canon in sports, particularly among veterans: Success comes not only with the ability to focus … but to refocus.

How Stumpie Got His Groove Back

July 2007

One would think that if one were to race triathlon, one would benefit greatly from sleeping the night before. Seems reasonable, doesn't it? Well, that's not how I approached my race yesterday in New York City.

Not that I didn't want to sleep—apparently the decaf coffee I had after dinner Saturday night wasn't as decaf as I'd hoped for. I lay in bed from 10:00 PM to 1:00 AM, flipping and flopping, breathing heavily, frustrated, Sharon sleeping semi-peacefully beside me in room 1309 of the Hilton on 6th Avenue. I turned on the TV and watched the day's rerun of the Tour de France, despite already knowing the outcome.

"You gonna watch TV all night?" Sharon asked, understandably aggravated.

"I'm wide awake, going crazy," I said.

"But what about me?"

I got up and decided to go for a walk. Sharon talked me back into bed, stating that all I needed was a cuddle; she would make things all better.

Didn't work. I practically bounced out of the bed, popped on a leg, and headed down the elevator. I didn't know where I was going, but I knew I couldn't lie there any longer. I headed north a few blocks on 6th Avenue, where I hit Central Park South and considered strolling through the park before my good senses directed me otherwise. I ended up on Broadway, where I strolled into a hotel to ask the concierge if there were any (respectable) movie theaters open at this time of night. (I was suddenly eager to see *Shrek the Third*). He didn't think so but directed me to 42nd and 8th just in case.

This brought me straight into the never-ending circus of Times Square. At 2:00 AM, the place was jammed with people of good and bad intentions—and what appeared to be many, like me, with no intentions whatsoever.

As expected, both the AMC and Regal cinemas were closed. McDonald's, however, was open, and I settled for a vanilla shake. Truth be told, I had to buy something in order to get *past the guards* to the men's room. Anyway, got my shake and continued the stroll. I stopped to enjoy a couple of street performers. I stood and watched those guys with the fast hands make quick acquaintance of the five dollars Mr. Passerby handed over when he thought he could guess which cup the ball was under. Another guy was collecting from another with a deck of cards. One stout little man offered me drugs. I'm sure I could have bought more than drugs from some of those women who were hanging out under that huge Coke sign.

By 3:00 AM, I was back in the room and managed to get some shut-eye by 3:15.

At 4:00, the phone rang as scheduled. By 4:20, I was making my way to 79th Street and the Hudson River for the start of the New York City Triathlon.

The race within the race is the Physically Challenged National Championships, and the fifty-eight athletes that showed up with parts missing, unresponsive limbs, or eyes not quite up to snuff constituted the largest number of disabled athletes to ever show up at a triathlon ever … in the history of the world! Great stuff—the stuff triathlon needs to get it included into the Paralympic Games sometime soon.

We all lined up on the pier sticking out into the Hudson, in line with 96th Street. The race director called us all into the water, directing us to hold onto the rope so as not to be swept downstream before the gun went off. As you might imagine, swimming downstream makes for fast swim times, and I got out of the water in personal record time, nearly two minutes faster than I had in my previous two races here. I was getting all excited, as it appeared I would be the first in my group out of the water—that's never happened before … in the history of the world. I climbed the exit pier ramp in a hopping-like fashion after covering the fifteen hundred meters in just over fifteen minutes. To my great dismay, BK Mike was already donning his leg. Bummer. (With the right eye of my goggles filled with water, I couldn't see too well on that side, and he must've been there.) I was nonetheless first out of transition and onto the bike to tackle forty kilometers.

The ride goes up the West Side Highway into Yonkers, and like past years, directly into a steady headwind. I was able to keep in the big ring most of the way out, but I granny-geared it on the one tough climb.

The course is an out-and-back, which affords competitors the opportunity to gauge their competition. Mine included not only the eleven other BKs but also the legendary One-Arm Willie. He and I have done battle in many races, and I've only beaten him once, on this very course in 2005.

I discerned a 1:30 lead at what was not quite the halfway point. With the wind behind me, I was able to lay it down well on the return. Before getting off the bike, the course passes transition and continues nearly a mile before another 180 turnaround. I then saw Willie and One-Arm Tommy (doesn't have quite the same ring) riding side by side about two and a half minutes behind me. At that point, I figured it was only a matter of time before Willie caught me. He typically runs under 6:30s to my 7:00s.

My transition was quick, and while I didn't have too much confidence, I learned long ago that pushing to the finish line is the surest way to win a race. I ran hard through the first three miles before Stumpie pain called for a reboot. Experience has also taught me that this type of pain is greatly reduced with a quick stop. I was able to get right back at it, at a slightly quicker pace, for another mile or so before the stomach cramps I've dealt with for over a decade grew to a point that I had to stop for five or six seconds to alleviate them and catch my breath. I continued up the steepest climb in Central Park as the stump pain gradually returned. At mile 4.5, I opted to pop the leg off but not the liner—not a complete reboot—for fifteen seconds to give the pain a break.

I looked back and didn't see Willie. At every mile marker I passed, I was quite shocked that he hadn't came past me yet—I had already considered it a small victory that I'd made it this far and continued to hold him off. I desperately wanted to make it in without further delays, but Stumpie was really starting to scream. With one last unavoidable reboot with half a mile to go, I saw the bloodshed by the quarter-sized blister at the bottom of Stumpie …

Still no Willie within the 150 meters I could see behind me. Got the leg back on and pushed it as hard as I could. At 300 meters to go, the race takes nearly a 360-degree loop, where I got a good view down the course, and finally, with 100 meters to go, I felt I had it. As stated earlier, pushing to the line is the best way to win.

I crossed the line a mere thirty seconds in front of a foaming Willie.

Rest suddenly seemed so overrated. The previous Wednesday, I flew to Florida for a Thursday round of golf, a thirty-minute run on the white sands of Panama City Beach, and a nice twenty-minute swim in the warm, salty gulf. On Friday morning, I spoke to a few hundred people at the Florida Society of Association Executives' annual meeting to remind them that attitude is everything. I made it home that evening and into bed at midnight. Up at 7:00 AM and on the road to New York City a couple of hours later. With a finish time of 2:15:22—fourteen seconds slower than my personal best nailed back in 1999—I was once again reminded that a little hard work goes a long way.

On the awards podium, it wasn't the athletes up there that would be remembered; it would surely be thirteen-month-old Jack in my arms, clapping with everyone else.

Good Race … Bad Race … Good Race

September 2007

A month ago, on the little vacation rock known as Block Island, Rhode Island, I raced the aptly named Block Island Triathlon. I did well.

Two weeks ago, at the popular vacation area known as the Lakes Region of New Hampshire, I raced the Timberman Triathlon 70.3. I did not so well.

On Sunday, in the northern city of Hamburg, Germany, I raced the Triathlon World Championships. I did well again.

Beware, this is a long one …

I'd been planning on that Block Island race for a couple of months, prodded by a friend, Donny Forsyth, whose family would be vacationing on the island—and he'd be racing as he does every year, actually winning the last two. Sharon and I were going to make a nice weekend out of it; we'd get in Saturday morning, enjoy the beach, spend the night, race in the morning, and go home. Seemed like a good plan.

Come Saturday morning at 7:08, I was confirming directions for the nearly two-hour ride to the ferry when I discovered that the race was not Sunday, but scheduled to start in just over four hours! Sharon shook her head and took charge. We were out the door with Jack in about ten minutes (luckily I packed the night before), looking to catch the 9:30 ferry, which itself takes a little more than an hour.

An aggressive drive south got us there about 9:10 and onto the ferry at 9:25. A slow loading led to a late departure, which put us on the island at 10:45. I pushed my way to the front, jumped on my bike with a bag of legs and race gear on my back, got to the race at 11:00, hurried my way through transition preparation, and was ready to go a few minutes before my 11:40 wave start.

I consistently create so much of my own stress for no good reason whatsoever.

The race opened with a one-hundred-meter soft sand run that the race director let me skip. I hung at the water's edge and hopped in when the boys came by. I jumped on my buddy Donny's feet, which helped me navigate past dozens and dozens in the slower waves in front of us. I exited the quarter-mile swim twenty seconds or so behind him, and I'm guessing second or third in my age group.

The bike was a two-looper with a couple of short but challenging hills. I felt strong and rode strong and truly enjoyed the hard effort for the thirty-something minutes on the bike. I managed not to get passed, which is always a good little stroke. The high temps and humidity made for a sweaty one; as I dismounted, my sloppily fitting leg came completely off, and a volunteer carried it the last twenty feet to my transition as I held the bike and hopped my way to the rack.

I was told I was in fourth or fifth place overall and knew it would be just a matter of time before I fell out of the top—I just can't run as fast as the big boys and girls.

The final leg started as a half-mile run to the right as you hit the beach from transition some fifty meters or so inland, then a couple miles in the reverse direction to another U-turn, which brought you back a mile and a half to the finish at transition. Running in soft sand is clearly more energy sucking than on the hard stuff, so I did my best to stay to the left early on. (The tide was such that waves were coming right up to the soft stuff, which had a six-inch lip, making it tough to select an efficient line.) That first line to the right situated my prosthetic on the low, left water side, remarkably easier than the flip side, which, of course, was exactly what I had to deal with on that two-mile run in the other direction.

Post U-turn, the energy required to keep a solid pace seemed to grow exponentially with each step! Again, the heat and humidity were ninety, my Össur Run-Flex was on the high side, and now I had to dodge all the kids running in and out of the water (I apologetically Heismanned one unsuspecting little boy). My heart rate was off the charts, pounding out of my chest like it was about to explode—I really wanted a top three age-group spot. A half dozen competitors had passed me at this point (with the help of a couple of reboots), and the turnaround couldn't come fast enough.

It eventually came, and with the new gimp side/hard sand juxtaposition, my pace must have gone from 9-minute miles to 7:15s in one of those heartbeats. I may have been passed by one or two more folks in that remaining 1.5 miles, but I also picked off a couple of my own. By now, my one Nike run shoe was soaked and packed with heaps of sand, so I popped it off and carried it to the finish line, crossing in one hour, twenty minutes.

I entered the race thinking this could be my first U.S. age-group podium finish—got third in Japan two years ago. Of the 458 starters, I finished eleventh overall and second in my age group! Without question, I was pumped to get up and receive my award with a big smile.

Of the eighty or so triathlons I've done over the years, wouldn't you know that this is the first one that awarded only the age-group first-place finishers!

The relative success left me marginally confident two weeks later, when the family headed north for a couple nights of campfires and a tent and the Timberman 70.3 Triathlon, my second half Ironman of the year.

Preparation couldn't have been any less focused: I got my hands on a thirty-foot ladder from a friend and opted to finish cedar clapboard siding our house. Up and down that godforsaken ladder for a week and a half took the snap out of the pistons, resulting in a sorrowful fifty-six-mile bike ride. The race started with a decent thirty-three-minute swim before that never-ending bike began. I actually felt okay on the ride until about the halfway point, when the juices dried up despite the ritual PowerGels. Early on, a couple of the young fast guys picked me off, nothing out of the ordinary. In the last miles, I must have been dispatched by twenty riders. That sucked. I don't like that. Don't want it to happen again. During that time, my head started getting all funny on me, questioning why I bother doing this stuff, why I put myself through it if I'm not willing to do it right, etc. Not the first time I've struggled both physically and mentally like this, and I'm sure it won't be the last.

Getting off the bike was heavenly. Sadly, this glory didn't last too long. Almost immediately on the run, my leg started getting loose and my intestines looser. I pulled up for a reboot and then went to a Porta-Potty (the one-piece race suit was suddenly deemed questionable). Back on the run but remaining quite belly-cramped, I couldn't get it going. I walked all the early aid-stations and didn't move too quickly in between.

By the second lap, my innards had recovered, and my leg suspension was solid since that early reboot. I was able to push hard and run a decent pace, but Stumpie decided to cramp hard every mile, forcing me to take many a reboot to relieve the pain. No question I wasn't terribly irritated by the built-in rest breaks. The finish line came with a healthy dose of disappointment, albeit acceptable and understandable—this was not the day I deserved to go fast.

(If you're wondering why I chose to side my house, the answer is twofold. First, the unfinished house is killing me. I just can't wait to get it done. Second, I have every intention of making the 2008 Beijing Paralympic Cycling Team, which will require much greater commitment and focus than I've put forth in the past three years. Getting a couple of projects done by the end of October is the immediate goal, and all this stuff trumps a late-season long race.)

Two-weeks after Timberman—whether or not I deserved to go fast can be debated—I sure wanted to do that at triathlon world championships. In preparation for a speedy race, my best bet was to get some rest and limit training to a few shorter workouts with some intensity thrown in. And that's just what I did. That and some golf.

On Thursday, I participated in the U.S. Paralympic Team's founding sponsor's golf tournament that raises money for the team. I can say I played fairly well, providing all the confidence needed for the big race three days later.

I headed off to Germany on Friday night, acutely aware of the pitfalls of arriving at an international race the day before. Namely, the prospect that one's bike doesn't make it.

You guessed it. Got to Hamburg at 1:30 PM, but the Griffen Vulcan rocket ship remained at JFK, and it didn't arrive until after the next morning's event. Remaining calm, a hallmark of my personality (cough), I knew I'd come up with *something* to ride; cruiser bike or not, I'd be competing.

Tim Yount, Team USA's director and my soon-to-be savior, is well known in this little circle for handling these things. I finally found him at 6:15 PM, and a scant three hours later, as I lay half-asleep in my hotel room (the situation at hand made actual sleep hard to come by), the knock on the door signaled something coming through. Brandyn Gates, wife of age grouper Trevor Gates, presented me with her near-perfect fit road bike!

Faith, ladies and gentleman. When you're a poor planner like I am, you gotta have faith …

Like the New York City Tri a little while back, I lay in bed rolling, flipping, and wrestling with the comforter as I tried to get some sleep. Jet lag, perhaps. In any case, I got about three hours in before eagerly jumping out of bed at 5:15. *Rrrrrrace day!*

Getting right to it (I know you, the reader, have things to do), the f-f-f-freezing cold swim, in water so brown you literally couldn't see your hand in front of you, took us under three bridges en route to the exit ramp—kinda cool. I exited the water behind, among others, fellow below-knee amputee Jeff Glasbrenner. I subsequently caught him at the halfway point of the bike and felt his presence the remainder of the ride. While doing so on the second lap, I was repeatedly disappointed to see the *packs* of young men passing me. The twenty to twenty-fours who started in the wave behind us were on the first lap and blatantly cheating; age-group triathlon is a draft-free sport, and these guys were committing the triathlete's cardinal sin: drafting!

Off the bike and switching legs, with Jeff just a couple of spots to my left, doing the same, I saw an Austrian BK run by me to start his final leg of the race. Now, we're the first wave, and there aren't a whole lot of us to begin with, so if another guy missing a leg passes me, I'm going to notice, and if he's in front of me on an out-and-back course, I'm going to see him at or near the turnaround.

As I comment on this aloud, Jeff tells me he saw the guy blaze by him in one of the packs. This set off the competitive juices, not to mention drew forth my R-rated vocabulary, and I took off after him. As I hit the 1k mark of the 10k run and was about to overtake him, the leg became loose. A few more of those words later, and I was back in the hunt. I caught him a bit past the 2k, but another reboot at 3k rescinded the lead. Same at 5k. At 7k, I was far enough ahead that upon the fourth reboot, I was back at it a step ahead of him. My temper was greatly tested, and many bad words came forth with another reboot at 9k. By then, the Austrian was off pace, and I was back to focusing on the winger in front of me, a German.

I caught him in the finish chute with one hundred meters to go and crossed the line first in my category, fourth overall, behind a very fast partially paralyzed arm guy and two visually impaired competitors.

I've been beyond fortunate to take part in my sixth ITU championship event, taking first in four of them. Thanks to all of you who made this happen for me and the rest of us. Thank you, Össur, for my prosthetic components, Nike for my shoes and apparel, CAF for their support, Griffen for the bike I didn't ride, A Step Ahead for building my legs, Xterra wetsuits for the wetsuit that was stolen from transition after the race (no joke), PowerBar for the energy, and to The Hartford, the company that has helped my family and me more than I can ever repay.

The Beginning of the End
March 2008

Today marked the start of the 2008 race season, what will most likely be my last push for Paralympic Cycling medals. (To that end, triathlon is on sabbatical this year.) The Beijing trials are in Colorado Springs in the first week of June, with a road time trial and the kilo and pursuit on the track. Since I haven't even seen a track in over a year, the chances of my qualifying on the oval could be considered slim. Indeed, it's the wife-in-anesthesiology-residency/two-boys-under-the-age-of-two thing that's kept me away.

I suppose this is a good time to get a plug in for the boys. They're doing absolutely fantastic. Luke is five months old, and is even more chill than Jack was at the same age. The big brother is now twenty months old and has survived the beatings I've laid upon him over the last couple of months. I guess I shouldn't call them "beatings." "Abuse" might be a better word; I dropped him on his head three times in a month …

The first one was his ice-skating debut. At eighteen months, he wasn't quite ready to take off on his own, so I tooled around the ice with him in my arms. Wouldn't you know that in the middle of a series of crossovers, my leg fell off and down we went. Most of the impact was to my forearm, but his forehead did make contact, and the egg followed.

The next day, as I pulled up his pants that had migrated south, he leaned forward, feet went out from under him, head hit floor.

The trifecta came while descending the stairs a couple of weeks later, sporting my new slippers. I soon found out why they call them *slip*-pers. With Jack in my arms, the good leg flew out from under me, the bad leg buckled, and Jack's ear rudely introduced itself to the edge of the oak tread.

His screams and tears left me feeling sincerely irresponsible and incapable of proper care of my own child.

A trip to the emergency room followed (Sharon had once seen something similar cause impotence in a monkey). Tests proved that all was fine, and the docs told us that his purple ear would soon return to its normal shade of pink, beige, or whatever color Caucasian skin is.

I'm happy to say he's doing just fine and was curbside along with the mini bugger little brother and their mother, cheering for his abuser a mere six hours ago, holding nary a grudge.

This morning's race was a 2.2-mile, eleven-lap circuit race on the beauteous peninsula of Marblehead Neck, a short skip north of Boston. In the thirty-five-plus Masters race, there were two of us representing the Union Velo Masters Team. Lucky for me, the McCormack brothers were in the mix (recently retired, successful ex-pro cyclists) so that when I would eventually win the race I'd have some serious swagger in my step. Unfortunately, the part where I win didn't actually happen.

What did happen was a consistent performance from yours truly—I made the same mistakes I've made in nearly every circuit or criterium race I've ever entered: I was in the middle of the pack on the first few laps, realized I had to get in position for a possible break away, got myself up front, faded back on the next couple laps, got back up front with a couple to go, faded back with one to go as the pace picked up and got stuck out of position for the final push, and, fittingly, chose Mr. SlowItDown's wheel, finishing in the middle.

The course was fairly challenging for a circuit race with one short, steepish hill, a downhill S-turn that kept everyone's attention and a 110-degree turn on narrow roads that demanded good acceleration on the way out. The finish line lay a couple hundred meters from the crest of the hill, which was a couple hundred meters from the sharp corner, so on the last lap, as competitors juiced it out of that turn, we had to go hard up the hill and, of course, hard again for the finish line. If you weren't in position—right up front—things got away from you, and the next thing you knew, the winner was winning … and the game was over.

That's pretty much what happened out there today for me. A bit anticlimactic, as bike races tend to be if you're not in the top ten.

Thanks to the Internet, the *VeloNews* article was posted moments ago (March 30, 2008) with this excerpt:

In a notable Masters 35 race, Team Fuji's Tobi Schultze got off the front in the last lap with teammate Frank McCormack, a multi-time national champion. *Schultze beat his famous teammate in the sprint and the pack was led in several seconds later by a third Team Fuji teammate, Frank McCormack's brother Mark, the recently retired former USPRO road champion.*

The good news is I felt comfortable most of the race, and at one point, I led the field up the hill. To top that off, after the race, I had a tasty beverage at the Salem Beer Works with an old friend from high school. I do try to see the bright side of every story—that's pretty much my MO.

April will bring me to two road races and a couple of local time trials and training crits, followed by a similar month in May. In the push for Beijing, please keep your fingers crossed for Jack and me, we can use all the help we can get.

Squirrels, Railroad Tracks, and Cellulitis
May 2008

Three weeks ago, I was spinning home through Framingham after a hard workout when I took note of a house across the street, recently gutted by fire. Poor fami ... *Slam!*

Much to my dismay, I had ridden over railroad tracks cutting diagonally across the road and my front tire lodged in the rail, abruptly driving my body into the pavement. Embarrassment was the greater pain as the nearby Brazilian street corner boys' array of comments registered: "Whoa!" "Chu okay, mayn?" "Ha-ha-ha!"

I was back in the saddle in ten seconds max, with a slight ache in my right hip and shoulder, wondering when I'd ever learn. Such is my life. Creating problems by making mistakes. Yet I'll be the first to tell you that I've done pretty well so far, which is a direct result of expecting to succeed in the first place, despite the bumps and bruises along the way.

I've made it my business to dig around to find the good stuff in any situation I face. In this latest drive on the bicycle, the challenges have once again found their way into my sphere, and I've managed to find something sweet within.

There I was, poor me, hanging out on a beach in Florida, holding one of my beautiful, healthy sons as we watched his beautiful, healthy brother play with my beautiful, healthy wife on the gulf water's edge. Poor me. I was all of a sudden having a self-pity moment. True story.

You see, I was stranded with Luke on my lap and unable to join the others because I was legless due to a recurring cellulitis infections on Stumpie. I wanted to walk over there and be part of the fun ... but I was disabled … The pity feeling came over me, and no sooner did it strike me that I was feeling down than something slapped my face, and I took in all the wonder that was my lot.

I'm the luckiest man in the world! I suddenly realized. (See beautiful/healthy sons/wife above.) That's how I feel 99 percent of the time. The other 1 percent is when I have to do any type of housework.

Further fortune provides overall physical well-being and enough motivation to continue pushing myself on the bike. At least for a couple of more weeks, although I *expect* for a few more months. (Who am I kidding? I hope to be pushing myself 'til the stone gets propped up overhead.)

Beijing Paralympic Trials take place on June 6 near Denver, Colorado, and with the race comes a new type of challenge for all the hopefuls this year: a limited number of Beijing team slots. Our formerly number one ranked team has sunk to number eight, resulting in a mere six spots given to USA men from the International Paralympic Committee, three of which are already spoken for. That leaves just three for the six or eight of us who stand a real chance of team membership. And the parity among the group makes it anybody's game.

As for me, training and racing have gone according to schedule. I've knocked off nearly all the workouts Coach Kathy has prescribed since November, and I've worked hard in the races I've done this spring. Since the season opener in late March, I've entered ten or so events, including road races, circuit races, crits, time trials, and even the Muddy Buddy while vacationing in Florida.

In case you're wondering: No, I didn't win any of them. Nor did I come anywhere near winning any of them. But I have made it a point to chase down breaks, create breaks, and just plain work hard for the sake of preparing myself for the first Friday in June. That's when it all gets laid down, and twenty minutes of riding will determine how much more riding I'll be doing in the immediate future.

One could argue without much resistance that I've been better prepared in the past, having put in more blue-collar saddle time yesteryear. But I believe things will go my way. This feeling was bolstered just yesterday, when I was telling a friend that trials will be tough and there's no guarantee. She said, "I have faith in you, Paul. The sun always shines on you."

Experience tells me that indeed it does. I'm telling you, I'm one lucky guy.

A few weeks back, I was riding along a residential road not far from home, in between ninety-second hill climb repeats. Up ahead, I saw a squirrel on the sidewalk, looking all worried about something. I noticed this squirrel before I noticed the one lying in the road. The poor little dude had just been hit by a car and lay there wondering, I imagine, what had just happened to him. I stopped and pulled him off to the sidewalk (wearing full gloves, rest assured, as it's still cold in New England in April), surmising that his leg was broken and he just might survive. *Just a squirrel*, I thought. *I'll leave him here so his pals can do whatever they do when one of their own takes a hit. I'm short on time, and Beijing calls for work to be done.*

I started off to repeat that hill, and I immediately felt a strong pull back to the rodent.

What to do? What to do?

My conscience got the better of me and the next forty-five minutes were spent on my cell phone, trying to discern which local official was responsible for injured wildlife. The best immediate answer I could come up with was a volunteer veterinarian about twelve miles away—and they don't pick up.

A nearby resident curiously came to our aid and provided a box for transport. With squirrel-in-a-box under my left arm, I abandoned my workout and made haste to the Phoenix Animal Hospital. It was Friday afternoon, and the wonderful folks who took the little guy said they'd do their best and have a prognosis for me by Monday. The weekend passed … and so did Mr. Squirrel. His crushed pelvis wouldn't allow a normal recovery to return to the wild, and so he was euthanized. My efforts were in vain …

Or were they not? I was told he had a much more pleasant departure than he would have experienced otherwise. And maybe, from above—or below or within or wherever—Mr. Squirrel appreciates my compassion and will be rooting for me when I need all that spirit energy I'm gonna need in a couple of weeks.

I'd like to think so. And thinking so is most often what brings it to bear.

I think I'm ready.

Good Grief

June 2008

The good news is that I have a summer full of options, so many things to do, so many weekends to spend as I like, doing whatever fancies me. Let's pretend Sharon has no say for a moment.

The bad news is that last Friday I failed to make the cut for a trip to Beijing.

Aaaah, crap …

That's certainly how I felt fifteen minutes after I crossed the finish line, when I learned that a couple of other guys had gone faster than I had. Can't say I was totally surprised; however, I think it's safe to say that I had a fair shot at earning one of the historically few slots available.

Rest assured, I feel good about my fitness, my approach, and my race. I didn't go out with a half-ass attempt. My finish time reestablished my Elite Team status, fast enough to remain in the top tier of American disabled riders. To make the Paralympic team, however, you had to be one of the three fastest riders relative to your disability standard (not counting the three guys who had already qualified, two of which also crossed the line ahead of me relative to their standards).

As mentioned in my last posting, Team USA was granted six cycling spots in total for men across all disability categories, including handcyclists (double amputees/quadriplegics/paraplegics). Three of those spots were claimed at last year's world championships by two handcyclists and a guy with some sort of degenerative muscular condition. Of the three spots left, two were grabbed Friday by other handcyclists and one by Ron Williams, my longtime compatriot and fellow below-knee amp. The first guy not to get a slot today was another guy in our class, Sam Kavanaugh—a finer man you'll struggle to find. (He'll get 'em next time; he's twenty-nine and only a few years into this whole one-legged thing.) Next guy not to qualify was a handcyclist. Next guy was me.

For those of you curious about these details, the standard is X unit of time per kilometer (which, of course, translates to a more familiar Y miles per hour). Those who qualified completed the course at a lower percentage of their standard. For instance, Ron finished in 18:50, which boiled down to riding 4 percent faster than our standard. Partial paraplegic handcyclist Oscar Sanchez, the first to qualify today, rode 5 percent faster than his standard, which is probably two to three miles per hour slower than ours.

My time of nineteen minutes, seventeen seconds on the tough 13.75k course was 2 percent faster than the standard. At 26.5 miles per hour, it was good ... but not good enough.

So what the hell am I gonna do now?

Tough question. Tough because I'm in darn good shape at the moment, and there's no sense letting it to go to waste. Tough because while I could go out and bike race for the rest of the summer, my true passion lies in triathlon, and there's a whole lotta races out there I'd love to do—but those would require making up for a whole lotta swimming and running I haven't been doing for the past nine months. Tough because I hope to play good golf someday soon, and if I just devote a little time ...

As I cathartically write these words, one thing I can be thankful for is that Sharon's mom came over from Australia to live with us for the summer. She timed it such that she could help mind the kids while Sharon works eight hundred hours a day and I deal with Beijing travel, training, and other pressures. Well, we know that the latter is no longer an issue.

Free babysitting for the summer.

Golf ... triathlon ... golf ... triathlon ...

But seriously. Ten years ago this month, the whole bike thing started when I showed up at national championships and won both the road race and the time trial. Since then, the bike has been very, very good to me, and there's not a single solitary thing I can complain about. More so, there's so much more good stuff to come. More than I can even imagine, I'm sure. Frankly, I'm still not quite ready to close the book on what, in some small degree, defines me.

Thanks for reading. Writing always makes me feel better.

Signing Off

The lessons one garners from another's life will vary from reader to reader. Some will see the author's path as beyond anything they will ever experience. Some will stir in the memories of similar works while others will be spirited with motivation to tackle the same. I expect no one to be amazed at the path I've chosen, I hope some will be inspired—I would be satisfied with amused.

These are a few of the philosophical bits I hope to have made clear in these pages:

Attitude, persistence, commitment, and work ethic will serve you well

- When choosing a path in life, let passion lead
- Everything you need is available—you just have to go get it
- Be willing to laugh at yourself and everyone else
- Seek love relentlessly and settle for nothing but The One
- To live the life you wish for, believe in yourself

It's safe to say I've had a good attitude most of my life. There were times as a teenager when I struggled to find the beauty in my circumstances; when drugs were a prominent player on the scene and success meant I couldn't remember how I got home. My little world improved after I admitted myself into a foster home at the beginning of my junior year of high school. This experience, I would later come to realize, taught me that we're not victims of our environment; we control it.

While the circumstances with my parents may have been at the root of my admission to foster care, my father has always been the example I hold myself to when it comes to work ethic—my mother that of compassion. The two years I spent as an ironworker taught me that I can—and choose to—work as hard as anyone. A lesson that has helped push me when I need a push.

Nevertheless, I had higher aspirations and chose to put my energy into academics. Five years later I earned a mechanical engineering degree from the University of Massachusetts at Lowell and in the process I learned I didn't want to be an engineer either!

Experience was teaching me that what I really enjoy is working with people and truly enjoy building relationships—that the analytical side of the engineering profession didn't stoke my fire. Upon graduation I accepted a position as a sales engineer for a welding equipment manufacturer, The Lincoln Electric Company. Six months later I lost my leg.

Following a few months of rehabilitation and prosthetic leg fittings, Lincoln sent me to the New York office to do what I was trained to do. The next three years were spent selling welding machines and testing my athletic abilities as a prosthesis-bound runner, skier and hockey player. You can probably guess in what direction my passions pulled my time, energy, thoughts and spirit.

Who knows what, if any, endurance sport ambitions I would have had had I not lost my leg. One thing I do know is that I had zero desire to run a marathon before the accident. When I woke up from the amputation my first thought was not, "Ahhhh, yes … it's all coming together … the missing piece of the puzzle … this is exactly what I needed to become a marathoner!" What we need we already have. What might be missing is the desire to groom it.

Nearly every sticky situation I get into is some fault of my own. I know that. I also know that a time tested remedy to avoid beating myself up over so many meathead moves is to laugh at myself and invite others to do the same. Laughter, as we all know, is Nature's answer to stress. On top of that, anyone can do it.

Just like anyone can be successful—maybe not everyone at the same thing at the same time, but there's no reason each and every one of us can't experience what it's like to have them raise the flag and play the national anthem. I'm not convinced, however, that it has ever happened to anyone who didn't *believe* he or she could.

It has been good run, I'm happy to say, and one that still isn't quite over. A year and a half after that Beijing qualification race, Sharon completed her anesthesia residency and we moved back to Colorado to settle in for the next segment of our lives. Outside of your basic child rearing and career duties, Sharon and I got right back at it: racing triathlons, bikes, marathons, 10ks, skiing, playing hockey and getting our kids into sports as well. Essentially, doing what we love to do.

My career as a professional speaker continues to bloom as I do my best to learn the ins and outs of the business. (Please visit HYPERLINK "http://www.paulmartinspeaks.com" www.paulmartinspeaks.com for more information on my programs.) This will be my path for the foreseeable future and I hope to write more books, both fiction and non-fiction. Choosing this long-term goal was not easy, yet somewhat natural. I'd written about the desire to head back to school to study law. What I didn't mention was that I didn't want to be a lawyer as much as I wanted to study something that interests me: the framework of U.S. litigation.

I opted out of law school primarily because Sharon and I wanted to start a family and to have the flexibility to keep one parent at home ... most of the time. Full-time anesthesia is a very demanding career, albeit a well-paying one. When the time comes that my speaking schedule consistently fills, we hope Sharon will be able to work part-time and spend those valuable hours with our children.

As of this writing our third child is well underway inside of Sharon and she's convinced it's another boy—like we did with Jack, our first-born, we're keeping this one a surprise. Not unlike the future, with so many surprises to look forward to and so many challenges to pursue.

With the packing of the bike after Beijing trials came a closing of the e-mail era. I've continued to write about my experiences living and racing and learning, these days via the Web site. Stop by the site now and again and I'll keep you up to date on the latest adventures, passionate causes and number of kids.

And remember, good things will happen.